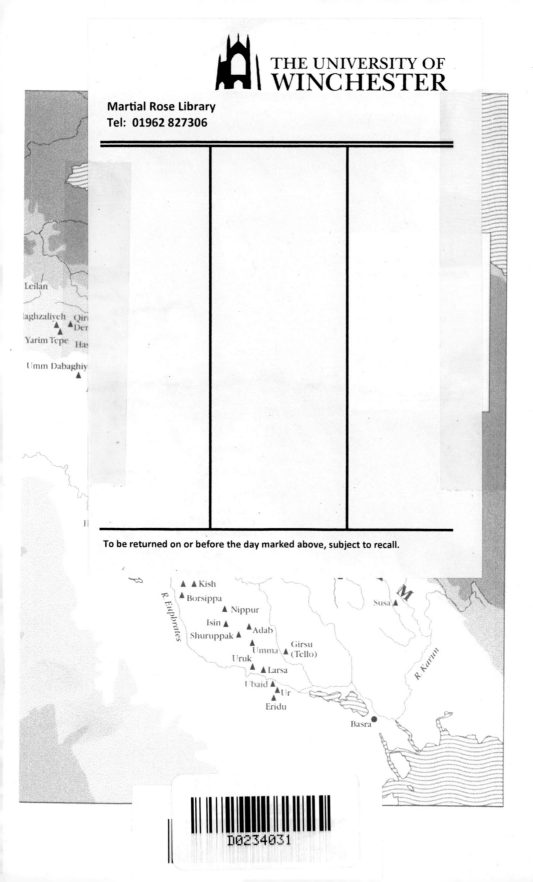

# THE UNIVERSITY OF WINCHESTER

Leilan

aghzaliyeh Qir
Der
Yarim Tepe Has

Umm Dabaghiy

Kish

Borsippa

R. Euphrates

Nippur

Isin

Shuruppak Adab

Umma Girsu
(Tello)

Uruk

Larsa

Ubaid Ur

Eridu

Susa M

R. Karun

Basra

# THE NEAR EAST:
## ARCHAEOLOGY IN THE
## 'CRADLE OF CIVILIZATION'

# EXPERIENCE OF ARCHAEOLOGY
## Series Editor: Andrew Wheatcroft

*The Archaeology of the Arabian Gulf*
Michael Rice

*The Near East*
*Archaeology in the 'cradle of civilization'*
Charles Keith Maisels

*Classical Archaeology of Greece*
*Experiences of the discipline*
Michael Shanks

# THE NEAR EAST: ARCHAEOLOGY IN THE 'CRADLE OF CIVILIZATION'

*Charles Keith Maisels*

Routledge
Taylor & Francis Group

LONDON AND NEW YORK

To my wife Jennifer
for being there

First published 1993
by Routledge
2 Park Square, Milton Park, Abingdon, Oxon OX14 4RN
Simultaneously published in the USA and Canada by Routledge
711 Third Avenue, New York, NY 10017

First published in paperback 1998

© 1993 Charles Keith Maisels

Typeset in 10/12 pt Palatino, Linotronic 300 by
Florencetype Ltd, Stoodleigh, Devon

*Routledge is an imprint of the Taylor & Francis Group, an informa business*

*British Library Cataloguing in Publication Data*
Maisels, Charles Keith
The near east: archaeology in the 'cradle of civilization'
I. Title
930.1

*Library of Congress Cataloguing in Publication Data*
Maisels, Charles Keith
The near east: archaeology in the 'cradle of civilization'/Charles Keith Maisels.
p.    cm.
Includes bibliographical references and index.
1. Archaeology–Middle East–History–19th century. 2. Middle east–Civilization–
To 622. I. Title.
CC101.M628M35 1992
939´.4–dc20    92-2777

ISBN 0–415–04742–0 (hbk)
ISBN 0–415–18607–2 (pbk)

# CONTENTS

# FIGURES, MAP, PLATES
# AND TABLES

## FIGURES

## MAP

## PLATES

All plates are reproduced by courtesy of the Trustees of the British
Museum.

## TABLES

# ACKNOWLEDGEMENTS

I wish to express my profound thanks to those who have helped give this work what merit it has:

To John Brockington, Kevin Hammond and Hushang Philsooph;

To Harriet Crawford, who read the whole work and provided invaluable criticism, especially in the interpretation of Mesopotamian archaeology and architecture;

To Douglas Baird, who also read the whole work and who, in addition to giving unstintingly of his time for wide-ranging and probing discussions, helped clarify my understanding of the Levant in general and the processes affecting the Pre-Pottery Neolithic in particular. This is especially appreciated, since it forms a part of his own Doctoral Thesis at Edinburgh. He has also specially drawn illustrative examples of projectile points.

To Michael Roaf, who kindly supplied the artwork illustrating the house he excavated at Tell Madhhur, and with whom I have had brief but informative discussion on related topics.

Finally to Ivan Boscov, engineer, who, as the 'educated layman' read the whole work very closely and critically. A better informed or more conscientious reader could not be wished for.

## NOTE TO THE PAPERBACK EDITION

In this edition I have confined myself to cleaning-up the text with a few corrections, deletions and additions (such as the definition of the state on page 195), and have also replaced Figure 5.1 with a similar but more comprehensive flow chart. The major change is the addition of a Glossary of physical terms.

A map of Mesopotamia and the Levant with some key sites appears at the back of the book.

Theoretical perspectives and apparatus are developed in Maisels (1990, 1993, 1995) and a fuller bibliography will be found in Maisels (1998).

# GLOSSARY

**Aggradation:** The 'building up' of the land surface (in Holocene times especially the lower reaches of river channels) by the *depositional* action of rivers, winds or seas (see next two entries plus loess). Its opposite is *denudation*.

**Alluvium:** Sedimentary deposits of eroded rock fragments laid by the action of rivers. Larger particles, notably gravels, are deposited upstream, while finer materials (usually called *silts*) are deposited downstream, sometimes right into waterbodies, where *alluvial fans* are formed. If offshore conditions are right, *deltas* are formed. Comprising unconsolidated (though usually deep and mineral-rich) material, alluvial soils are a type of *immature*, *skeletal* or *azonal* soil, manifesting poorly developed *horizons*, which are levels of different structure and organic activity.

**Anastomosing:** A condition of rivers, in which, due to excessive *deposition* (see above) there is little gradient (slope) in the rivercourse, encouraging the main stream to break up into a network of branches or braids, the number and location of which shift over quite short periods of time. *Levees*, which are broad raised banks, can also result.

**Biome:** An ecosystem covering a significant proportion of the earth's surface, land or water. Tundra, Boreal (i.e. northern coniferous) forests, tropical rainforests and savannas are examples of biomes. A dominant life-form structures each – mosses and lichens in the case of tundra – hence Biomes have also been called 'formation types'. However, the dominant life-forms (on land) are themselves a consequence of latitude, precipitation and altitude.

**Caprid:** Goat. *Caprini* is the *tribe* including both sheep and goat. *Capra aegagrus* is the Bezoar goat, the wild progenitor of the domestic goat, while *Capra ibex* is a type of goat (the ibex) specializing in high altitude and desert conditions.

**Climax:** Two senses: (1) the most massive species of plant that a territory can sustain, e.g. oak; (2) the final stable plant community, e.g. oak–ash forest, reached after a process of *succession* from simpler/lower/less massive/less woody plant types. Thus primary succession from tundra to broadleaf and coniferous forests occurred in Britain after the Last Ice Age, and secondary succession, which takes place after climax has been removed, is spontaneously towards renewed forest cover. Moisture, temperature, seasonality, light and soils are determinants of what species represent climax for particular locations.

**Dendritic:** Tree-like branching, for instance of watercourses in the 'fan' type of drainage basin (q.v.).

**Dendrochronology:** tree-ring dating.

**Drainage basin:** The area from which a river, its tributaries and their feeder streams drain the rainfall left after evapotranspiration (q.v.). Drainage basins are separated by watersheds.

**Distal:** Situated farthest *away from* the point of attachment or connection, the converse of *proximal*, nearest.

**Ecotone:** The transitional zone between two biomes.

**Epiphysis:** Peculiar to mammalian vertebra and limb bones, this is the separately ossified end of a growing bone (the *diaphysis*). Separated by cartilage, the two only become unified at maturity.

**Evapotranspiration:** The rate of water loss from surfaces of (a) the ground and (b) leaves and stems; a function of temperature and wind speeds. The water balance (positive or negative) of an area is the rate of evapotranspiration set against rainfall plus any exogenous supply (see below).

**Exogenous:** Coming from without. Thus the Nile in Egypt is fed from drainage basins which lie in areas of adequate rainfall outside Egypt. A substantially positive water balance (see above) is required for rivers to originate, otherwise only wadis form (q.v.).

**Fractal:** Describes similar forms repeated at different scales, most often in natural phenomena. Thus trees, mountains, clouds and coastlines manifest fractal symmetry: leaves have similar forms to branches and branches have similar forms to whole trees (by affine transformation). Small stones in close-up resemble large rocks and the form of individual rocks resembles mountains. Coastlines have similar 'ragged edge' interactions between land and water at every scale from, say, a 1:4,000,000 map, down to that of rockpools. The Mandlebrot Set is a well-known demonstration of fractal process.

**Hydric/hygrophyte:** Plants which require large amounts of moisture and which therefore only thrive in/by water or in humid regions (c.f. mesic and xeric below).

**Isohyet:** A line joining points that receive the same amount of rainfall. Analogous to isobars, which are lines of equal atmospheric pressure, and points of equal height (contours). All are *isopleths*, lines joining points of equal value.

**Loess soils:** Sometimes called 'brickearth' soils from their sandy-yellow colour, hence the 'Yellow River' (Huang He) from the sediment it carries. Consisting mainly of fine quartz particles in deep layers, the loess soils of north China are rich in lime and form a good *loam* for agriculture. Loess soils are analogous to alluvial soils, but are primarily wind-deposited (aeolian), compacted and thus more cohesive, being able to sustain vertical banks when rivers cut down (as they always do in loess). Loess soils, being free-draining, do not waterlog. Russia's fertile 'black earth' (Chernozem) soil is loess with a high humus content. Such soils also occur in a long swathe from Saskatchewan through North Dakota to Texas.

**Mesic/mesophyte:** Temperate climate plants requiring moderate amounts of moisture.

**Metacarpal bones:** Corresponding to the palm-region in man, those are the rod-like bones of the fore-foot in tetrapod vertebrates, usually one corresponding to each digit (finger or toe). *Metatarsals* are the same bones in the hind foot (sole).

**Nucleation:** A settlement type which has its buildings clustered tightly together leaving little space between (only squares, greens or plazas, not fields and farms).

**Obsidian:** (Rhyolite) 'Volcanic' glass in extrusive igneous (i.e. *magmatic*) rocks. Like glass, obsidian takes a very sharp edge.

**Ovicaprids:** Sheep (*Ovis*) and goat together, used particularly where differentiation from skeletal remains is difficult. However, wild sheep (e.g. *Ovis orientalis*, or Mouflon, the progenitor of domestic sheep) and goat have different environmental preferences and tolerances, goat being tougher and more versatile.

**Palynology:** Pollen analysis. Since many pollens were originally airborne and all are different, identification and counting of different types in sedimentary and peaty deposits can reveal changing vegetation types over time; e.g. from woodlands to grasslands where man has cleared for farming and grazing.

**Phytoliths:** Silica deposits in soil from plant cells, notably grasses. The morphology of the deposits is related to transpiration and so can indicate water availability.

**Prairies:** Longer mid-latitude grasslands found in both North and South America (prairies and pampas). Natural grasslands are a function of 'interiority' (distance from coasts) and wind direction. Much of the Argentine pampas is only *situational climax* (a function of species availability) as trees will thrive when introduced. (See the discussion of grass as climax in Maisels 1995: 51–9.)

**Savanna:** Low-latitude grassland, often containing trees such as baobab (*Adansonia digitata*), acacia and euphorbia. The Llanos and Campos of South America are savannas and it covers much of Australia. However the regime is often referred to as 'Sudan-type' as it extends right across sub-Saharan Africa from the White Nile to the Atlantic. See steppe.

**Steppe:** Short grassland, most extensive in mid-latitudes. A belt extends all the way from the Ukraine to northern China.

**System:** A system is a pattern of interaction between nodes or elements. Nodes can be anything from simple switches to complex sets of sub-systems, such as living cells. A system that seeks out its own energy is alive. Energy is the capacity to do work, and work is the capacity to produce changes of condition, that is, of state or position.

**Wadi:** An intermittent watercourse without baseflow and thus only running after rains or storms (carrying runoff). Not to be confused with a Palaeochannel, which is a course abandoned by a river for geological or energetic reasons (cf. anastomosing above). A wadi is more like a large erosion gully than a river.

**Xeric/xerophilic/xerophyte:** Trees like tamarisk, baobab and acacia ('gum', 'wattle' or 'thorn' trees) and other plants such as cactus (succulents) which can thrive in arid conditions. In addition to a simple lack of soil moisture, excessive transpiration caused by heat *or* wind (or both) produce xeric conditions. Thus pines and marram grass (on dunes) are xerophytes. Responses to periods of intense or prolonged drought can have significant consequences for radiocarbon dating.

# 1

# INTRODUCTION

Everyone wants to know how the present situation – and thus their current condition – came about. Everyone needs to understand their own existence as individuals in society. And since people sense that histories consist in chains of cause and effect, they usually want to know how things began, in a sense what the first 'cause' was. Of course, the very first cause was the Big Bang at the origins of the universe and any subsequent cause always has causes preceding it, resulting in a chain of causes and effects which form a trajectory in time.

But this is not a book about the Nature of Time, the Universe and Everything. As a work in prehistory and early history it describes three 'firsts': the earliest approach to a settled life after the 40,000 years during which modern humankind had pursued a hunting-and-gathering way of life in small groups. This experimental regime was the Natufian culture of the Levant which flourished as modern climatic conditions were becoming established there some 12,000 years ago. The second 'first' was the formation of the world's earliest village farming cultures – the Hassuna, Samarra and Halaf cultures of Mesopotamia – which led on in only a few millennia to the first sustainable cluster of cities in the world: the third 'first'.

Villages existed elsewhere prior to Hassuna ones but not recognizable village *cultures*. Likewise, towns such as Jericho in the Jordan Valley (Levant) and Çatal Hüyük in Anatolia (Turkey) existed before the cities of southern Mesopotamia, such as Uruk, Eridu, Ur and Nippur. However, the earliest large settlements were not cities as they lacked urban structure – density and diversity of activity manifested in the built environment – and consequently there were no urban societies until their advent in Sumer (southern Iraq) during the fourth millennium BC. Sumerian urbanism in turn produced a whole cascade of 'firsts' – those conventionally associated with civilization – literacy, numeracy, monumental building, organized religion, organized warfare and the state.

In Sumer, for the very first time, we have sources of information that supplement archaeology, indeed that are strictly speaking 'historical',

*Plate I(A)* A Fara-type tablet (*c.* 2600), recording numbers of workmen.

for historiography (the writing of history) is an enterprise dependent upon the existence of texts. Those are cuneiform documents (overwhelmingly economic), written with a stylus on clay, and, in earliest pictographic form, dating from around the end of the fourth millennium. When writing first appears it represents the Sumerian language – one with no known affiliations – but later in the third millennium Akkadian and Eblaite are represented by the same means, thereby becoming the earliest Semitic languages to be recorded (Plate I, A and B).

The study of cuneiform tablets in Sumerian and Akkadian is the province of Sumerologists, philological specialists, and one eminent scholar who has been active in this field for over half a century is S.N. Kramer. In his book *History Begins at Sumer* (1956, 1981), he lists no fewer

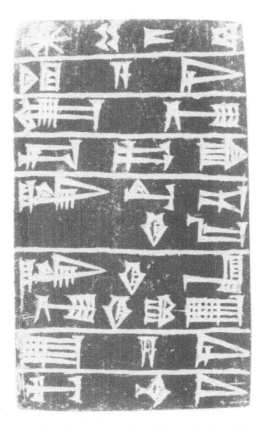

*Plate I(B)* A later but clearer example of the script: a tablet of King Shulgi (2094–2097) of the Third Dynasty of Ur (2122–2001), from the temple of Dimtabba at Ur.

than '39 Firsts in Man's Recorded History' which he has recognized from Sumerian texts. Those range from the first schools through the first 'Noah' (Ziusudra) and the first Farmers' Almanac to Man's First Cosmogony and Cosmology. He might also have added the earliest formal organizations known, namely the *oikos* household and the temple, which were (it is argued below) crucial to Mesopotamian social evolution.

More strictly literary is certainly the earliest narrative tale known – the 'quests' of Gilgamesh – the earliest literary debates, plus the first recorded proverbs and lamentations. All this and yet more. However, the point is not to list (even though many Sumerian texts are lists of professions, plants, places, animals, mores, etc.) but to understand how all this came about.

There are two aspects to this. The first is to see how all those elements of civilization fit together in a functioning society, embodied in the city-states of Sumer and Akkad (the area of the alluvium adjoining Sumer to the north). The other is to see how that society evolved from earlier ones. In the case of Sumer we know that its immediate precursor is the Ubaidian culture, so named from a site in the extreme south of alluvial Mesopotamia, south even of the River Euphrates which, with the Tigris, was responsible for depositing most of that silt.

Indeed, it is the still controversial argument of this book that the Ubaidian culture, which so successfully colonized the alluvium, owed that success, based upon irrigation, to its pioneering Samarran fore-bears. It is further argued that the specific form of economic production and social reproduction developed in that endeavour – the *oikos* house-hold – was the key not only to secure and highly productive irrigation farming in a semi-desert, but that this household form (large and stratified) gave the emerging city-states their social and political charac-ter. In turn, the products of this character (for the ancient world dy-namic and democratic) were seminal to subsequent developments in the Near East and ultimately the world.

Later (e.g. Iron Age) developments and interconnections have been traced in my previous book *The Emergence of Civilization* (Maisels 1990) where a fuller bibliography and more extensive notes will be found. Here I concentrate on a more straightforward developmental account showing how the data for this emerged piecemeal from the labours of many archaeologists working under many different circumstances, all of them difficult. However, archaeologists do not find facts, they find artefacts – things like flints, seeds, pots, bones, cylinder seals, hearths, refuse pits and mud-brick walls – which all have to be *interpreted*. The artefacts are certainly data, but they do not speak for themselves, so archaeologists must speak for them. Accordingly, I have also tried to indicate how different pre-occupations – Biblical, Classical, Antiquarian – caused different questions to be posed, different data sought and different answers given.

In the process, and not in isolation from other sciences, modern archaeology has emerged as the basis for a prehistory which, like the rest of History now, is no longer just 'one damned thing after another', any more than modern Geography is merely 'one damned thing next to another'. On the contrary, both are essential to the space-time grid upon which any rational view of the world must be based, and it is to the promotion of such a framework that I hope my work contributes.

Biological evolution has provided us with memory and curiosity. As biological individuals we have no option but to exercise those faculties to construct perspectives; we are quite unable to float in a timeless present, for we are aware that the present ever recedes, that there are gener-ations before us and hopefully after us and that the present state of affairs is transient, as our lives are. Therefore we have to keep track and trace connections.

Accordingly, all known societies have accounts of how things came to be. Without the disciplines of History and Geography, Archaeology and Anthropology, our accounts will remain mythical and social evolution a matter of blind stumbling, as chaotic in the future as in the past.

If we are to escape the tyranny of the past we have to demythologize History. This means comprehending it as a complex of processes – chains of causes and effects – driven by biological and cultural forces. By knowledge we might actually get to grips with the motive forces and so control them, rather than they us.

# 2

# AN ARTEFACTUAL BASIS FOR THE PAST

Toward the end of the twentieth century it is hard for us to conceive the extent to which European social–historical–cultural thinking was formed on the twin axes of the Bible and Classicism.[1] Both streams were of course transmitted from antiquity, though differentially, providing an invaluable, quasi-ethnographic, contrast to extant conditions while supplying an historical, quasi-evolutionary perspective. Christianity, in the form of Eastern and Western churches, and with them patristic writing of late antiquity, survived the collapse of empire so well that within a relatively few centuries the Western church was able to Christianize Dark Age Western Europe, where the church alone remained literate.

Classicism, the cultural legacy of the (pre-Christian) Graeco-Roman world, had a more partial and spasmodic recovery to independent existence. Not only was the greater part of written material in Latin lost with Roman collapse (finally in AD 476) but so too was widespread literacy, which perhaps had reached around 20 per cent (Harris 1989). The widespread recovery of the classical legacy is conventionally dated after 1453, when Byzantium fell to the Ottoman Turks, and many scholars bearing manuscripts and with, of course, a perfect knowledge of Greek, fled west. There they encountered in Italy, and also in northern Europe, city-state regimes where Classicism was already fostering Humanism, a secularized form of Christianity. This process of the revival of learning inspired by classical sources and stimulated by widening geographical horizons and technological competence, was later termed 'the Renaissance'.

If the emerging Humanism reinforced by intellectuals from the New Rome (Constantinople = Byzantium) strengthened awareness of the Graeco-Roman world (the Byzantine Empire was always Christian and Greek-speaking), the Bible kept alive awareness of and interest in the history and geography of the Near East. So much so, indeed, that at the launch of the Palestine Exploration Society in London, on 22 June 1865, formed, as its founding statement relates 'for the purpose of investigating the archaeology, geography, geology and natural history of the Holy

Land', no less a personage than the Archbishop of York, the inaugural meeting's chairman, could declare that 'This country of Palestine belongs to *you* and *me*, it is essentially ours. . . . It is the land towards which we turn as the fountain of all our hopes; it is the land to which we may look with as true a patriotism as we do this dear old England, which we love so much' (cited Lipman 1988: 51).

Formed by the remarkable George Grove (also the moving spirit of the standard *Dictionary of Music and Musicians*, the short title of which is just 'Grove's') with a mix of church and scientific luminaries, the Palestine Exploration Fund was the first permanently organized body devoted to long-term research in archaeology. Like Grove's dictionary, the PEF thrives to this day, with Her Majesty the Queen as its Patron and His Grace the Archbishop of Canterbury as President. The PEF's explicit purpose was Biblical exegesis, to collect *facts* surrounding the composition of the Bible and thus to facilitate better comprehension. The key thing was that by 1865, a broad spectrum of the Church of England could agree with historians and scientists that systematic exploration and excavation was the way forward. This was an archetypal expression of the 'scientific' spirit of the times, in which the geology of Lyell (*Principles of Geology* 1830) and the natural evolutionism of Darwin (*Origin of Species* 1859) had supplied decisive disproofs of Creationism – the doctrine that God had made the world all-of-a piece at a certain time.[2] Based on biblical genealogies, Archbishop Ussher of Armagh calculated 4004 BC and rabbinical authorities at about 3700 BC; but all were heretofore agreed that the world was not of long existence and indeed had most of its time already behind it. Also most of the world's existence was 'historical', reaching from Creation itself to the Roman Empire in Biblical accounts, then the Dark Age interval, then medieval and modern times.

Darwin's outlook was informed by the work of Charles Lyell, the foremost geologist of his day, who, a reconstructed Catastrophist, came to accept (and, in his *Principles of Geology* 1830–3, provided a mass of evidences for) the Uniformitarian ideas outlined by the physician James Hutton, originally contained in a paper to the Royal Society of Edinburgh in 1775. Hutton argued (in an approach that became famous as 'Huttonianism', but was only generally accepted a quarter of a century later) that the geological processes currently observed are those which have always and everywhere operated (= uniformitarianism). Those processes were and are fundamentally of two sorts: igneous, the primary source, coming from the earth's interior, of which vulcanism is a manifestation; and the other a consequence of erosional deposition on the ocean floor (sandstones, limestones, clays, etc.), which are subsequently uplifted and folded to form dry land and mountain ranges, all driven by the agency of heat (Gillispie 1959: 47).

Under Creationism, by contrast, there is no prehistory, for the Bible is an accurate historical record of everything fundamental from the origin of the world and mankind to the establishment of God's church on earth. But if there is to be a narrowly defined 'prehistory' within creationism it is located 'before the Flood', in the dreamtime extending from the Garden of Eden to the major cleansing of Ut-napishtim's (aka Noah) Flood, as the Akkadian sources had it from Sumerian, where the original 'Noah' is Ziusudra. Ironically, the Biblical Flood had supposedly occurred in 2349 BC, which we now know as the end of the Sumerian Early Dynastic Period. The Euphrates floods are the bases of the stories which may reach right back into the pre-literate Ubaidian period of the fifth millennium when the southern alluvium was colonized, no doubt reinforced by subsequent heavy flooding to which that river is prone. Nonetheless, the church-father Tertullian (AD 155–220) declared that fossils in rocks were proof of extinctions wrought by the Flood, and this was a strong belief which existed until the nineteenth century.

> Although, during the Middle Ages, there was a tendency to dismiss fossils as mere freaks of nature – as effigies in stone which bore a fanciful resemblance to living plants and animals – by the seventeenth century it was widely accepted that they were in fact organic in origin, and that they represented the petrified remains of creatures destroyed in the Flood. About this time, however, the Danish geologist Nicolaus Steno, and the Italian naturalist Antonio Vallisnieri, drew attention to the significance of stratification in rock formations, as providing an indication that one layer had been deposited upon another. This, in turn, suggested that above and below could be interpreted in terms of after and before – the now familiar law of superposition. Moreover the importance of this observation was enhanced by the findings of Count de Buffon and others, which indicated that they could be classified according to the particular rock strata they occupied, the deeper layers containing examples for which no living counterparts were to be found.
>
> (Cleator 1976: 32–3)

Thus in its day and in its (totally empirical) way, Hutton's uniformitarianism (developed further by 1795 in his *Theory of the Earth, with Proofs and Illustrations*, 2 volumes, Edinburgh), was as revolutionary as Darwin's in the mid-Victorian period; indeed they are each part of a continuing revolution in cosmology which makes mankind a (small) part of a dynamic autonomous universe of matter in motion. Hutton's account convinced the likes of Lyell because it alone accounted for all the data without forcing or ignoring any. Thus Gillispie (1959: 48–9) observes that

certain consequences of Hutton's views became immediately

apparent. Most obvious was the vastness of geological time which his theory demanded. No observed change had taken place in all of recorded history. Throughout how many inconceivable ages, then, must this endless rising and falling of continents have been proceeding! Dr. Hutton offered no evidence for a creation and no denial of it either; he simply had nothing to say about it. Life, however, had to be very ancient, as old as the rocks which preserved its residues. And the whole concept hung upon the proposition that the cumulative effects of minute forces and infinitesimal changes can produce results of those equal to those of any sudden cataclysm [though this last was never stated] superseding the necessity for any divine intervention.

This provided the basis of, but did not yet supply, a prehistory for mankind. In Bibliological terms there was really no place for a prehistory of mankind. For if the Bible is treated as an historical account, everything from the Creation itself through to the Kingdom of Israel and beyond to the Rome of the New Testament is fully historical; that is, textually recorded. And what was not actually stated in the Bible could be inferred analogically. Thus the peopling of the earth could be conceived of by diffusion from a 'heartland' of wandering 'tribes' such as the Israelites were at several periods. Indeed distance from the Near East was held to account for the 'loss' of both revealed religion and the agro-pastoral techniques and ways of life reflected in the Bible.

In the role of finally instituting a human prehistory, Jacques Boucher de Crevecoeur de Perthes (1783–1868), a customs supervisor, poet, dramaturge and antiquarian, is prominent. In 1838 he argued to the Société Impériale d'Emulation at Abbeyville in the fateful Somme Valley, that man had been contemporaneous with animals now extinct. Two years later he produced stone hatchets from the Somme gravels to prove human presence during the Pleistocene era. However, as de Perthes related in 1860, the year after (as he thought) his final vindication: 'Practical men disdained to look; they were afraid; they were afraid of becoming accomplices in what they called a heresy, almost a mystification: they did not suspect my good faith, but they doubted my common sense', and so they called his work 'amateurish'. That just cited is Lowie's (1937: 7) translation in his *History of Ethnological Theory*. He continues:

A treatise 'De l'Industrie Primitive' [1846] made no impression on the learned until Dr. Rigollot [1854], a former antagonist examined the sites from which the tools had been secured and announced his conversion. Still the guild of savants remained unconvinced. There were those who pronounced the hatchets as hardly older than the advent of the Romans. Some thought the tools had sunk to

Pleistocene depths by their own weight. Others doubted the human origin of the flints, assigning their shape either to volcanic or glacial action.

It has to be said that good evidence for the presence of prehistoric man in Britain had been reported to the Society of Antiquaries as early as 1797 by John Frere (1740–1807), a Fellow of the Royal Society as well as of the Society of Antiquaries. Though dated 1797, the letter was not published until 1800, when it appeared in the thirteenth volume of the Society's periodical *Archaeologia* (pp. 204–5). As this is the earliest coherent account delivered to a scholarly body, Frere's letter is worth reproducing in full:

Sir,

I take the liberty to request you to lay before the Society some flints found in the parish of Hoxne, in the county of Suffolk, which, if not particularly objects of curiosity in themselves, must, I think, be considered in that light from the situation in which they were found. . . .

They are, I think, evidently weapons of war, fabricated and used by people who had not the use of metals. They lay in great numbers at the depth of about twelve feet, in a stratified soil, which was dug into for the purpose of raising clay for bricks.

The strata are as follows:
1  Vegetable earth 1,1/2 feet
2  Argill 7,1/2 feet
3  Sand mixed with shells and other marine substances 1 foot
4  A gravelly soil, in which the flints are found, generally at the rate of five or six in a square yard, 2 feet.

In the same stratum are found small fragments of wood, very perfect when first dug up, but which soon decompose on being exposed to the air; and in the stratum of sand were found some extraordinary bones, particularly a jawbone of enormous size, of some unknown animal, with the teeth remaining in it. I was very eager to obtain a sight of this; and finding it had been carried to a neighbouring gentleman, I inquired of him, but learned that he had presented it, together with a huge thighbone, found in the same place, to Sir Ashton Lever, and it therefore is probably now in Parkinson's Museum.

The situation in which these weapons were found may tempt us to refer them to a very remote period indeed, even beyond that of the present world; but, whatever our conjectures on that head may be, it will be difficult to account for the stratum in which they lie being covered with another stratum, which, on that supposition, may be conjectured to have been once the bottom, or at least the shore, of the sea. The manner in which they lie would lead to the persuasion that it was [the] place of their manufacture and not of their accidental deposit; and the numbers of them were so great that the man who carried on the brickwork told me that, before he was aware of their being objects of curiosity, he had emptied baskets full of them into the ruts of the adjoining road. It may be conjectured that the different strata were formed by inundations happening at distant periods, and bringing down in succession the different materials of which they consist: to which I can only say that the ground in question does not lie at the foot of any higher ground, but does itself overhang a, tract of boggy earth, which extends under the fourth stratum; so that it should rather seem that torrents had washed away the incumbent strata and left the bog earth bare, than that the bog earth was covered by them, especially as the strata appear to be disposed horizontally, and present their edges to the abrupt termination of the high ground.

If you think the above worthy of notice to the Society, you will please to lay it before them.

I am Sir,
with great respect
Your faithful humble Servant,
*John Frere*

A remarkably clear and concise account whose consequences were obvious, once the concepts were in place. It ought to have led to a conceptual revolution, but this had to await the dogged persistence of Boucher de Perthes. Indeed, the significance of Frere's observations seems only to have registered when Prestwich, in his paper to the Royal Society on 26 May 1859, referred to it as additional evidence (to which *his* attention had been drawn by Evans) supporting de Perthes' claims. Even so, in this paper, an abstract of which appeared the next year in the *Proceedings of the Royal Society of London*, Prestwich was not unequivocal in the conclusions he drew from a comparison of Frere's site and finds with those of Saint-Acheul:

The author purposely abstains for the present from all theoretical considerations, confining himself to the corroboration of the facts:

1 That the flint implements are the work of man.
2 That they were found in undisturbed ground.
3 That they are associated with the remains of extinct Mammalia.
4 That the period was a late geological one, and anterior to the

surface assuming its present outline, so far as some of its minor features are concerned.

He does not, however, consider that the facts, as they at present stand, of necessity carry back Man in past time more than they bring forward the great extinct Mammals toward our own time, the evidence having reference only to relative and not to absolute time; and he is of the opinion that many of the later geological changes may have been sudden or of shorter duration than generally considered. In fact, from the evidence here exhibited, and from all that he knows regarding drift [i.e. surface] phenomena generally, the author sees no reason against the conclusion that this period of Man and the extinct mammals – supposing their contemporeity to be proved – was brought to a sudden end by a temporary inundation of the land; on the contrary, he sees much to support such a view on purely geological considerations.

(cited from Daniel 1968: 67)

So much for the paradigm switch to the new geology! Such switches seem always to be less sudden and much less complete than imagined later.

Other early reports, such as John McEnery's concerning Kent's Hole in Devon and Schmerling's at Liège, were resisted out of Bibliological prejudice, even by geologists, as Lyell's remarks on Schmerling in 1833 demonstrate: 'He has found human remains in breccia, embedded with extinct species, under circumstances far more difficult to get over than I have previously heard of . . .' (cited Stocking 1987: 72). As late as 1855 Lyell was still maintaining 'we have every [sic!] reason to believe that the human race is extremely modern' (ibid.: 73); but by 1858 circumstances arose which proved impossible 'to get over'. This was Brixham Cave, near Torquay and not far from Kent's Hole, newly opened by quarrying. Its excavation was overseen by an eminent committee, including no less than Charles Lyell, appointed by the Geological Society of London (Stocking 1987: 73). When those excavations revealed numerous human artefacts *in situ* with extinct animals (ibid.: 74), the case for human prehistory could no longer be resisted and Boucher de Perthes' earlier conclusions would have to be accepted. Indeed Lyell himself did so in his 1863 publication: *The Geological Evidences of the Antiquity of Man*.

In his Preface to *Marriage, Totemism and Religion: An Answer to Critics*, published in 1911, John Lubbock, Lord Avebury, wrote:

Rather more than fifty years ago I had the advantage of examining the river gravels of the Somme with Sir John Evans, Sir Joseph Prestwich, and Mr. Busk, and we convinced ourselves that the flint implements discovered and described by M. Boucher de Perthes were really of human workmanship.

Shortly afterwards I visited the Danish Shell Mounds, the Swiss Lake Dwellings, and the caves of the Dordogne, and described them in a series of articles in the *Natural History Review*, subsequently collecting and expanding them in my work *Prehistoric Times* (1865) and comparing the modes of life they indicated with those of existing savages.

So, rather than any one site or set of artefact associations or (museum) seriations or publication(s), it was this coming together of international evidences from the Palaeolithic, Mesolithic and Neolithic (and, as Lubbock states, its ethnographic parallels), that by the 1860s amounted to incontrovertible evidence for the antiquity of man, and for his organic and social evolution over long, that is, 'geological' time periods.

Indeed,

The first use of specific prehistorical dating, as distinct from the vaguer 'primaeval', came in the *Archaeological Journal* of 1870 with the use of the term megalithic, and in 1877 in the *Journal of the British Archaeological Association* again with a reference to the mega-lithic period. The two journals bore articles referring to the palaeo-lithic for the first time in 1880 and 1881 respectively. The gradual integration of prehistory and its eventual elevation to an almost defining role within archaeology was thus of major importance in determining the development of the subject in an academic context.

(Levine 1986: 95)

De Perthes' vindication by Evans, Prestwich and others, following on from the palaeontologist Hugh Falconer's visit to him in 1858, came at the Aberdeen meeting of the British Association for the Advancement of Science in 1859, the same year that Darwin's *Origin of Species* was published. However, by a bitter twist, de Perthes' finds of flint axes with a 'prehistoric' human jawbone at the pit of Moulin-Quignon in 1863, which were to have proved his full and final vindication, were shortly revealed by John Evans to be frauds perpetrated on Boucher by his own workmen.

Nonetheless the case was already made and a great conceptual block-age removed. For as Stocking (1987: 172) relates, 'it was only when Brixham Cave established the great antiquity of man, and Darwinism linked man to some antecedent form, that this interest was translated into a systematic investigation of human sociocultural origins'; that is, launched the modern social anthropological enterprise, subsuming and supplanting the earlier 'ethnological' (data-gathering) tradition associated

13

most notably with J.C. Pritchard, and also the long established tradition of philosophical anthropology. The new approach, at its formation epitomized by John McLennan (1827–81), Edward Burnett Tylor (1832–1917) and Sir John Lubbock (1834–1913), the latter a close friend and neighbour of Charles Darwin,[3] may be regarded as an outgrowth of the utilitarian tradition, with each of the three informed, for example, by John Stuart Mill's *Logic of the Moral Sciences* (Stocking 1987: 171).

The classical sociocultural evolutionists: McLennan, Tylor, Lubbock and his father-in-law after 1884, Lane Fox (Pitt-Rivers), regarded themselves as engaged on a single 'naturalistic' project, but subsequent generations have assigned the first two to be founding fathers of Social Anthropology, the last two of Archaeology.[4] Certainly Pitt-Rivers pioneered rigorous excavation techniques on inheriting the Cranborne Chase estates, and John Lubbock (MP) was largely responsible for the passing in 1882 of the Protection of Ancient Monuments Act (under which the first inspector was none other than Pitt-Rivers).

This formed the mental climate for the emergence of Archaeology as a discipline, but actual digging for antiquities did not, unfortunately, await such developments, nor for decades after did it really respond to them.[5] Not only had sporadic digging occurred in Europe prior to this, but by the 1840s major digs had even been undertaken in Egypt and Mesopotamia, the latter by names famous in their own times and subsequently, such as Paul Emile Botta and Henry Layard. For the Bible and the Classics, especially Homer, made known to educated nineteenth-century Europeans, names such as Babylon, Nineveh, Jericho and Troy. Here the antiquarian and the literary traditions fused in the endeavour to make legendary places and times palpable through the recovery of monuments and artefacts.

Antiquaries were those dilettantes (not a profession but an interest of men of education and means) who sought to unravel the meanings of monuments and reliques of past times (inferred either from older sources or from their manifest non-contemporaneity).[6] This could be considered merely an historical interest but it betokened more than this, for what aroused their curiosity (and a scientist is but someone with a trained curiosity) was the meaning of *objects* for which there was no evident purpose – such as 'antediluvial' hand-axes, fossils, meteorites – every type of object for which there was no manifest explanation. To such inspired empiricism Stonehenge or long barrows (in contrast, for example, to Roman forts or baths) were just unknown artefacts on a grand scale. As usual, the clearest exposition of the difference between traditional (literary) historians and antiquarians, is provided by Momigliano (1966: 3) who observes that:

(1) historians write in a chronological order; antiquaries write in a

systematic order; (2) historians produce those facts which serve to illustrate or explain a certain situation; antiquaries collect all the items that are connected with a certain subject, whether they help to solve a problem or not.

Antiquarianism is thus a form of 'pure research', while for most of its existence historical writing has served instrumental purposes: basically political or moral instruction, or indeed political justification, a purpose it still too often serves.

Whereas an historicist approach would endlessly have scoured texts for clues to the meanings of such artefacts, the archetypal antiquary wished to interrogate the objects themselves and to do this he had to go out of the library or the cabinet into the field to measure, sketch and try to find new artefacts that might throw light on his perplexity. This is not to say that antiquarians were antithetical to history or poorly read in it; on the contrary most were practitioners of both approaches. The novelty of antiquarianism, however, resides in its implicit assertion of the full autonomy and worth of the extra-textual, that is, the physical, despite the fact that 'no single methodology lent coherence to antiquarian work' (Levine 1986: 23).

Nonetheless, by the late seventeenth and early eighteenth centuries non-literary evidence (numismatics, diplomatics, epigraphy and iconography) had become, in Momigliano's words (1966: 16) 'especially authoritative'. So much so indeed that, in its concentration upon 'objective data' antiquarian approaches revolutionized what was considered to be the basis of reliable historical accounts.

And of course de Perthes was an antiquarian. As late as the mid-Victorian period, such a background was also that of Sir William Matthew Flinders-Petrie (1853–1942), the founder and longest-ever practitioner of scientific Egyptology (or indeed of any branch of field archaeology) who relates (1932: 8) that as a child

> From my mother's collection I soon knew a hundred minerals, and found garnet-granite and serpentine in the gutter-linings of the streets, which I howked up and chipped for specimens. I soaked in old Allan's *Mineralogy* till I knew every page of it, a delightful book not devitalized by abstract science. Minerals naturally led to testing specimens, and so to chemistry, and I collected the testings of every element I could get, to make comparative tables. I revelled also in dozens of pots and bottles with various messes, and in electro-typing, and tried everything that I could start on, out of Miller's *Inorganic Chemistry*.

Later,

> Stimulated by a bit of earthwork on Blackheath Common, where

15

we lived, I made myself a working sextant with cardboard and looking-glass, and then my father let me have his sextant, and I began planning earthworks. In pursuing this, I followed a plotting process more accurate than had been used before, with three-point survey. The detail of this I published long afterwards [1904] in *Methods and Aims in Archaeology*.

(ibid.: 13)

However, it is Petrie's *Inductive Metrology* of 1877 that Levine (1986: 89) designates 'a milestone' in the shift from *a priori* deduction to inductive analysis, by his exposition of rigorous quantitative methods, especially in surveying. Indeed, without exact survey methods there can be no archaeology, for there can be no proper (i.e. three-dimensional) excavation. And without the establishment of those three dimensions, the fourth, time, cannot logically be introduced.

Obviously one would have to be buffered from the exigencies of subsistence in order to pursue interests so apparently useless, which would accordingly have to be self-financed; and as Trigger (1990a: 56) has rightly remarked, both education and opportunity made antiquarianism properly so-called (as distinct from upper-class collections of *objets d'art*) a middle-class concern. C.J. Thomsen himself was the son of a merchant and supported himself through the family business; while one of Flinders-Petrie's grandfathers was the explorer after whom the Flinders Range, Island and River in Australia are named. Thus, although there was some interest from this quarter, it is not the case that antiquarianism was a pastime of the landed elite. On the contrary, the overwhelming majority of its practitioners were employed, but in occupations demanding higher education, not those requiring constant personal attendance or too much physical labour. Therefore, with an awareness of 'pasts' derived from a training in the classics (even 'grammar schools' meant Latin grammar), minds were open to the lure of objects that might relate to times, places and events referred to in classical or historical texts, or in the Bible, or beyond either.

Early efforts were largely literary:

The membership of the Academy for the Study of Antiquity and History founded in 1572, provides a commentary on the state of antiquarian studies in Elizabethan England. Here peers and country gentlemen, sat side by side with courtiers, heralds, lawyers, judges and MPs, meeting frequently (until they were dissolved by James I [in 1604] who suspected them of subversive purposes) to read and discuss papers on every aspect of British antiquities.

(Moir 1958: 783)

However, Moir (op. cit.: 782) points out that 'the emphases of these early works is topographical; their approach still largely uncritical. They contain in fact more or less whatever pleased their authors'; which is scarcely surprising since whatever profession the authors had, 'antiquarian' was not one of them, so the authors merely followed their own inclinations.

A comprehensive topographic work which ended this early phase by confining itself to field survey and excluding the usual mass of disparate information, was the *Britannia* (1586) of William Camden, a founding member of the Society of Antiquaries of London. Intended, as he said, 'to restore Britain to Antiquity and Antiquity to Britain', it necessarily included Scotland and Ireland, as well as Shetland and the Isles of Scilly. This made it

> impossible for him to see all this himself and he was therefore compelled to turn to a band of local correspondents, and to seek that cooperation of the country gentry which has always remained one of the most familiar characteristics of English antiquarian writing.
>
> For it was with a highly informed and critical public in mind, and frequently with their active support, that these works were written. An interest in antiquity, in genealogy or heraldry was the common pastime of the age, and numberless country gentlemen were engaged in the study of their locality. . . .
>
> For the investigation of origins fascinated more and more, and an informed interest in anything with an antiquarian flavour encouraged the advances made in all branches of antiquarian scholarship.
>
> (Moir 1958: 782)

Already in the seventeenth century a rational prehistory was being given to Man by the Bordelais Calvinist, Isaac de la Peyrère, who produced, in the words of his own title, *A Theological System upon the Pre-supposition that Men were Before Adam* (the 'Praeadamitae', 1655, London and Amsterdam). For there maintaining, *inter alia*, that the so-called 'stone thunderbolts' (lithic tools) were those of this 'pre-Adamic' race of humans, 'he and his book were seized by the Inquisition, the book publicly burnt in Paris, and the author forced to recant' (Daniel 1976: 37). Indeed, he was induced to retreat to a monastery while a flood of books and pamphlets sought to exorcise his thought.

Classical authors did not have to work in a monotheistic straight-jacket, and so Lucretius (Titus Lucretius Carus, *c.* 95–*c.* 55 BC), in his famous poem *De Rerum Natura*, which developed Epicurean materialism

17

into a coherent ('atomist') worldview, could straightforwardly posit an evolutionary stage of stones, wood and fire, being succeeded by one of copper that in turn gave way to iron. However, such a scheme's rediscovery in Europe depended in part upon the force of examples from living societies in other continents, whose practices could not be denied. Here the North American examples were especially potent, for there were a lot of Indians in sustained, centuries-long contact with a lot of literate Europeans, inducing Locke to remark that 'in the beginning all the world was [like] America' (cited Stocking 1987: 13).

Thus, as related by Daniel (1976: 37):

> In the year following the publication of de la Peyrère's book, Sir William Dugdale (1605–86) in his *The Antiquities of Warwickshire* (1656: 778) describes and illustrates a stone axe and refers to the finding of several of them 'curiously wrought by grinding in some such way . . . being at first so made by the native Britons . . . were made for use as weapons, inasmuch as they had not then attained to the knowledge of the working of iron or brass to such uses'. Dr. Robert Plot [1640–96, Dugdale's son-in-law], the first Keeper of the Ashmolean (in Oxford, probably the world's first public museum[7]) based on the collection of John Tradescant, published his *History of Staffordshire* in the year of Dugdale's death, and in it he had no doubt of the true nature of stone implements. He described an axe of speckled flint with a ground edge, saying that either the Britons, or Romans, or both made use of such axes, and says 'how they might be fashioned to a helve may be seen in the Museum Ashmoleanum, where there are several Indian ones of this kind fitted up in the same order as when formerly used'.

Further, the polymathic antiquarian Edward Lhwyd (1660–1708), who succeeded his tutor Dr Robert Plot as Keeper of the Ashmolean, wrote in 1699 after a tour of the Scottish Highlands in which he encountered arrowheads used by the natives as amulets:

> As to this *elf-stricking*, their opinion is, that the fairies (having not much power themselves to hurt animal bodies) do sometimes carry away men in the air, and furnishing them with bows and arrows, employ them to shoot men, cattle etc. I doubt not but you have often seen these Arrow-heads they ascribe to elfs or fairies: they are just the same chip'd flints the natives of New England head their arrows with at this day; and there are also several stone hatchets found in this kindom, not unlike those of the Americans . . .

(cited in Daniel 1968: 28)

## ARCHAEOLOGY'S FIRST PARADIGM – THE THREE AGES SYSTEM

The importance of museum collections, facilitating direct comparisons rather than relying on verbal accounts or rare illustrations, can clearly be noticed. Although such ideas as typological succession reflecting different phases of antiquity were about for centuries following the Renaissance, it was the need to make chronological sense of museum collections that was to prove decisive in establishing a basic temporal framework for archaeology. It is also logical that this should take place where (a) extensive, non-local collections were housed under one roof; and (b) where classical literary presuppositions did not swamp the artefacts, since this area had not been part of the Roman Empire.

Such an area was Scandinavia, specifically Denmark, and the conceptual apparatus is basically the work of Christian Jurgensen Thomsen, in charge of the recently formed (1807) National Museum in Copenhagen, inspired by Rasmus Nyerup's protests (in a book – *Oversyn over Faedrelandets Mindesmaerker fra Oltiden* – published in 1806) at the destruction of the nation's monuments. Nonetheless even there Nyerup confessed that 'everything which has come down to us from heathendom is wrapped in a thick fog; it belongs to a space of time which we cannot measure'.

To Thomsen the numismatist and man of independent means, we owe the first application of the 'Three Age System' of Stone (Palaeolithic, Neolithic), Copper (Chalcolithic), and Iron.[8] For as Daniel (1976: 39) states:

> One can be sure that in England, despite Plot, Dugdale, Lyttleton and Frere, no specific concept of three technological ages emerged [prior to Thomsen], and that Colt Hoare, after ten years of digging barrows in Wiltshire, was forced to confess 'total ignorance as to the authors of those sepulchral memorials: we have evidence of the very high antiquity of the Wiltshire barrows, but none respecting the tribes to whom they appertained that can rest on solid foundations'.

Colt Hoare, an indefatigable fieldworker, was a contemporary of Thomsen. Yet, in a letter of 1825 to the antiquarian J.G. Busching, Thomsen could write:

> It seems clear to me that in an early period, all of northern Europe – Scandinavia, most of Germany, France and England – was inhabited by actually very similar and very primitive races. They were war-like, lived in the forest, were not acquainted with metals (or only sparingly so), divided themselves into large groups, and

were partly slain, partly subjugated and partly pushed back into hinterlands and remote areas.

(Rodden 1981: 58–9)

So why did the promulgation of such a system have to await the publication of Thomsen's museum guidebook in 1836? (The book was called *Ledetraad til Nordisk Oldkyndighed*, which appeared in English in 1848 as *A Guide to Northern Antiquities*). If Colt Hoare could be so much in the dark, the formulation of the Three Age System could not be a matter of 'obvious common sense', though that is what we take it to be now, as indeed the concept of 'prehistory' as such. From the early 1820s, when the National Museum moved from the library of Copenhagen University to the royal palace of Christianborg, Thomsen had grouped the artefacts of Stone, 'Brass' or Bronze and Iron Ages into separate rooms (Daniel 1981: 59). In the *Ledetraad*, he defined the periods as:

*The Age of Stone*, or that period when weapons and implements were made of stone, wood, bone, or some other kind of [natural] material, and during which very little or nothing was known of metals. . . .

*The Age of Bronze*, in which weapons and cutting implements were made of copper or bronze, and nothing at all, or very little was known of iron or silver. . . .

*The Age of Iron* is the third and last period of the heathen, in which iron was used for those articles to which that metal is eminently suited, and in the fabrication of which it came to be employed as a substitute for bronze.

(cited in Daniel 1981: 59)

Thomsen's insight was manifest, not only in seeing that the materials characterizing his Ages successively supplemented without necessarily replacing those previously used; but also in his most perceptive observation that, concerning northern Europe:

No instance is known to us of writing being found on any specimen belonging to the Bronze Age, although the workmanship in other respects evinces such a degree of skill as would lead us to suppose that the art of writing could not have been unknown at that period.

(cited in Daniel 1968: 84)

Thomsen's scheme was, however, persuasive because it was not merely a nominal sequence, but a set of stages formed from find-associations, and therefore related materials *within* periods at the same time as differentiating *between* periods. Thus,

Thomsen knew, for instance, that silver was used in the Iron Age,

20

but never in the Bronze Age or Stone Age. But he also knew that gold, like bronze, was already in use in the Bronze Age and even as early as during the transition from the Stone Age to the Bronze Age, and that the use of bronze continued into the Iron Age (Thomsen 1836: 32, 58ff; 1848: 30, 64ff). He dated glass vessels in the Iron Age but he also noted that glass beads had not been used in the Bronze Age and even in the Stone Age (1836: 38, 60ff; 1848: 64ff, 68). He had observed that amber was used in the Stone Age . . . and that pottery had been produced during each of the three ages . . .

(Gräslund 1981: 47–8)

In other words, his was a directly operational scheme, not merely a notional one about 'what must have been', or 'what we may safely assume'.

So why was archaeology's first, and still basic paradigm, developed then and in Denmark? Gräslund (1981: 547–8) answers that

The Copenhagen museum simply was the only museum at that time where you could easily get a survey of sufficient prehistoric material from a large enough area to allow for a chronological synthesis. Christian Jurgensen Thomsen was the first person ever to have had this opportunity and he also had the qualifications to make use of the situation.

It is therefore not coincidental that the world's first professional archae-ologist – Jens Jacob Asmussen Worsaae (1821–85) – started out as Thomsen's assistant at the National Museum, subsequently becoming its Director, Inspector General of Antiquities in Denmark and also Professor of Archaeology at the University of Copenhagen (Daniel 1968: 85).

However, a paradigm does not a discipline make. That requires the existence of parallel knowledges that illuminate other areas of the natu-ral and social world (e.g. geology and anthropology), plus specific institutional supports, such as learned journals and universities, where different disciplines can be pursued together. Behind, and as a condition of these, however, there must exist a cultural climate which sees the world as open to and, positively benefiting from, the acquisition of new knowledge.[9] All of those were coming together in Europe during the second half of the nineteenth century, but the developed discipline of archaeology would still have to develop a corpus of practical technique which would then have to be imposed upon excavators through train-ing, peer-pressure and public opinion. This signally failed to happen during the nineteenth century, and was only realized with great diffi-culty and unevenness in the twentieth century. Central to the problem was the ideological barrier that could (perhaps grudgingly) admit an evolution of forms of *society*, since such a sequence could be fitted into a post-Garden-of-Eden scheme (either of degeneration or ascent or both, for more and less-favoured 'nations'); the real stumbling-block was the *evolution of Man into society from a position in (even at the top of) the animal world*, for that conception removes mankind from a 'specially created' condition and inserts him into the 'natural order' with the flora, fauna and geomorphology upon which all depends.

Thus Stocking (1987: 41) in his history of Victorian anthropology, writes that

> however much of Victorian sociocultural evolutionism was implicit in [J.S.] Mill's program, it was not yet evolutionist in the biological sense. The environmental plasticity of the human mind did not imply its simian origin. Few British [or indeed any!] thinkers in this period publicly entertained such a notion, and the most notable advocate – the Scotsman Robert Chambers – published his work anonymously. The controversy precipitated in 1844 by his *Vestiges of the Natural History of Creation* is thus a final crucial element in contextualizing the problem of civilization on the eve of Darwinism.

Chambers's *Vestiges* saw the origin of man and the early progress of human civilization as part of a broader, cosmic developmental sequence in which it had 'pleased Providence to arrange that one species should give birth to another, until the second highest gave birth to man'. But such manifest deism did not save Chambers from violent attack, and although both Darwin and Huxley found the biological argument naïve in the extreme, the reaction of many scientists was clearly conditioned by non-scientific ideological factors. As the geologist Adam Sedgewick, writing in the *Edinburgh Review* in 1845, put it, 'the world cannot bear to be turned upside down'. The 'glorious maidens and matrons' of Britain must not 'poison the springs of joyous thought and modest feeling' by listening to the 'seductions' of an author who argued that

> their Bible is a fable when it teaches them that they were made in the image of God – that they are the children of apes and the breeders of monsters – that he has *annulled all distinction between the physical and the moral* – and that all the phenomena of the universe
> (original emphasis)

were merely 'the progression and development of a rank, unbending, and degrading materialism'. If the *Vestiges* were true 'the labours of sober induction are in vain; religion is a lie, human law is a mass of folly [and] morality is moonshine'.[10]

And this in 1844, long after the specific political context had ceased to exist that, with counter-revolutionary paranoia and reactionary Bibliolatry, had caused the reviling of Erasmus Darwin during the Napoleonic Wars, and William Lawrence (for his *Lectures on the Natural History of Man* (1819)) even after war had ended. Nonetheless, the attention which its odium drew upon Chambers's *Vestiges* caused it to go through twenty editions by 1860 (Stocking 1987: 45); and by then, as the latter remarks, the cultural context was rapidly changing.

## OFFICIALS, MUSEUMS AND EXCAVATORS

Flinders-Petrie first went to Egypt in 1880 to survey the pyramids in order to check the bizarre obscurantist notions of a family friend who was Astronomer Royal for Scotland, Piazzi Smyth.[11] This particular piece of pyramidiocy (currently in print!) was disproved by actual measurement: Flinders-Petrie stayed on to excavate, horrified by the despoliation all around him. Peasants dug sites to use mud-brick and organic remains for fertilizer (*sebakh*) and stone for houses. If they found artefacts made of precious metals they could be sold for their bullion value. Other artefacts could be sold on the antiquities market. But the European excavators, often acting for museums, were little better, interested mainly in *objets d'art*, the more exotic the better, and not caring what they wrecked in getting them.

Even the British Museum was not exempt; on the contrary, when Flinders-Petrie, a model of energy and integrity, in 1887 found excellently preserved iron tools from around 600 BC in the Delta,

> All the best were sent to the British Museum, and on my enquiring to see them, some years later, I was told that 'Mr. Newton said they were ugly things and he did not want them, so they were thrown away'. All the other examples were thrown away in a general smash-up of the objects which I had arranged for distribution. The perils of discoveries are by no means over when they reach a museum. Thing after thing has been spoilt, lost, or thrown away after it seemed safely housed.
>
> (Petrie 1932)

Flinders-Petrie, who was self-financed and who only associated with Miss Amelia Edwards's Egypt Exploration Fund (she opposed him at the outset) in order to obtain some official status, was under no obligation to supply the British Museum. Yet the curse of the 'Fine Arts' was upon them all, since all museums saw themselves, in their heart of hearts, as art galleries. Accordingly, Petrie (1932: 86) states:

> The ideas of museum management are a serious danger. In one of our larger English museums, a great number of necklaces were all

hung up in pretty festoons, and the labels neatly stacked in the corner of the glass case. After some years I was asked to sort them out, and settle which was which. In another museum they imitated the British Museum and the Louvre, in plastering up stone tablets against the walls, where the damp works through and brings all the salt out on the face, and the sculpture perishes in powder. Sculpture has also had scant treatment at the hands of the Treasury. Franks applied for many years for a grant to glaze over the Indian sculptures on the staircase, but was always refused. At last he paid for the glazing himself, at a cost of £500. Such an interference with fiscal authority was not to be tolerated, and he received a severe letter, winding up with the desire that such irregularity should not occur again.

Museums in the countries of origin were yet worse, even those instituted and run by Europeans, as was that of Egypt under Auguste Mariette, appointed 'Conservator of Egyptian Monuments' in 1858. As Director of the Antiquities Service until 1881, Mariette and his successors, Maspero and Grébaut, required all antiquities to be cleared by them through Cairo, whether the finds came from rigorously exact excavations by Flinders-Petrie, or the horde of pillaging antiquity-seekers whom they licensed to ransack sites, when they were not 'excavating' on their own account. Thus, according to Flinders-Petrie (Petrie 1932: 25) in 1881

Mariette most rascally blasted to pieces all the fallen parts of the granite temple [at Gizeh] by a large gang of soldiers, to clear it out instead of lifting the stones and replacing them by means of tackle. The savage indifference of the Arabs, who have even stripped the alabaster off the granite temple since Mariette uncovered it, and who are not at all watched here, is partly superseded by a most barbaric sort of regard for the monuments by those in power. Nothing seems to be done with any uniform and regular plan, work is begun and left unfinished; no regard is paid to future requirements of exploration, and no civilized or labour-saving appliances are used. It is sickening to see the rate at which everything is being destroyed, and the little regard paid to preservation.

Of course, similar vandalism characterized most nineteenth-century excavations – the mid-century activities of Hormuzd Rassam in Assyria are notorious, and even Botta and Layard's methods were more destructive than productive – yet they were well-intentioned pioneers. In Egypt, matters were worse due to the very accessibility and visibility of ancient monuments. Egyptian antiquities were accessible because Egypt was part of the Mediterranean littoral, with easy river access inland, in contrast to Mesopotamia, geographical and political access to which was always difficult. Thus, in his first year in Egypt (1881) Flinders-Petrie observed at the Gizeh pyramids visitors' graffiti, over sixty of which were earlier than 1700. The problems consequent upon easy access are exacerbated because in the Nile Valley itself, monuments and artefacts are overlain by fine particulate sand which is all too easy to clear away.

This antiquity-hunting resulted in an attitude compounding the worst aspects of *laissez-faire* and fickle autocracy, reflected in both the resources of the Cairo museum and the conduct of its officials. They gathered the choice pieces they fancied, let rot what they could not be bothered with, and sold, through well-known local dealers, much that would fetch good prices on the antiquities market.    Just one encounter of many by Flinders-Petrie occurred in 1888. Having spent his usual eighteen-hour days excavating in the Fayum (a large depression to the west of the Nile Valley)

> the cargo to Cairo was sixty cases. At the Museum, Grébaut as usual delayed, the cases were laid out in the garden, without any cover, a violent storm came on, and next morning I found them standing in three inches of water. To wet such perishable organic material was almost fatal, yet to take out wet mummies to dry was impossible, as there was no shelter.
>
> The charges imposed by the Museum in a single year would have paid for a shelter, yet so far as I know, antiquities taken to the department for examination have never [written 1932!] been protected from the storms frequent about May, nor put under lock for the night. I went back by long sea [route] with the cases, and had several out on deck and dried the mummies in the sun.
>
> (Petrie 1932: 88–9)

As Flinders-Petrie wrote in his diary at the time:

> When passing the things [for export], Grébaut appreciated the portraits immensely, insomuch that he bagged all the finest female portraits and the two best men. He took a dozen in all, and we had not one left which could compete with the best half dozen of his. When he had apparently done, I asked if he was now content; he hesitated, and then said that 'he once knew a young lady like that', and therefore took one more of the best. He also took the whole of the finest textiles.
>
> (op. cit.: 89)

Despite papyrus finds of the very greatest significance, for example parts of the *Iliad* and Plato and Euripides (1887–9), Flinders-Petrie was no better served by scholars than by museum functionaries. Having found two large and perfect Byzantine land deeds in 1889, he 'lent them to Sayce[12] to publish, [who] deposited them for safety in the Bodleian Library, and since then they have not been found' (ibid.: 97). This, however, was all too tragically typical. For example, excavating houses of Roman age in the Delta in 1884, and by his usual fastidiousness having saved baskets-full of carbonized papyri, he got them to London: 'one, copied by Griffith, was a unique schoolbook of signs with their names; the other, copied by me, was a design for astronomical and geographical decoration of a temple' (ibid.: 51). However,

> Of demotic [Egyptian] papyri there were 228, beside 38 Greek. These were then sent to Revillot, whom Poole much admired. He never did anything with them, and though several times in the last forty years I have tried to get some of the Committee of the Exploration Fund to make enquiries and claim the papyri, no one would ever take the trouble. The greater part of results of the year were therefore wasted.
>
> (ibid.)

And that year (1884), as ever, the Cairo officials were greedy for their cut:

> Maspero was agreeable about the larger things that I produced, but he and Brugsch [Keeper of the Cairo Museum] were greedy for small valuables; two good figures of apes, in sets of figures, were both taken, though I counted eighteen already in the museum. A silver chain and various other nice things were also kept. The objects which I was allowed to retain I showed in London, at the first of a long series of annual exhibitions which has done much to educate and interest the public.
>
> (op. cit.: 51)

One often hears archaeologists (and anthropologists too) disparage any suggestion that they ought to expend some effort to 'educate and interest the public'; the excuse being lack of time and/or money. For his entire adult life Flinders-Petrie was far busier than they would ever be, and he also found time, and his own money (£60–80 on each) to mount his own public exhibitions. To put this into perspective; in the early 1890s he had 'only £110 of fixed income for living and travelling, and precarious additions from museums in return for some things in my share of antiquities' (op. cit.: 132), at which point he had already sunk £100 in publications; and in 1891 alone, anticipated spending a further £150 for publication (ibid.: 133). The income from booksales took years to even approach what he had earlier expended on publication.

In 1890 a row blew up in London and Cairo over the ransacking of Egypt and the complicit role of the Antiquities Department in this. Matters were brought to a head in Cairo by Grébaut, Director of the

Department of Antiquities, changing the regulations to make excavation even harder for archaeologists, but easier for dealers, who were more accommodating. This was just too much, so after much politicking the notorious Museum Committee was shelved and Flinders-Petrie's proposals adopted instead: '*sans pareil* definition [of things taken for the Museum], compulsory presentation to Museums, publication, and an alternative for dealers of giving half to Government' (ibid.: 123). As a consequence, 'We have definitely pushed archaeology into the political situation as a thing to be guarded, and not to be thrown away' (ibid.: 124). We could do with his unswerving dedication and integrity in Britain now. Unfortunately however, whereas James Henry Breasted founded Chicago's Oriental Institute to continue and extend his own painstaking work in Palestine, Flinders-Petrie left no equivalent in Britain (University College, London, does however, possess a Petrie Museum of Egyptian Archaeology – not the same thing). Yet he it was who, amongst other things (such as the recovery of so many papyri and demonstrating the evolution of the pyramids from the mastaba), alone recognized the true nature of Mycenaean pottery in Egypt and dated it correctly; confirmed Herodotus on the seventh-century Greek settlements of Daphne and Naucratis; excavated Egyptian, Greek, and Roman houses, some in whole villages; excavated also Akhenaten's capital, Tell el Amarna, on whose texts (found by a peasant woman) we are dependent for most information on Great Power relations during the Bronze Age; and between 1894 and 1897 at Qift (on the western side of the Nile north of Thebes) at Deshasheh and at Dendera north of Cairo, discovered the first prehistoric cultures of Egypt, notably that named after Naqada (near Thebes), developing the process of pottery sequencing to date them, a procedure which became the central technique of archaeology. In addition to his crucial emphasis on pottery and small finds, the list could go on for his unmatched three-quarters of a century in archaeology, in every year of which he made significant contributions, not the least being the training of generations of archaeologists. 'On the whole . . . the general cultural sequence that Petrie worked out has stood the test of time remarkably well' (Trigger *et al.* 1983: 5). He ought to be a national hero on the strength of any one of those achievements, made substantive by the establishment of a well-funded Oriental Institute bearing his name.

## THE SOCIAL PRECONDITIONS FOR ARCHAEOLOGY

From this we can see the sort of milieu from which archaeology eventually emerged at the end of the nineteenth century. It is, again, the peculiar synthesis of the historical with the artefactual that generates the need for new factual sources, necessarily extra-textual. Thus archaeological thinking, with its long and slow evolution, could not have had the early start that Anthropology gained from the Greek historians and geographers, notably Herodotos (*c.* 484–*c.* 420 BC) 'the father of history' (and, logically, the first to write a major work in prose); and Strabo (*c.* 63 BC–AD 21 or later) the 'father of systematic geography' (Herodotos also discussed geographical topics). Being organized into competing city-states (*poleis*) no two of which were alike in their social morphology, Greeks were alert to social variation within the Greek-speaking world, and even more so between it and their neighbours, notably Persia and Egypt. Indeed Herodotos devoted a whole book to Egypt and no less than nine books to the wars between Persia and Greece, analysing them as a clash of sociocultural morphologies.

Curiosity about, and a certain openness to, different forms of social organization are then sufficient to generate ethnological accounts, once the conceptual apparatus has been put in place by literacy. In Greece this had occurred late in the eight Century BC (cf. Maisels 1990: Appendix E), and as early as the *Works and Days* of Hesiod (*floruit c.* 700 BC) a small-farmer and writer is trying to conceptualize successive social states in the descent from a Golden Age. By the time of the Roman historian Tacitus (*c.* AD 55–*c.* 120) we find the myth of the 'noble savage' (Britons and Germans) already developed in his works *Germania* and *Agricola*, describing the conquest of those remote regions (his *Annals* and *Histories* were not recovered until the Renaissance).

However, it is the opinion of Evans-Pritchard (1981: 3) that Social Anthropology begins with Montesquieu (1689–1755), thanks to

> his insistence on the scientific, comparative study of society; the use of the data of as many societies as possible; the inclusion of primitive societies as examples of certain types of social systems; a need to start with classification or taxonomy of societies based on significant criteria – the way zoology and botany, for example have begun; the idea of inter-consistency between social facts (social systems), and that any social fact can only be understood by reference to other social facts and environmental conditions, as part of a complex whole; and the idea of this interconsistency being of a functional kind. Also we find clearly stated in the *L'Esprit des Lois* the idea of social structure and of dominant values which operate through a structure.
>
> (op. cit.: 11)

Commenting on Kames (1696–1782), Evans-Pritchard (ibid.: 14–15) remarked that to some extent it could be said 'that all the Scottish moral philosophers wrote the same books' (cf. Stocking 1975), so what he found in Kames can also be found in some form in the others, namely:

28

his basic criteria for a classification of types of society are bionomic, based on modes of production such as hunting and collecting, pastoral, and agricultural; and like Ferguson, Condorcet, and others, he makes . . . the point that as population increases various social consequences follow.

And while Adam Ferguson's *Essay on the History of Civil Society* (1776) embodies many of the basic assumptions of modern social anthropology, in the estimation of Evans-Pritchard (1981: 20) it is in John Millar's *The Origin and Distinction of Ranks* that we find the use of the Comparative Method[13] to classify societies into four distinct types or conditions: hunters and fishers, pastoralists, agriculturalists, and the 'commercial' (Evans-Pritchard 1981: 30). But while Ferguson conceived of unilineal social evolution whereby societies moved at different rates (or not at all) down one set course of advance, Millar did not. Accordingly the *Origin* is 'in many respects nearer to a modern sociological treatise than any other eighteenth century book' (Evans-Pritchard 1981: 33).

However, while John Millar established his 'modes of production' as a potential basis for the emergence of social anthropology in the next century, no such organizing framework was yet available to archaeology. Indeed, there was as yet no archaeology. In 1799 the French expeditionary forces in Egypt uncovered, and immediately recognized the importance of, the Rosetta Stone, a metre-high slab of basalt on which was inscribed the same message – a decree issued at Memphis by Ptolemy V – in three scripts: Greek and Egyptian hieroglyphic and demotic. Of course the Greek, well-known since the Renaissance, was to prove the key to the hitherto unread Egyptian, which by 1822 had been largely deciphered by Jean-François Champollion from Figeac. But the Rosetta Stone (lost to France on the abandonment of Egypt, but now in the British Museum) was discovered by accident during building, not archaeological operations, at Fort Julien (near Rosetta). Yet the Commission 'studied and measured every [*sic*] site and every visible monument, and finally published their great work, *La Description de l'Egypt*, which appeared between 1809 and 1816' (Montet 1964: 286). In Rome too, between 1809 and 1814, great archaeological works were undertaken by the French.

While antiquarianism – the collection of 'simply interesting or curious' data about the past – can be said to have its origins in Greece during the late fifth century BC in the work of Hippias, Hellanicus, Damastes and Charon, who 'collected traditions of the past and took pleasure in erudition as such' (Momigliano 1966: 4), archaeology as such – that is as an excavating discipline – like the natural sciences had to await the emergence of instrumentalities: interlocking apparatuses, conceptual and practical.

# 3

# DIGGING BEFORE EXCAVATION

I

When, in the first of seven editions of his book *Pre-historic Times, as Illustrated by Ancient Remains, and the Manners and Customs of Modern Savages* (1865), Sir John Lubbock (1834–1913) introduced the distinction between Old and New Stone Ages, that is between Palaeolithic and Neolithic, the English-speaking world had already accepted the new way of thinking about antiquity using the 'Ages System'. However, this was not the position in the German-speaking world, where, as late as the 1880s, scholars were unwilling to accept the idea of distinct Bronze and Iron Ages (Graslund 1981: 49), despite Thomsen's *Ledetraad* having been translated into German only a year after its publication in Danish. Indeed for nationalistic reasons 'the Germans maintained their opposition to the system more or less to the end of the century, although the number and importance of the antagonists decreased' (Sklenar 1983: 88–9). This while the great Swedish archaeologist Oscar Montelius (1843–1921), in the 1880s and 1890s was subdividing Neolithic, Bronze and Iron Ages into periods by the seriation of closed finds, and thus forming clusters of association that in turn enabled him to establish regional and pan-European chronologies (Trigger 1989: 157).

The probable reason for this is that Britain was the country then pioneering Anthropology as a discipline, and the early archaeologists were either anthropologists themselves, or were close friends of and in continuous contact with the seminal evolutionary anthropologists of the 1860s and after.[1] Among such were McLennan, Tylor, Lubbock and Lane Fox (who became Pitt-Rivers); the first two now assigned as founding fathers of Social and Cultural Anthropology, the last two of Archaeology. Thus speaking of the Anthropological Institute of Great Britain and Ireland – formed during 1871 from a merger of the populist Anthropological Society with the older and now Darwinian Ethnological Society – Stocking (1987: 261) remarks that

For the first decade of its existence during which Lane Fox was the leading figure, the Journal was so heavily archaeological that presidents of the Institute (themselves predominantly archaeologists) were occasionally somewhat apologetic. When an exploration committee was founded in 1875, it was for archaeological enquiries, and a number of the research committees organized by the anthropological section of the British Association were also archaeological.

Lubbock was made Lord Avebury, after the famous henge site which he studied and later bought to secure against despoliation. In the same year as *Prehistoric Times* first appeared (1865), E.B. Tylor, generally regarded as the founding father of Social Anthropology, published his seminal work *Researches into the Early History of Mankind.* In the spring of 1868 Lubbock delivered a series of lectures at the Royal Institution, which described 'the social and mental condition of savages, their art, their systems of marriage and of relationship, their religions, language, moral character and laws' (Preface to *The Origin of Civilization and the Primitive Condition of Man*, 1870). Published only one year before Tylor's *Primitive Culture*, which is usually reckoned to be the *Grundrisse* of Social Anthropology (Radin 1958: xiv–xv [Introduction to Tylor 1871]), Lubbock's subject-matter was the same as the leading anthropologists of his day, especially Tylor, whose 'remarkable work on the Early History of Mankind, more nearly resembles that which I have sketched out for myself' (Lubbock 1870: vii). Accordingly Lubbock cites contemporary anthropologists throughout, as well as their predecessors of the Franco-Scottish Enlightenment, notably Kames's *History of Man* and Montesquieu's *Esprit des Lois*, 'both of them works of great interest, although written at a time when our knowledge of savage races was even more imperfect that it is now' (op. cit.: vii).

Lubbock grossly fails, however, to cite his contemporary Daniel Wilson, whose two works: *The Archaeology and Prehistoric Annals of Scotland* (1851) and *Prehistoric Man* (1862) 'developed the framework of a science of prehistory' and whose ideas Lubbock shamefully cribbed (Kehoe 1991: 472). Thus while 'In contrast to John Lubbock's cobbled together *Prehistoric Times*, Wilson's book [*Prehistoric Man*] is well organized', Kehoe (1991: 472) explains. 'In *Prehistoric Man*', he continues,

> the systematics of ethnographic comparison are laid out to comp-
> lement the systematics of archaeology already presented. A
> marked difference between Wilson's work and that of Lubbock
> and, to a lesser degree Tylor, is that Wilson's use of the compara-
> tive method involved field experience on both sides of the pro-
> cedure [i.e., both archaeological and ethnological fieldwork]. His
> statements are clearly tempered by his firsthand observations of
> Ojibwa on the western Ontario frontier and of prehistoric sites in

the American Midwest. Lubbock and Tylor read *Prehistoric Man*; Tylor cited it, as well as *The Archaeology and Prehistoric Annals of Scotland* in his *Primitive Culture* (1871: 187, 265). Lubbock, reviewing *Prehistoric Man* in conjunction with four Smithsonian Institution publications on North American archaeology in the January 1863 *Natural History Review*, failed to list it with the other publications or give its title in the footnotes.

(Kehoe 1991: 472–3)

Due, however, to his position in London society and Wilson's as an outsider (Edinburgh and Toronto), Lubbock got himself recognized as a 'founding-father', while Wilson, who even introduced the term *prehistory* into English usage in 1851, has been consistently ignored.

What made Tylor the founding father of Social Anthropology was how he defined its subject-matter: as Culture. Indeed the term 'primitive culture', in the sense we now understand it as describing what is characteristic because enduring and thus socially structuring, is the significance that he gave to the concept of *culture*, enabling it then to serve as the organizing principle of a discipline to which his predecessors and contemporaries (such as Maine, Morgan and McClennan) made specific, but not decisive contributions. The definition of Culture, accordingly, constitutes the very opening lines of Tylor's *Primitive Culture*:

Culture *or Civilization*, taken in its wide ethnographic sense, is that complex whole which includes knowledge, belief, art, morals, law, custom, and any other capabilities and habits acquired by man as a member of society.

(1958 edn: 1; my emphasis)

This is the core concept for the practice of Social Anthropology. But that it can also serve Palaeoanthropology (Prehistory/Archaeology) in that capacity, is immediately apparent from the ensuing lines:

The condition of culture among the various societies of mankind, in so far as it is capable of being investigated on general principles, is a subject apt for the study of laws of human thought and action. On the one hand, the uniformity which so largely pervades civilization may be ascribed, in general measure, to the uniform action of uniform causes: while on the other hand its various grades may be regarded as stages of development or evolution, each the outcome of previous history, and about to do its proper part in shaping the history of the future. To the investigation of these two great principles in several departments of ethnography, with especial consideration of the civilization of the lower tribes as related to the civilization of the higher nations, the present volumes are devoted.

(ibid.)

Thus reports from contemporary societies of the simpler sort were to be concentrated, compared and analysed to determine their organizing principles ('the uniformity which so largely pervades civilization'); they could then be used to analyse both contemporary complex societies and historic ones of greater or lesser degrees of complexity. The relevance of this to an emerging discipline of archaeology is obvious; that is, to a discipline which wishes to recover lost forms of society from artefactual evidence, and is not merely seeking curios and *objets d'art* from past time. Indeed, Tylor, in his Preface to the second edition (1873), declares that his success depended upon 'collecting wide and minute evidence, so that readers may have actually before them the means of judging the theory put forward'. He reacts to comments on the absence of discussion of the works of Darwin or Herbert Spencer (whose *Theory of Evolution*, in which social life is made analogous to organic life in its development of complexity through time, was published in 1852), by saying that *Primitive Culture* relies on ethnographic evidence for its argument and conclusions. Similarly Darwin, aware of, and no doubt affected by the writings of Lamarck, Buffon, and most of all, his grandfather Erasmus's *Zoonomia*, nonetheless derived his hypothesis of descent with modification through the natural selection of numerous successive, slight, favourable variations, 'like a true scientist, through his own dealings with Nature, patiently pursued through more than twenty years, in the light of what was at first a wild surmise, but which was verified at every turn by the facts' (Willey 1961: 10).

Previous generations produced more or less helpful conjectures, but it was a sufficiency of information allowing a new factual edifice to be constructed, 'selecting against' the less well-grounded hypotheses, that enabled natural and social evolution to be rendered scientific almost simultaneously, and in the process constituting anthropology and archaeology as disciplines.

## II

Not only were *Prehistoric Times* and the *Early History of Mankind* both published in 1865, but as already mentioned, the Palestine Excavation Fund (PEF) was formed that year, constituting the first permanent archaeological research body (the Egyptian Fund was formed in 1882). That Palestine should be so selected was, in the nineteenth-century context, almost inevitable. At university even Darwin was intended for the ministry and Woolley (born 1880) was the son of a reluctant clergy-man. Piggott (1981: 20) notes that already in the seventeenth and eigh-teenth centuries, 'the Mosaic narrative seems to have been regarded more as an historical document far earlier than, but comparable to, Herodotus or Livy, than as divine revelation'. The more so in the nineteenth century when much superior means of travel and communi-cation made exploration and physical investigation increasingly attract-ive.[2] So to illuminate the 'historicity' of Biblical accounts, the Palestine Excavation Fund aimed to launch its activities with a campaign right at the heart of the Holy Land, namely in Jerusalem. The consequences of this decision have been graphically described by a former Director of Excavations for the Fund, R.A.S. Macalister. As what he critically remarks about his own organization's activities applies equally to other nineteenth-century campaigns, his observations in *A Century of Excavation in Palestine* (1925: 31–4) deserve quotation without editing:

> The claims of Jerusalem for special attention were too insistent to be disregarded; with the exuberance of enthusiastic youth, the society boldly tackled some of its obscurest problems. It is easy – and proverbially futile – to be wise after the event. While we recognise this, we must yet permit ourselves to describe the premature assault on Jerusalem as a fundamental mistake. One of the many minor sites in the country should have been attacked first, and worked out thoroughly, in order to learn the general character and chronology of the antiquities of the country. *Excavation is necessarily destructive. Facts are torn from the ground, to be transferred to the explorer's notebook. If not so transferred they are lost for ever.* If the excavator has not sufficient knowledge to interpret the facts, their value is proportionately diminished. In 1867 nothing was known about the development of pottery in the country, which is now recognised as being the chief clue to the dating of Palestinian sites and strata. Without potsherds, there is little or nothing to discriminate between a wall of 100 BC and a wall of 2000 BC: there is marvellously little difference in the masonry. A site of first importance, such as Jerusalem, ought therefore to have been left alone, until the excavators had learnt their business on the *corpus vile* of some place less important, the destruction of which would have involved less serious loss.
>
> A further mistake was made in the instructions issued to Lt. Warren [afterwards Sir Charles Warren] who had been selected to carry out the work at Jerusalem. It was expected that the projected excavations would settle, once and for all, the controversies regarding the Holy Places. A programme sufficient for several lifetimes was laid before the man who was to work for three years.

It is almost pathetic to look back to those early days, and to read the eager hopes that problems of this nature would be solved by the expenditure of a few hundreds of pounds, and the turning over of some spadefuls of earth. But the essential mistake lay not so much in the magnitude of these expectations, as in the drawing up of a definitely conceived programme, of whatever nature. A true excavator will attack his chosen site with but one intention – to find out what it contains. Few questions are more irritating, and more unanswerable, than the stock enquiry which any excavator may expect to be asked by any casual tourist who happens to pay him a visit – 'What do you expect to find?' An obsession as to what ought to be in a site will blind the excavator as to what is actually there. In his disappointment at unrealised hopes, he is apt to forget the gifts, often rich enough, that the gods actually send him. We can give striking illustration of this from Ireland. Certain worthy folk got it into their heads that the Israelite Ark of the Covenant lay hidden under one of the mounds on Tara Hill, where, they professed to believe, it had been concealed by the prophet Jeremiah. We shall leave the reader the pleasure of making the comments appropriate to a theory of this kind, and merely record the facts of the case. In the pursuit of this chimaera they dug up and destroyed the mound. They did not find the Ark, but, it is understood, they did find certain objects or structures which would have been of value for local history. Not being interested in local history, they paid no heed to them, and these were lost. It is almost a universal experience that an excavation will mock the expectations that are entertained of it, while at the same time give the excavator rewards of which he never dreamed, if only one is prepared to receive them.

(my emphasis)

This should prove salutary to those for whom 'problem-oriented archaeology' is of more than heuristic value. But Macalister was also horrified by the methods employed:

Warren's work at Jerusalem was carried out mainly by tunnelling – the most unsatisfactory of all excavation processes. Vertical shafts were dug to a certain depth, after which horizontal galleries were driven through the soil in the required direction. Sometimes this method of working is inevitable. A cantankerous or greedy landowner, a building that must not be removed, a cemetery still in use – all these are obstacles that cannot be surmounted, and therefore must be circumvented by some means. But only under compulsion of the kind is tunnelling justifiable. It is very costly work; it is also slow, as the labour of carrying the waste soil through the ever-lengthening gallery is very expensive. The super-vision of workmen is next to impossible; a man digging at the inner extremity of a narrow tunnel could conceal within his garments an object of obvious value, with but little fear of being detected in the act by his foreman, however vigilant the latter might be. In any case the chance of finding antiquities is reduced to a minimum, as only a very small portion of the soil is touched; and the superposition of chronological strata cannot be studied at all.

Which means that archaeology cannot be pursued at all! To know what people were doing, we must know what is found with what; in other words the juxtaposition of contemporary things as they were deposited. Thus each stratum must be gridded if contemporary inter-relationships are to be established. Grid-lines must therefore be pegged out on a site, within which (for instance) a metre-square frame, strung at 100 mm intervals, is moved linearly, starting from one of the corners. The draughtsperson, looking down vertically upon the frame with its internal stringing, transfers what appears within and across the 100 mm squares to graph (i.e. squared) paper. Thus all features are drawn to scale.

This is a very fast and relatively accurate method. It can be faster though less accurate than triangulation by standard surveying methods (which Flinders-Petrie took to such a pitch). However, the potential accuracy of triangulation, which requires that the measured grid on site be permanently marked out by pegs, and tied into the national grid, means that its use is often restricted to important finds, key features, or points of departure. Thus it is usual that triangulation is combined with coordinate gridding, which should be imposed upon, and thus situated by, a triangulation grid. Gridding is the indispensable basis of exca-vation. Even if, as is now too often the case, 'excavation' is restricted by time and money to a few trenches, no modern archaeologist worthy of the name would proceed without gridding and surveying, accompanied by drawing and photography.

Indeed, before commencing a contemporary excavation, a site's sur-face is extensively 'levelled' (i.e. spot heights are taken), in order to draw up a contour plan. As work proceeds each surface exposed is levelled, as also are all the datum points used to produce section drawings. And all such measurements need to be logged separately, only later transferred to the main plans. An archaeological dig is to collect as wide a range of data as possible, not artefacts (which are only a narrow subset of the data), and therefore the earth covering a site is itself data and not dirt obscuring it. The (mis)conception of soil as a general overburden needing simply to be 'cleared' to reveal the wonders beneath, accounts in large measure for the absence of data on the economic basis of sites (e.g. bones and seeds) prior to about the middle of this century.

However, the Fund seems to have sensed what a disastrous start had been made. Warren's diggings ended in April 1870, and in the subsequent twenty years little excavation took place in Palestine (Macalister 1925: 39). But something more fundamental was done: from 1872–78 a British expedition, led by C.R. Conder and H.H. Kitchener (later of Khartoum), made a thorough inch-to-the-mile survey of western Palestine, missing very little, so that it 'remains indispensable for the archaeologist and topographer' (Albright 1960: 27).

In 1870 an American–Palestine excavation society was established on the lines of the British one, and subsequently dispatched two expeditions to survey Transjordan. However, due to local difficulties and chronic underfunding nothing was achieved (Albright 1960: 28).

Of course, the possibilities of sustained excavation did not originate with the PEF. Rather it was inspired by what had been occurring for decades prior to its establishment in Mesopotamia, particularly the spectacular excavation of Nimrud (Biblical Calah) opposite Mosul in Iraq, by Austen Henry Layard (pronounced Laird; 1817–94); and by work in the same area (Assyria, of which Nimrud was the capital from 880 BC), by Paul Emile Botta, the discoverer (in 1843) and first excavator of Khorsabad.

Accordingly, Grove, the prime mover of the PEF, having made great efforts to secure its ecumenical nature, also ensured that Layard, a great celebrity, was present and spoke at the foundation meeting in Willis' Rooms, St James, on 22 June 1865. At that meeting A. C. Tait, Bishop of London, read the prayers and then gave a speech declaring 'exegetical theology' to be the theology of the age. Exploration of the Holy Land would give exegesis a solid basis. He was followed by Layard, who

> Moved a resolution on the importance of exploration for throwing light on 'the archaeology of the Jewish people'. He cited discoveries of archaeological excavations in Assyria and said that excavation in the Holy Land could do the same for the history of the Jewish people. He also wanted to investigate the possibilities of finding links with the arts of Egypt and Assyria, already revealed

(Lipman 1988: 50)

Thus the PEF was formed by two sorts of people: those interested in biblical exegesis, and scholars (such as Grove and Layard) whose interests were secular and historical. What enabled the latter to gain the support of the former, and so take the whole British establishment along with them, was the long tradition of British antiquarianism (the Society of Antiquaries, formed as the Tavern Society in 1707, was the second oldest scholarly society in the world, the first being the Royal Society, 1662); plus the by then general permeation of the Whig philosophy of history, which meant that an exact knowledge of the past would inform us of just how far we had advanced.

So reporting the efforts of Lieutenant Charles Warren of the Royal Engineers, 'with the assistance of Sergeant Birtles and one or two other non-commissioned officers, employed during the last two years by the Palestine Excavation Fund', the *Illustrated London News*, which has provided continuous archaeological coverage since its first year of operation (1842), stated in 1869, that:

> The fund is raised by a society whose objects are the accurate and systematic investigation of the archaeology and topography, the geology and physical geography, and the manners and customs of the Holy Land; with a view to Biblical illustration, but with a view no less to the general interests of historical and scientific enquiry. Its undertaking is therefore one that deserves the aid of persons of the most diverse religious opinions, associating their efforts in the common pursuit of that knowledge which is desired by every intelligent mind.
>
> (Bacon 1976: 42)

The *Illustrated* goes on to 'recommend this enterprise to the liberality of our readers' and provide illustrations by a 'Special Artist'.

### III

Layard's activities caught the attention of the British public to such an extent that he was given an honorary doctorate by Oxford in 1848 during the interlude between his first and second campaigns, while, after the second, he was given the Freedom of the City of London in 1854. Writing in March 1850 of relief panels from Nimrud which had been on display in the British Museum for the previous couple of years, the *Illustrated London News* wrote:

> That the interest raised by the exhibition of these remarkable monuments of a remote historic period does not decline, is fully proved by the number of visitors who daily throng the room at the British Museum in which they are deposited.
>
> (Bacon 1976: 23)

And from the point of view both of stimulating the interest of the British and French publics, and the requirements of scholarship, it is indeed fortunate that the earliest digs in Mesopotamia were undertaken (by Layard, Botta and Place) in the very large mounds of the Assyrian north, where they dug up and removed pictorial panels of the first millennium

BC; and not earlier remains from the south (Sumer) where all the twentieth-century excavation and conservation skills of a Leonard Woolley were required to do justice, for instance, to the 'Royal Tombs of Ur', dating from early in the third millennium BC.

Austen Henry Layard was neither an oriental scholar nor an antiquarian, but a young man of 22 undergoing legal training. However, in 1839 he left England taking an overland route for Ceylon with the intention of practising as a barrister, having for the previous five years been articled to his maternal uncle, Benjamin Austen (Saggs 1970: 5). His attitude, a concentrated blend of what was best in early Victorian Britain, comes out clearly in the opening lines of his famous and popular work *Nineveh and its Remains* (1849):

> During the autumn of 1839 and winter of 1840, I had been wandering through Asia Minor and Syria, scarcely leaving untrod one spot hallowed by tradition, or unvisited one ruin consecrated by history. I was accompanied by one no less curious and enthusiastic than myself [E.L.O. Mitford]. We were both equally careless of comfort and unmindful of danger. We rode alone; our arms were our only protection; a valise behind our saddles was our only wardrobe, and we tended our own horses, except when relieved from the duty by the hospitable inhabitants of a Turcoman village or an Arab tent. Thus unembarrassed by needless luxuries, and uninfluenced by the prejudices and opinions of others, we mixed amongst the people, acquired without effort their manners, and enjoyed without allowance those emotions which scenes so novel, and spots so rich in varied association, cannot fail to produce. . . . I had traversed Asia Minor and Syria, visiting the ancient seats of civilisation, and the spots which religion has made holy. I now felt an irresistible desire to penetrate to the regions beyond the Euphrates, to which history and tradition point as the birth place of the West. A deep mystery hangs over Assyria, Babylonia and Chaldea [i.e. Mesopotamia from north to south as then understood]. With these names are linked great nations and great cities dimly shadowed forth in history. After a journey in Syria the thoughts naturally turn eastward; and without treading on the remains of Nineveh and Babylon our pilgrimage is incomplete.
>
> (Saggs 1970: 65–6)

But Layard's 'pilgrimages', full of adventure and misadventure, soon became so complete that he became attached to the staff of Sir Stratford Canning, British Ambassador to the Istanbul court which then ruled virtually the whole Near East. In the process of his travels, he also spent many months in Khuzistan, and lived with the Bakhtiari tribe, producing what is in effect the first ethnology of a Near Eastern people. This was incorporated in a Memoir, published in the journal of the Royal Geographic Society in 1846, for which he received the Society's gold medal (Lloyd 1980: 92).

While Layard was working for Canning at Istanbul, Botta (1802–70), who was an orientalist and the son of a famous historian, had begun his excavations at Kuyunjik in December 1842, moving on to the more promising site of Khorsabad (which turned out to be Sargon II's city of Dur Sharrukin) fourteen miles to the north, in March 1843 (Lloyd 1980: 96–7).

Botta and Layard were friends, having met during Layard's travels, and Botta permitted both Canning and Layard to read his periodical reports to Paris which, of necessity, passed through Istanbul. Canning's failure to get any official position from London for Layard, prompted him to proffer some money of his own to get Layard started on digging in Assyria. Layard took only twelve days to reach Mosul, and on 9 November 1845 (Saggs 1970: 44) having initially hired six Arab labourers, set to work at the sixty-acre site of Nimrud, the ancient Kahlu, the second capital of Assyria after Assur which was the formative centre.

Locally adverse political conditions were removed with Pasha Keritlo Oglu over Christmas 1845. This, and the general stability that followed, allowed Layard to move with his labourers, who now included thirty 'Nestorian Chaldeans' from Salamiyah to a village close by the mound itself. Layard, now joined by Hormuzd Rassam, the brother of the British vice-consul, writes of this period that:

I had now uncovered [parts of five walls] belonging to the palace on the S.W. corner of the mound. In the centre of the mound I had discovered the remains of the two winged bulls; in the N.W. palace [I had uncovered], the great hall Y, the chamber A, and the two small winged lions forming the entrance to chamber BB. The only additional bas-reliefs were two [from the S.W. palace]. The slab on which these bas-reliefs occurred had been reduced in size, to the injury of the sculpture, and had evidently belonged to another building. The slabs on either side bore the usual inscription, and the whole had been so much injured by fire that they could not be moved.

My labours had scarcely been resumed [in 1846] when I received information that the Cadi of Mosul was endeavouring to stir up the people against me, chiefly on the pretext that I was carrying away treasure; and, what was worse, finding inscriptions which proved that the Franks [a generic name for Crusaders] once held the country and upon the evidence of which they intended immediately to resume possession of it, exterminating all true believers.

(Saggs 1970: 92–3)

In this the Cadi was ably assisted by the Mufti, so upon the request of the new Pasha, Ismail, work was suspended. Layard thus ceased digging until 9 February 1846 (Saggs 1970: 95), when trenches were opened in the southwest palace. Another wall, q, bearing relief slabs in the style of Khorsabad, was found, but again having been reused from elsewhere. The best preserved, separated from one above by a band of cuneiform inscriptions, showed a tiara-wearing king triumphant, with his enemies underfoot. The rest of this consisted of gigantic winged figures, sculpted in low relief, but almost entirely defaced (ibid.). Further trenches yielded other poorly preserved and often deliberately defaced slabs. Many, however, carried inscriptions.

Since none of those slabs would bear removal, Layard abandoned this corner, and shifted his attention to the edge of the mound in the north-west, which already had a ravine cutting into it (Saggs 1970: 96). Here,

> In two days the workmen reached the top of a slab which appeared to be both well preserved, and to be still standing in its original position. On the south side I discovered, to my great satisfaction, two human figures, considerably above the natural size, sculptured in low relief, and still exhibiting all the freshness of a recent work. In a few hours the earth and rubbish were completely removed from the face of the slab, no part of which had been injured. The figures appeared to represent divinities, presiding over the seasons, or over particular religious ceremonies. The limbs were delineated with peculiar accuracy, and the muscles and bones faithfully, though somewhat too strongly, marked. An inscription ran across the sculpture.
>
> (ibid.)

This led to the discovery of other reliefs, one an eagle-headed human figure bearing offerings; but a day later the most striking prize of all was uncovered. It consisted first of a gigantic, bearded human head wearing a cap with three horns, which on full excavation turned out to be a winged human-headed 'bull' with the musculature again well delineated. In fact there were a pair of fourteen-foot high, twenty-ton 'bulls' and they formed an entrance. Accordingly, from the front they were carved in full three dimensions, but from the side only in high relief. Fortunately for their purpose as museum exhibits (they ended up in the British Museum) the pair were perfectly preserved.

However, while those discoveries added to Layard's fame amongst the mobile Arab tribes with whom he was on good terms from the outset, in Mosul itself, the reported discovery of 'Nimrod' gave the Cadi, Mufti and Ulema the opportunity to press the Pasha again to have such sacrilegious work stopped. This he requested Layard to do, so he again ceased excavation in March. But not entirely. He dismissed all the workmen, but two continued to dig quietly, and by the end of March another pair of winged, human-headed lions had been discovered, in this case with the human torso continuing to the waist (ibid.: 101). Again, the state of preservation was excellent, but most important, the inscriptions, which covered all of the slab not pictorially carved, were in perfect condition, 'not a character wanting in the inscriptions' (ibid.: 102).

In May 1846, Canning finally managed to get Layard official permission to excavate, in the form of a Viziral letter. However, at this time the Mufti of Mosul's provocations became such that Layard broke a stick over his head, causing uproar not only in Mosul, but also in Baghdad. Nonetheless, during the early summer, Layard succeeded in floating the first of the sculptures by raft on the Tigris to Baghdad; no less than twelve slabs being on view in the British Museum by August 1847. One bull and one lion were floated down the Tigris on 22 April 1847, but then remained at Basra for two years (Saggs 1970: 54–5). However, now officially sanctioned and increasingly famous abroad, the trustees of the British Museum commissioned Layard to undertake excavation on their behalf from September 1846 until June 1847. In early July 1847, Layard ended his first expedition, and left Nimrud for England, accompanied by Hormuzd Rassam, who intended to undertake education there (ibid.: 56). Layard, however, did not leave until he had staked Britain's claim to the mound of Kuyunjik by a fortnight's excavation, which partly uncovered eight chambers. This is the mound that was to yield the centrally important collection of more than 20,000 cuneiform artefacts which comprised tablets and fragments from Sennacherib's invaluable library; and upon which, as Saggs (ibid.: 56) states, Assyriology as a textual discipline is based.

But *not* yet the decipherment of the cuneiform script, which had to proceed from at least bilingual texts, of which one would need to be in a language already known. And such a document, it turned out, was already on public display, though where only the determined could read it.

What the French expedition's *Description de l'Egypte* did for serious antiquarian interest in Egypt, was done for Mesopotamia by the *Memoir on the Ruins of Babylon* of Claudius Rich (1786–1821), the remarkable Resident in Baghdad of the East India Company. Rich made an important collection of antiquities, manuscripts and cuneiform texts (subsequently the basis of the British Museum's collection) and initiated some digging at Babylon, whose surface features he sketched. With the publication in 1818 of his *Second Memoir on Babylon* and his survey sketch in 1820 of the ruins of Nineveh, Rich had indeed, in the words of Lloyd

(1980: 65) 'virtually exhausted the possibilities of inference without excavation'.

Though he died of cholera at Shiraz in 1821, his later replacement was exactly the right man to take full advantage of his location, and accordingly served as a vital collaborator of Layard. This was Henry Creswicke Rawlinson, a soldier and a considerable scholar, not least in Persian. Though the Baghdad Resident during Layard's excavations, Rawlinson had originally been sent with a mission from the Indian army to Kermanshah in 1835 in order to modernize the Persian army. Being naturally active and enquiring, he soon visited and began copying the great trilingual inscriptions carved into the cliff face of Bisitun (Behistun), about twenty miles east-northeast of Kermanshah. *This* was the Rosetta Stone of 'Assyriology', not the material collected in Layard's *Inscriptions in the Cuneiform Character* (the principal texts from Nimrud with some others, published between his first and second campaigns); nor was Rich's collection, in which, of the £7000 paid to his widow Mary, no less than £1000 represented the inscribed material.

A promising start in deciphering cuneiform (neither the signs nor the language it represented being known) was made in 1802 by G.F. Grotefend, a schoolteacher whose work was ignored by the German academic establishment because of his lowly status. Rawlinson worked directly from the Behistun inscriptions in what turned out to be Persian, Elamite and Babylonian, carved into the rockface 122 metres above the Hamadan-Kermanshah road in 516 BC, in order to glorify the name of the great king Darius Hystaspes (521–485 BC). Rawlinson began visiting the rock in 1835 in order to copy the inscriptions, and

> By the end of 1837 he had succeeded in making a translation of the entire first two paragraphs of the inscription, which he sent as a paper to the Royal Asiatic Society. It was on this paper and a subsequent one written in 1839 that Rawlinson's claim to be considered the 'Father of Cuneiform' rests.
>
> (Lloyd 1980: 77)

However, this was merely a translation from Old Persian, an easily accessible Indo-European language, though in 1846 he published a complete translation in two volumes: *The Persian Cuneiform Inscription of Behistun*. But the Babylonian and Elamite texts still eluded translation, as is clear from Rawlinson's exchanges with Layard. Nonetheless, others – Dr Edward Hincks, Oppert and Fox-Talbot (the inventor of the standard negative/positive process in photography) – also worked on the Babylonian inscription, such that, by 1857 all could make independent but agreeing translations of a cylinder of Tilgath-Pileser I (1115–1077 BC). Indeed

It was this decipherment (demonstrated to the Royal Asiatic Society, whose President received the translations in sealed envelopes), that enabled the mounds across the river from Mosul to be identified by Rawlinson as Nineveh, Sinkara to be the ancient city of Larsa, Tell Mukkayar to be Ur-of-the-Chaldees and Tell Abu-Shahrein the Biblical Eridu. Rawlinson found himself as famous as Layard: he, too, was given an honorary doctorate by the University of Oxford, and was knighted in 1856.

(Daniel 1981: 80)

Layard's *Nineveh and its Remains*, which appeared early in 1849, went through four editions by July, and by the end of the year had sold 8000 copies (Lloyd 1980: 101), a remarkable figure given the then population of Britain. Even secondary works had a large market. By 1853 a work by Joseph Bonomi – a Briton who had been on Robert Hay's scholarly expedition to Egypt between 1828 and 1839 to which he contributed accurate reproductions of hieroglyphic inscriptions and scenes from the wall of tombs (Wortham 1971: 63) – was already in its second, expanded edition. Bonomi was also artist/illustrator on K.R. Lepsius's expedition to Egypt from 1842–5, which had been promoted by Alexander von Humboldt and (well) financed by Wilhelm IV of Prussia.[3] Entitled: *Nineveh and its Palaces: the Discoveries of Botta and Layard, Applied to the Elucidation of Holy Writ* (429 pages, 'with numerous additional engravings, and the results of the most recent discoveries'), Bonomi's work concludes with a chapter on 'The latest Proceedings and Discoveries in Assyria', and recounts the independent progress being made by Rawlinson and Hincks in deciphering Babylonian script.

Layard's popular account of his second expedition, beginning in the autumn of 1849, had appeared under the title *Discoveries in the Ruins of Nineveh and Babylon* in 1853. Financed to the tune of £1500 by the British Museum, he was able on this occasion to employ the services of a doctor and an artist. Prior to the establishment of photography as a portable medium, all recording had to be by drawing, and complex designs called for a trained artist. In his earlier work Layard, who was not so trained, desperately tried to record his more volatile finds by his own sketching, but neither time nor training allowed him to do this to his own satisfaction. And when, for the second expedition, to do justice to the inscriptions in particular, he did get the services of an artist, both he and the doctor turned out to be useless, proving that technical competence is no substitute for zeal, and forcing Layard to complain that he got on better when on his own.[4]

At Sennacherib's palace in the mound of Kuyunjik – where British claims had been kept alive in Layard's absence by H.J. Ross and Christian Rassam keeping a few men at work over the intervening period – Layard certainly made great progress within only a few months of his return. He states:

> In this magnificent edifice I had opened no less than seventy-one halls, chambers, and passages, whose walls, almost without exception, had been panelled with slabs of sculptured alabaster recording the wars, the triumphs, and the great deeds of the Assyrian king. By a rough calculation, about 9,880 feet, or nearly two miles, of bas-reliefs, with twenty-seven portals, formed by colossal winged bulls and lion sphinxes, were uncovered in that part alone of the building, explored during my researches.
>
> (cited in Lloyd 1980: 125)

But better was yet to come. Two large chambers were covered about 30 cm deep in cuneiform tablets in what proved to be nothing less than the palace archives and library. Not only did the texts concern contracts and state correspondence, but historical literature, the king's private library and the Temple library (Lloyd 1980: 126). The particular importance of the library texts is that they contain copies of earlier literature, often reaching back to early Sumerian times and constitute the first, sometimes the only, transcriptions of certain works. It is as if the Library of Alexandria had survived. Three years later Hormuzd Rassam, also tunnelling, discovered the other part of those archives in the palace of Sennacherib's grandson, Ashur-banipal (who reigned only a year or two around 668 BC, and whose father was Esarhaddon, 680–669 BC). All the key Sumerian *topoi* are represented, as the first modern excavator in Sumer, R. Campbell-Thomson made plain:

> Myths are represented by the Seven Tablets of the creation, wherein is described the beginning of all things and the creation of Man [i.e. the *Enuma Elish*, a translation of the parts then recovered appeared in 1876 as *The Chaldean Account of Genesis*, by George Smith, of whom more below]; the twelve tablets of Gilgamesh, who seeks to solve that problem which has exercised the mind of man from time immemorial, what will happen after death, and how to obtain eternal life: the legend of Etana, who was carried up like Ganymede, on an eagle's back: Adapa, who, having broken the wings of the south wind, was hauled before Anu to answer for his crime against Nature, as we shall too. . . . Science held high place: medicine proper (distinct from magic) is accorded due position on some 500 tablets, which give good, honest, practical prescriptions for every ill under the sun, from ear-ache and ophthalmia to childbirth and the restoration of the apparently drowned, showing a knowledge of some five hundred drugs: botany had recorded some hundreds of names of plants, with a vast display of knowledge

of their properties: the chemist had already discovered the practical use of a large number of minerals from red lead to magnetic iron ore, and he has left an invaluable treatise on the components for glass and the glazes for pottery. The charlatan of the observation of the future by omens is equally represented: but as it gives us an insight into the tremendous knowledge of the heavens, the sun, moon and stars, it deserves in part to be promoted to the category of science. Philology too has its abundance of dictionaries.

(1929: 135–6)

But Assyria is in the northwest of Mesopotamia. Archaeology in what was Sumer owes its origins to another member of the Turko-Persian Boundary Commission, this a geological one, in the person of William Kennett Loftus. Having scouted the sites on the southern alluvium at the end of 1849 while the rest of the Commission was being moved by river to Mohammerah (the site of the dispute that brought the Commission into being), Loftus's report allowed him to be detached to undertake small-scale excavations at the mound called Warka. This was done over a three-week period initially, and two years later, when in the employment of the Assyrian Excavation Fund, over a three-month period. Loftus found no such 'artistic monuments' as were then so plentiful in the north, but rather inscribed bricks, tablets, plaques and bullae that enabled Rawlinson, who had returned in 1851 to a second Residency in Baghdad as Political Agent, to positively identify Warka as Uruk, and Sinkara as Larsa. There terraces of kiln-fired bricks were identified as belonging to the temple and ziggurat of the sun-god Shamash (Lloyd 1980: 133). And Loftus's book *Travels and Researches in Chaldaea and Susiana* (1857) added to the educated public's interest in Mesopotamia in general and the south in particular. It must be remembered that until this time 'pre-Babylonian' Sumer and Akkad were not known.

While Rawlinson's tenure was renewed in 1851, Botta was replaced by Victor Place (1822–75), architect and antiquarian, and Bonomi concludes his book with this upbeat account of Place's activities, taken from *The Athenaeum* for 18 September 1852:

Letters received in Paris from M. Place, consul at Mosul, report further excavations and successes among the mounds of Nineveh. Among the recent gains from this rich mine of antiquities [sic], besides a large addition of statues, bas-reliefs in marble, pottery, and articles of jewellery, which throw light on the habits and customs of the inhabitants of the ancient city, the French explorers have been able to examine the whole of the palace of Khorsabad and its dependencies. In so doing, they are said to have elucidated some doubtful points [*sic*], and obtained proof that the Assyrians were not ignorant of any of the resources of architecture. M. Place has discovered a large gate, 12 feet high, which appears to have been one of the entrances to the city – several constructions in marble – two rows of columns, apparently extending a considerable distance – the cellar of the Palace, still containing regular rows of jars, which had probably been filled with wine, for at the bottom of those jars there is still a deposit of violet colour. The operations have not been confined to the immediate vicinity of Khorsabad. M. Place has caused excavations to be made in the hills of Bashika, Karamles, Tel Lauben, Mattai, Kara Kush, Digan, etc., on the left bank of the Tigris, within ten leagues of Khorsabad. At Mattai, and at a place called Bar Tau, M. Place has found bas-reliefs cut in the solid rock; they consist of a number of colossal figures, and of a series of full-length portraits of the kings of Assyria. M. Place reports, that he has taken copies of his discoveries by means of the photographic process; and he announces that Col. Rawlinson has authorised him to make diggings near the places which the English are engaged in examining.

(original punctuation)

Such optimism was, however, short-lived. In 1855, 300 cases of this material – supplemented by the relatively scant finds of Fresnel and Jules Oppert in Babylonia, with material from Kuyunjik that Rawlinson had allowed Place to select for the Louvre, and also a consignment of antiquities intended for the Prussian government – were loaded onto rafts (*keleks*) and floated down the Tigris toward Basra. At Qurnah where the Tigris and Euphrates join to form the Shatt al-Arab, the flotilla was intercepted by Arab brigands who, not finding the 'treasure' they imagined, sent the lot to the bottom. Fortunately Felix Thomas, who had latterly been working with Place at Khorsabad, had meticulously recorded reliefs from there, but Boutcher's drawings of the lost slabs from Kuyunjik were actually lost in England prior to publication (Lloyd 1980: 140)! Twenty-six remaining pieces reached the Louvre on 1 July 1856. Place's excellent draughtsmanship of the buildings on top of the Khorsabad mound, albeit rendered somewhat conjectural due to walls being traced by tunnelling, appeared in 1867 as the three volumes of *Ninevé et l'Assyrie*. Between 1857 and 1863, Oppert published in two volumes (plus an atlas) an account of the work done under government auspices in Mesopotamia by Fresnel, Thomas and Oppert himself. His paper of 1869 to the French Society of Numismatics and Archaeology correctly identified the non-Semitic inhabitants of 'Babylonia' as Sumerians, the first such identification.

## IV

In 1854 the Crimean War broke out, with Britain and France fighting Russia in the Black Sea in order to prop up the decayed Ottoman Empire which Russia was trying to dismember. Though only fought in the Crimea, the outbreak of hostilities induced a twenty-year hiatus in the archaeology of Turkey's Mesopotamian provinces.

However, in 1871 George Smith, a self-taught Assyriologist and former engraver employed by the British Museum to join broken tablets from the Nineveh libraries, published *The History of Ashur-bani-pal Translated from the Cuneiform Inscriptions*. Much more interest was created by a paper which he read on 3 December 1872, before the Society of Biblical Archaeology, where he announced that amongst his fragments he had encountered a clear 'portion at least of the Chaldean account of the deluge' (cited in Lloyd 1980: 146), the part relating the coming to rest of the ark on the mountains of Nizur, and the sending forth of a dove which returned having found no resting place (Daniel 1981: 73). But a piece of the tablet (which is an episode in the Gilgamesh cycle) was missing, and so the *Daily Telegraph* put up £1000 to finance an expedition, led by Smith, to find the missing part.

Although Smith had never been to Mesopotamia, and indeed had never excavated anything, within five days of beginning work at Kuyunjik in 1873, he had found the missing part. As is the way with far-sighted British financing, at this point the *Telegraph* promptly withdrew its support, causing Smith to return to England. And although the British Museum subsequently paid for him to return to Kuyunjik, he could never regain the lost momentum in the face of Turkish obstruction, and he died at Aleppo in 1877 on his way home from the third season of excavation.

However, his *Assyrian Discoveries* and especially *The Chaldean Account of Genesis*, were immensely popular, and kept the subject of archaeology high in public interest and esteem. References, as in the above title, were still largely to Assyria, and Mesopotamian textual and epigraphic studies were being referred to as 'Assyriology', but the prominence of Assyria is late (first millennium BC) and its language Semitic, which certainly assisted translation. The seminal language of Mesopotamia, however, is Sumerian (not only a non-Semitic language but one with no known affiliations), something that Oppert had already postulated in 1869. Again it was a French vice-consul based at Basra, Ernest de Sarzec, who in excavations at Tello from 1877 until 1900, recovered the first extensive corpus of Sumerian material. He it was who recovered, along with many late third-millennium statues, the deservedly famous bust of *Gudea*, **ensí** of Lagash, and the Early Dynastic fragment called 'Stela of the Vultures' showing the earliest formation of infantry (phalanx; cf. Maisels 1990: 178). No matter that they wrongly identified Tello as the eponymous capital city, Lagaš; and that the true centre was at Al Hiba, fifteen miles to the southeast, while Tello is in fact the site of the city of *Girsu*, within the territory of the state of Lagash; the real problem was that poor on-site security both in de Sarzec's time and after (1903–31) allowed, *inter alia*, 35,000–40,000 tablets to appear for sale by Baghdad dealers, along with many statues, some in pieces. It was to acquire some of this material for the British Museum that Wallis Budge, having purchased a part of the Tell el-Amarna tablets in Egypt, travelled on to Baghdad via Basra.

Also in 1888 an expedition sponsored by Pennsylvania University, under its field-director, the Reverend Dr John Punnett Peters, began excavating at the site of Nippur, 'the navel of Sumer'. Relationships with the locals were abysmal, and the expedition was soon burned out. Nothing daunted they returned in the new year of 1890, and had more success, for although *their* approach had changed somewhat, local circumstances had drastically changed: the population of the Afaq marshes had in the interim been devastated by cholera, and survivors were keen to work for wages.

While quite methodical, neither de Sarzec's nor Peters's excavations could be described as scientific. However, three long seasons' work at Nippur did yield in excess of 30,000 tablets, crucially most in Sumerian and spanning a millennium (Lloyd 1980: 164). Of those about 2100 were literary texts, and presently constitute the largest corpus we have of literary texts *in Sumerian*; otherwise we should be dependent on late copies in other languages, where such were even made.

Hormuzd Rassam, who became Layard's successor – after an earlier career in which his workmen had 'examined' a plethora of mounds within a 200-mile radius of his native Mosul (the Aleppo pashalik) largely in order to forestall the French (even at Tello when de Sarzec had already started there) – was commissioned by the British Museum in 1876 to renew excavations, which he did from 1878 until 1882 (Lloyd 1980: 149). The British Museum was particularly keen that he gather more tablets from the library of Assur-banipal at Nineveh. In the meantime Layard had followed a distinguished and varied career in the diplomatic service and in Parliament. Accordingly, when Rassam was seeking his firman from Istanbul, he had the benefit of Layard's presence (then knighted and from 1877 Minister Plenipotentiary to the Porte), to get him permission not only to excavate unconditionally all the crown lands in the pashaliks of Baghdad, Aleppo and Van, but even permission to retain all his finds other than duplicates (ibid.). Finding his instructions too tame, he dug many sites including at Abu Habbah, some twenty miles southwest of Baghdad. There he found the inscribed marble stela of Nabu-apla-iddina (*c.* 870 BC), showing in relief the sun-god Shamash with his ministrants. From the inscription in front of the shrine of the temple in one chamber of which the stela was located, reading: 'Image of Shamash the Great Lord dwelling in Ebabarra in the city of Sippar' (Lloyd 1980: 156), it was apparent that this was the site of that highly important Sumerian city. Rassam uncovered about 170 (of 300) rooms surrounding a ziggurat in the city-centre, and from them recovered, in his own estimate, 40,000–50,000 tablets and inscribed cylinders, markedly degrading their condition in the process. Most fittingly, one of the cylinders contained an inscription of Nabonidus (555–539 BC), the last native king of Babylon, who dedicated himself to antiquarian research and whose informed excavations make him the first archaeologist.

From 1899 onwards, scientific excavation began in Mesopotamia with the Deutsche-Orient Gesellschaft (D-OG); foreshadowed by Flinders-Petrie in Egypt, by Pitt-Rivers (self-financed) at Cranborne Chase in Dorset and indeed, by the German Archaeological Institute themselves, who began their well-financed work at Olympia in the Peloponnese as early as 1875. Between 1899 and 1914, the D-OG dug not only at Borsippa (Birs Nimrud) and Shuruppak (Fara), but also at Babylon, upon which Koldewey concentrated while Andrae excavated Assur (Qalat Shirgat), taking its history back to its origins as a peripheral city-state in the third millennium. This was achieved by the planning, photographing and recording of *each stratum* as it was exposed; and, at Babylon, with the lines of mud-brick walls properly traced for the first time, enabling a whole city-plan (of the Neo-Babylonian period, of which Nabonidus was the last king) to be laid out.

(A thorough and detailed list of excavations in Iraq between 1842 and 1965 can be found in A.R. Al-Haik (1968) *Key Lists of Archaeological Excavations in Iraq, 1842–1965,* ed. Henry Field and Edith M. Laird, Florida, Field Research Projects.)

# 4

# PRACTICAL PIONEERS AND THEORETICAL PROBLEMS

One of this century's key pioneers is Dorothy A.E. Garrod, the first female professor at Cambridge, who laid the basis for modern studies of the Upper-Palaeolithic/Epipalaeolithic both in the Zagros and in the Levant. In the highly risky, unsettled conditions of Iraq in the late 1920s, Dorothy Garrod, with a small team that comprised the zoologist Dorothea M.A. Bate and Mr F. Turville-Petrie, based themselves near the RAF camp at Suleimaniya. The first site they investigated from there, a small cave in the Surdash area on the drainage of the lesser Zab river in southern Kurdistan, gave its name – Zarzi – to what Braidwood and Howe (1960: 180) saw as 'the terminal aspect of the pure food-collecting way of life (if it is conceived of as an ideal type) in Iraqi Kurdistan'. Forced to move about with an armed escort, Garrod's team managed to excavate for only nine days at Zarzi cave, with another nine spent excavating one of the caves at Hazar Merd. Despite this, her excavations of 1927–8, were not followed up until 1948, when a team led by Robert J. Braidwood began work on what became the 'Iraq Jarmo Project', sponsored by the Oriental Institute of the University of Chicago (the major world centre for ancient Near Eastern research), in association with the American Schools of Oriental Research.[1]

In addition to Zarzi itself and Hazar Merd, Zarzian occupations have been found at Palegawra, Pa Sangar, Warwasi, and Shanidar Cave, the last an important cave site excavated by other archaeologists of the 'pioneering modern' post-war period, namely Rose L. Solecki and Ralph S. Solecki. Zarzian culture is estimated to commence around 20,000 BP (Before Present) (Hole and Flannery 1967: 152) and to end around 11,000 BP (Braidwood and Howe 1960: 156). Although Braidwood and Howe refer to the Zarzian as the latest period of 'pure' food-collection, what is meant is 'hunting and gathering' with the emphasis, given the then climatic regime, very definitely on the hunting, and of large herbivores at that.

From Palegawra rock-shelter which overlooks the Bazian valley from the southern slopes of the Baranand Dagh, Turnbull and Reed (1974:

140) found that no less than 99.5 per cent of consumable meat was provided by only seven genera of megafauna: *Equus* (horse), *Cervus* (deer), *Ovis* (sheep), *Capra* (goat), *Gazella* (gazelle), *Sus* (pig) and *Vulpes* (fox; neither herbivore nor megafauna), while *Equus* and *cervus alone* supplied 76.6 per cent of consumable meat. If such proportions are at all representative, and to date the Palegawra faunal sample is the fullest we have for the Zarzian, then the contrast between it and the Natufian, with which it is coeval for the last millennium or so of its long duration, is strongly marked. Nonetheless, if the Zarzian, which succeeds the Baradostian in the Zagros, is anything like as long-lived as appears to be the case – it is on these dates contemporary with the Kebaran, the Geometric Kebaran and most of the Natufian – then internal evolution is inevitable. Indeed, in the Late Zarzian, geometric microliths appear, principally in the form of scalene and isosceles triangles, along with microburin technique.

In the Zarzian levels of Pa Sangar, Hole and Flannery (1967: 160) recovered two large scallop shells, and encountered numerous fragments of *Dentalium* shell, which they took to be the remains of personal ornaments. This parallels the extensive use of dentalium for similar purposes by the Natufians, to the awareness of whom also, we are further indebted to Dorothy Garrod. She first encountered this culture in the cave of Shukba (28 km northwest of Jerusalem), on the western slope of the Judaean Hills during two months' work in 1928, undertaken with the Americans, George and Edna Woodbury. Shukba is a very large cave with a vault some 22 m high, situated 22 m above the present streambed of the Wadi en-Natuf.

Excavation revealed a top layer, A, which varied between 80 cm and 3 m in thickness, containing pottery ranging from Early Bronze Age to Byzantine. Beneath this was an uneven layer, B, consisting

> of a layer of black hearths containing very abundant microlithic industry. This rested on the very irregular surface of a red breccia containing Mousterian implements, which rose in hummocks from the floor of the cave. The breccia [coarse-grained angular sedimentary rock] had obviously been extensively eroded by water action and in places had been removed right down to the bedrock
>
> (Garrod 1932: 257)

Obviously it was this layer, B, which was significant, and which provided the characteristic artefacts of what Garrod in this article (op. cit.: 261) named the 'Natufian'. Diagnostically,

> the most abundant form is the small lunate with blunted back . . . ; in addition to these, there are a few triangles rather roughly made . . . but other geometric forms are absent. A typical tool is a small

parallel-sided blade with blunted back and ends retouched obliquely, the back often showing marked concavity. . . . Larger blunted-back knives are fairly common, but not very typical; end-scrapers . . . are rare, core scrapers . . . very abundant. Bone points are abundant, the majority being made of metacarpal or metatarsal bones of small ruminants with the articular surface left untouched – a type common also in the early Bronze Age. There are a few rather coarse bone needles, one of which has the eye at the point, and a fragment of a bone plaque decorated with groups of parallel incisions engraved obliquely along its edge

(1932: 258)

Against the background of rather indifferent lithics one thing stands out: what would now be called 'sickle-sheen' on the 'larger blunted-back knives', which comes from reaping grasses. Indeed, at the very next cave examined – the Mugharet el-Wad, the largest of a group lying at the foot of Mount Carmel near Haifa – actual sickle shafts of bone were found, one with two flint blades still in place, leaving no doubt that it was a sickle. On discovery they were, and have remained, the earliest class of sickles known. And at the cave called Mugharet el-Kebarah, 15 km south of Mugharet el-Wad, excavated (at the suggestion of Garrod who had spotted it from a train) by F. Turville-Petrie in 1931, he reported that 'Of the flint implements . . . the most numerous were sickle blades', over a thousand being found (Turville-Petrie 1932: 271–2), along with two intact sickle-blade hafts. One was 38 cm in length, and decorated at the handle with the carving of a goat's head; the other was 23 cm long. There were also many fragmentary hafts, represented by carvings of a bovine and a deer. But this was itself an aspect of a highly-accomplished bone-working industry at Mugharet el-Kebarah, where harpoons and fish-hooks were also numerous; likewise 'bone-points', combs, pendants and beads (ibid.: 276). Cult objects included phalli of limestone and of flint, while the importance of gathering is reinforced by the presence of no less than five basalt mortars with a number of pestles.

Rescue archaeology is not a new phenomenon. The excavation of Shukba was postponed after only a couple of months' work at the request of the Department of Antiquities, so that the team from the British School of Archaeology in Jerusalem might excavate the Mugharet el-Wad before it was quarried, amazing as that seems. Due to disturbance, the stratigraphy of the cave was even more complex than at Shukba. The terrace, which was excavated over a wide area, again divided into an A and a B layer. A, which was from 0.5–2 m thick, contained everything from Early Bronze age to recent material. Layer B is the 'Mesolithic' (i.e. Epipalaeolithic) layer, from 0 m to as much as 3 m thick, resting on bedrock in the upper part of the trench, and on a sterile layer in the lower.

It was possible to distinguish two subdivisions in B, corresponding to a well-marked typological differentiation. Of these the lower, B2 [0–2.5 m in thickness] contained an industry identical with that found inside the cave, while the upper, B1 [15–60 cm in thickness], more closely resembled Shukba B. By this time it was abundantly clear that we were dealing with a microlithic culture that would not fit exactly into any of the pigeon holes already existing, and therefore I decided to give it a label of its own, adopting the name *Natufian* from the Wady en-Natuf at Shukba. Layer B2 would thus correspond to the Lower Natufian, and Layer B1 together with Shukba B to the Upper Natufian.

(Garrod 1932: 261)

The lower level, B2, contained more and better-worked bone than B1, including single-row barbed harpoons of delicate construction, double-ended points which were probably gorgets, plus pear-shaped and other pendants. Sickle hafts have already been mentioned, but also found in B2 was the statuette of a young deer carved on the end of a long piece of bone, and a small human head roughly carved from a piece of banded calcite (hard chalk). Again, phalli were shaped from flint and pestles from basalt (a fine-grained igneous rock). Two limestone mortars were found in B2, plus some vessels also in basalt. A number of the pestles showed their use in grinding red ochre (ibid.: 266).

At Mugharet el-Wad human burials were common throughout layers B1 and B2, but had their greatest frequency in B2, with at least forty individuals represented.

Two skeletons, lying close together to the north of the rock platform, had head-dresses of dentalium shells, and one had also a necklace of curiously shaped bone pendants strung in pairs. The skeleton of a young child, close at hand, had the remains of a cap of bone pendants.

(Garrod 1932: 267)

At Shukba, Garrod (op. cit.: 258) found eleven human burials in the B layer, of which three were the skeletons of children. 'In one case an adult male skeleton was found in a sitting position under a large fallen rock, with the remains of two children on his knees, the bodies being packed into position with fragments of limestone.'

At the Mugharet el-Kebarah, Turville-Petrie (1932: 271) found a collective burial pit, closely resembling those at el-Wad, again including several infants. He concludes that

If we try to correlate the Mugharet el-Kebarah culture with that of

54

the two other known Natufian sites, namely Shukba and Mugharet el-Wad, it will be found that it most closely resembles that of the Lower Natufian or B2 level at Mugharet el-Wad and therefore represents the earliest Natufian phase at present known. This phase seems to be characterised by the absence of microgravers so abundant in the Upper Natufian layer at the Mugharet el-Wad, *by the preponderance of sickle blades over crescents* and the finished workmanship of the former implement, by the preponderance of the oblique sharpening retouch over the ordinary flat back technique, and finally, by the amount and variety of worked bone.

(op. cit.: 276; my emphasis)

Indeed beneath the B level at el-Kebarah, Turville-Petrie (1932: 271) encountered a 'second Mesolithic level, C, with a fairly uniform thickness of 25 cm all over the cave'. This turned out to represent the immediate Palaeolithic predecessors of the Natufians, since those finds called *Kebarans*.

Garrod had great difficulty in dating her finds. She knew that the Natufian was clearly antecedent to the Early Bronze Age in Palestine, and indeed that 'it ante-dates the appearance of pottery in Palestine' (Garrod 1932: 268). Rejecting any direct comparison with Egyptian material, she nonetheless provisionally dated the Natufian between 4000 and 5000 BC, broadly on the basis that she considered 'the Natufian to be at least as old as the Badarian – probably in view of the absence of pottery, somewhat older' (ibid.). Now, thanks to her own pioneering, we know that even the higher figure suggested has to be at least doubled, with a recent summary estimation (Henry 1983: 137) giving the Natufian a span from 12,750 BP to about 10,450 BP. But the trail-blazing quality of Garrod's work can be seen clearly in the title of the JRAI article (Garrod 1932) from which I have been citing extensively: 'A new Mesolithic industry: the Natufian of Palestine'.

From subsequent work building on that of Garrod and Turville-Petrie, as also on that of René Neuville who was then working in the Judaean desert and who discovered the important rock-shelter of el-Khiam, we now see clearly that the Natufian culture is Epipalaeolithic; that is, it spans the period from the ending of the last Ice Age into the beginnings of the present post-Glacial conditions, the Holocene. The term 'Mesolithic' is now reserved for transitional, but quite distinct developments in western Europe, where the Mesolithic cultures were replaced only after several millennia by the spread from the Near East of the farming way of life (cf. Maisels 1990: Appendix C).

## THE NEAR EAST IN GEOGRAPHY

Crucial to those developments is of course the geography of the Near East as a region, and the Near East is the one bridging Asia to Africa and Europe. It comprises the contemporary states – clockwise and from the north – of Turkey, Syria, Iraq, Iran, the states of the Arabian Peninsula, Egypt, Israel, Jordan and Lebanon.

The region is bounded by five seas, which are, again clockwise: the Mediterranean, Black Sea, Caspian Sea, Persian Gulf and the Red Sea. As the Near East is the region with the most uninterrupted insolation (direct sunlight) in the world (Fisher 1978: 69), the presence of those seas is the difference between merely arid and true desert conditions (like the Sahara, which is an interior or continental continuation). For most rainfall in the Near East is a product of air masses moving westward in winter from the Atlantic along the length of the Mediterranean. Accordingly, as Fisher sums it:

> The distribution of rainfall in the Middle East is largely controlled by two factors: topography and the disposition of land and sea in relation to rain-bearing winds. It must be remembered that the Middle East is predominantly a continental area, influenced only in certain regions by proximity of relatively small areas of sea. Hence air masses reaching the Middle East from the west, even though of oceanic origin, have lost some of their moisture; and it is only where a sea track has allowed partial rejuvenation [i.e. from the Mediterranean] that considerable rainfall can develop.
>
> (1978: 65)

This of course means that the zones nearest to, or best exposed to, the winds from the eastern Mediterranean have the most rainfall (e.g. Lebanon), excepting the special conditions along the southern shores of the Black Sea.

Climatic conditions termed 'Mediterranean' are those of winter-wet and summer-dry. Such a regime, defined by levels of winter precipitation exceeding by three or more times the rain falling in summer, characterizes most of the Mediterranean basin. Such ratios are well exceeded in the Near East, where summer drought and great diurnal and seasonal temperature ranges are the norm.

Those are caused over much of the year not only by the absence of cloud to retain daytime heat, but seasonally by exposure to very cold northeasterly air masses moving in from Siberia. Indeed at Mosul in northeastern Iraq snow is not uncommon, and the Tigris has been known to freeze here (Brice 1966: 39). At other times the region, as far north as the southern shores of the Caspian, can experience tropical air systems moving in over the Gulf. The southern shores of the Caspian are also prone to earthquakes, due to the movements of the plates. The Zagros mountain arc is another consequence of a plate collision boundary running up the Gulf.

## THE NEAR EAST AS THE INTERSECTION OF CONTINENTS

Although the layman thinks of geographical configurations (if at all) as a kind of accidental jumble, topography is never accidental but contingent, being a determinate product of very definite forces. Thus the Near East is what it is, and, for example, has the oil that it has, as a consequence of the movement of crustal plates bearing the continents (and the seas). This process of the movement of continents across the surface of the planet during geological time (measured in hundreds of millions of years) is called continental drift, produced by convection currents in the underlying mantle of molten rock, driven by a superdense and hot core.

In Triassic–Jurassic times (*c.* 200 million years ago) all the present continents were bunched together, separated only by a long north–south trench that was to become the Atlantic; and in the centre by an ocean (filling a broad geosyncline) called the Tethys Sea, partly closed off at its eastern extremity by Australia. This sea was to become the Mediterranean and the Indian Ocean with the subsequent northward anticlockwise rotation of Africa. However, the latitude and relative closure of the original Tethys Sea produced the abundance of marine organisms whose remains form the oil deposits of the Middle East and East Indies.

The northern hemispheric grouping of North America and Eurasia is called Laurasia; the grouping of South America, Africa, India, Antarctica and Australia is called Gondwanaland. To this day each grouping contains related species of plants and animals, which are distinct from the other grouping. Pivoting as they moved north, the collision with Eurasia of the plates carrying Africa and India, caused great chains of mountains to be thrown up right along the southern margins of Eurasia. Those chains now extend from the Atlantic to the Pacific, its central and highest range being the Himalayas, formed by the impact of the plate carrying both India and Australia (there are seven major and twelve minor plates).

As the African continent rotated during the Cretaceous period, which began around 135 million years ago (the period during which dinosaurs were at their peak), plate fragments became detached from its northeastern corner. Those, called 'proto-Iranian', impelled by spreading action, became attached to Laurasia, with Tethys sediments trapped as interior basins. By the Cenozoic era (Tertiary period) around 65 million years ago, another plate, the Arabian, had become detached from the same region of the African plate, and impacting the Iranian plate already part of Laurasia, threw up the main Zagros ranges which also largely consist of Tethys sediments.

Thus the Arabian plate, central to Near Eastern landforms, is now a part of Eurasia, but not yet fully detached from Africa. However, a major spreading fault is marked by the Red Sea, which continues northward as the Jordan Valley until it more or less terminates in the Orontes Valley adjacent to the Hatay Hills of coastal Turkey.

Although all of the Near East, lying as it does below 40° North (Istanbul is 41°N, Muscat 24°N), is in those latitudes receiving maximum insolation, all else, from landforms to rainfall, shows great variation.[2] Precipitation in parts of Turkey consistently exceeds 1000 mm (van Zeist 1969: 42) as indeed in the vicinity of Beirut also, while none at all will occur in some years in Arabia. On the coast of Israel the 13 km long Mount Carmel receives 700 mm presently; and while the west-facing slopes of the northern Zagros are well-watered enough to support forest (with, for example, Lake Zeribar at 1300 m in an intramontane valley receiving 600–800 mm), the interior (eastern) ridges are fairly arid, as also are those nearer the Gulf. For perennial rivers to originate requires rainfall in excess of 100 mm above the rate of evapo-transpiration (i.e. the rate of surface evaporation plus the moisture transpired by plants); which in those latitudes means rainfall amounting to at least 600 mm per annum (Fisher 1978: 31). Thus the Tigris and Euphrates, the region's main rivers, originate in eastern Turkey; but the annual rainfall at the major town of Diyarbakir, not far south of the originating zone, is only 457 mm (the same at Ezerum, further north but to the east), indicating the great variability obtaining over quite short distances (i.e. the presence of a high *zonality* within *areas* composing the Near Eastern *region*).

Wigley and Farmer remark that:

> The climate of the eastern Mediterranean/Near East (M/NE) is influenced by the main middle to high latitude westerlies to the north and northwest, the mid-latitude subtropical high pressure systems which generally extend from the Atlantic to the Sahara, and the monsoon climate of the Indian subcontinent and east Africa. In winter, the region is affected by the strong thermal high pressure system which covers a large part of the Asian continent (the Siberian High). All of those factors may be modified by the Mediterranean itself (as a heat and/or moisture sink or source) and by local topographic effects. Any discussion of M/NE climate must include a review of these larger scale features of the atmospheric circulation which begins with hot air rising from the equatorial belts.
>
> (1982: 4)

Accordingly the winter precipitation that is characteristic of the Levant, with 70–80 per cent of annual amounts falling between November and February, is a consequence of its exposure to cyclonic circulation belts, while the summer aridity is due to the area coming under the influence of subtropical descendent (and thus dry) air-masses.

Wigley and Farmer conclude, however, with the cautionary statement that despite the undoubted importance of the large-scale circulation features, relatively small changes in *any* of which 'might cause significant regional climate changes', smaller-scale 'local effects (topography, land–sea temperature contrasts, the oceanic water source itself, etc.) and possible changes in variability are extremely important and need to be given due weight in any analysis of palaeoclimate data' (1982: 35).

## FARMING IS HARD: WHY DO IT?

In the nineteenth century and the first part of the twentieth, the superiority of farming as a way of life was assumed to be so self-evident that it was generally felt that any population which could, would certainly take up farming. All, therefore, required for this great leap forward, was for some 'genius' to 'discover' plant domestication and/or animal husbandry and his grateful kinsmen and neighbours would leap at the chance of seasonal overextension followed by seasonal underemployment. However, the fixed abode and routine were assumed to more than compensate for drought, flood, pests and all the risks crops are exposed to. Of course hunter-gatherers are also exposed to risks which include drought, flood and pests; but they have coping strategies not available to most farming communities, the most important being the ability simply to move further than they normally do, or in a different direction than is seasonally usual.

By the middle of this century more deterministic explanations were being sought, especially as it was becoming plain from ethnological fieldwork that hunter-gatherer existence was not necessarily nasty, brutish and short, but could on the contrary be congenial (in terms of variety) and even affluent (in terms of the work required to procure subsistence). This realization that hunter-gatherers were capable of leading rich lives and not ones always teetering on the brink of disaster was given substance in the seminal *Man the Hunter* colloquium held in Chicago in 1966 (and published under that title by Richard Lee and Irving de Vore in 1968), while it was given further theoretical expression by Marshall Sahlins in his *Stone Age Economics* (1974). Understanding the actual way of life of real live hunters and gatherers is probably the biggest debt archaeology owes to anthropology.

Beginning with ⋮ Gordon Childe, the most influential and widely read archaeological theorist of the mid-twentieth century, explanations for the adoption of agriculture have been sought in some kind of compulsion: environmental, social, demographic, or in some combination of these. Accounting for the Neolithic Revolution (his term) in his influential work *Man Makes Himself*, originally published in 1936, Childe argued that environmental desiccation following from the ending of the Ice Age forced man and animals together at oases:[3]

> the period when the foodproducing economy became established was one of climatic crises adversely affecting precisely the zone of arid sub-tropical countries where the earliest farmers appear, and where the wild ancestors of cultivated cereals and domestic animals actually lived. The melting of the European ice-sheets and the contraction of the high pressures or anticyclones over them involved a northward shift in the normal path of the rainbearing depressions from the Atlantic. The showers that had watered North Africa and Arabia were deflected over Europe. *Desiccation set in*. Of course the process was not sudden or catastrophic. At first and for long, the sole harbinger would be the greater severity and longer duration of periodical droughts. But quite a small reduction in the rainfall would work a devastating change in countries that were always relatively dry. It would mean the difference between continuous grasslands and sandy deserts interrupted by *occasional oases*.
>
> (1966: 77; my emphasis)

Childe was right about the northward shift in the rainbearing storm tracks across the Mediterranean. He was, however, wrong about timing and whether the rainbearing winds reached the Levant at all. They were not displaced into Europe but – and this is crucial – during the progress of the Holocene, they swung progressively north into Anatolia leaving the southern Levant highly arid (Henry 1989: 46–7). Of course, in a region as diverse as the Near East no tendency is uniform in application: in this case the southern Levant's loss was the northern Levant's gain. However, at the crucial period of the onset of the Holocene the overall tendency was for greater amounts of available moisture and not toward greater desiccation.

The conventional date for the ending of the last Ice Age and thus for the beginning of the Holocene (see table from Whitehouse 1983: 417) is 8300 BC, or 10,250 BP where 'present', used for radiocarbon calculation, is fixed at AD 1950, the time when the technique of radiocarbon dating became generally available (having been developed in 1948 by Willard

Libby). However, the Near East was not directly affected by the Ice Sheets that extended over much of northern Eurasia, and so climatic amelioration began in the Levant around 13,000 years ago (Henry 1983: 110). 'Pollen recovered from Late Natufian and Harifian deposits indicates that drier conditions began to replace the Early Natufian moist phase by about 11,000 BP, and persisted until after 10,000 years ago' (ibid.). Nonetheless, even then 'the environment remained more lush than the modern setting, as evidenced by Dama [i.e. deer] remains from the Late Natufian site of Rosh Zin in the Negev' (Henry 1983: 113). Though the occurrence of megafauna is not good evidence (especially at one site), as the remains may represent only a small relict population, it may be that more free water was available in the millennia immediately *prior* to the onset of the Holocene temperature elevation, making more moisture available then than subsequently.

Beginning, therefore, around 12,500 years ago, surface temperature increased by from 6–8°C, producing warmer *and wetter* conditions in the Near East, although in the more northerly and easterly areas, namely in the northern Levant, Taurus and Zagros mountains and the Caspian shores, cold-dry conditions obtained until about 11,000 BP, 'by which time a relatively drier phase had begun in the central and southern Levant' (Henry 1983: 114).

From the study of pollens found in specially bored cores, Van Zeist and Bottema (1982: 282) conclude that 'between 11,000 and 10,000 BP, forest vegetations (such as *Quercus, Olea* and *Ostrya/Carpinus orientalis*), must have expanded rapidly in northwestern Syria', while 'the pollen evidence suggests that forest vegetations reached their greatest expansion [there] in the period of *c*. 10,000–8000 BP'.

In the *southern* Levant, by contrast, 'the considerable expansion of oak in the period of 14,000–10,000 BP which coincides with the Late-Glacial, points to an amelioration of climate' (1982: 283). However, 'after 10,000 BP open vegetations gained terrain at the expense of oak forest. The greater climatic dryness was probably caused by a rise in temperature which was not sufficiently compensated for by an increase in precipitation' (ibid.).

Generally speaking then, the Holocene has been characterized by the spread of trees (mostly oak) and grasses throughout the Near East, until impacted by man.

Accordingly,

in the *Quercus ithaburensis* [Tabor oak] and *Quercus brantii* formations and related park-forests that stretch from Palestine[4] to south Turkey and Iraqi and Iranian Kurdistan, one finds extensive 'natural fields' of wild cereals. Conspicuous examples of such massive wild stands occur on the basaltic plateaus and the hard limestone slopes of the eastern Galilee and the adjacent Gilead and Golan.

(Zohary 1969: 56)

The full range of what were to become the cultivated grains is here present extending for miles over uncultivated slopes. Indeed

in their growth and total mass, these wild fields of wheat, barley and oats are not inferior to their cultivated counterparts. Those robust wild forms can be favourably compared with their culti-vated relatives in grain production also.

(ibid.)

Contrary then to a post-Pleistocene desiccation leading to the necessity of, and opportunity (through propinquity at oases) for domestication and agriculture, the Pleistocene/Early Holocene has been characterized by elevated biomass levels produced by increased moisture and tem-perature. Van Zeist (1969: 45) reckons that both trees and the wild cereals would have begun to spread from their refuge areas as early as 14,000 BP, reaching a distribution by 10,000 BP not much different from that obtaining today (apart of course from the progressive drying of the southern Levant, more or less completed by 5000–4400 BP). Importantly, Van Zeist (ibid.) also points out that, if the relatively drier episodes between 10,000 and 6000 BP meant that autumn, winter and spring rainfall was the same as at present, but that *summer* rainfall was less, this would not seriously affect the growth of *annuals*, such as the wild cereals.

The abundance of 'fields' of wild cereals is obviously attractive to hunter-gatherers, but making intensive use of this resource demands making stores of harvested grains and either staying close by to use and protect them, or storing them and making periodic revisits. What con-sumption strategy is adopted will depend upon the value of the grains in the annual procurement system, and it seems from their ready and widespread incorporation into subsistence strategies across their areas of natural occurrence, that a high value was placed on this resource that was easy to harvest and store. This process is detailed in the next chapter. Here another form of 'compulsion hypothesis' should be dis-posed of, that of population-pressure, since I am arguing for an inducement-led process for the emergence of permanent settlement and farming. It will be noted that population-pressure is the direct inverse of the environmental deterioration hypothesis, since it turns on the dimi-nishing proportion of resources to people, while the former turns on the consequences of an increasing number of people to be sustained by lagging resources.

## THE CIRCULARITY OF POPULATION PRESSURE AS AN EXPLANATION

Since the 1970s the most prominent proponent of population pressure as the engine of social evolution has been M.N. Cohen. In his influential work *The Food Crisis in Prehistory* (1977), explicitly subtitled 'Overpopulation and the Origins of Agriculture', he set out

> to argue that human population has been growing throughout its history, and that such is the cause, rather than simply the result, of much human 'progress' or technological change, particularly in the subsistence sphere. While hunting and gathering is an extremely successful mode of adaptation for small human groups, it is not well adapted to the support of large or dense human populations. I suggest therefore that the development of agriculture was an adjustment which human populations were forced to make in response to their own increasing numbers.
>
> (Cohen 1977: 14)

The methodological fallacy here should be immediately apparent: one starts from the fact that populations have grown, then one posits a problem about subsistence resources supplying those populations and then, as if this had really been shown to be a problem, one can plausibly (*but not logically!*) claim that certain observed changes in economic patterns were *a response* to the problems that have merely been *inferred*!

With such problems of logical circularity I shall not attempt here (as I did in 1990: 25–31) a full empirical refutation of Cohen's thesis on the Near East Epipalaeolithic. In general he maintains

> that sedentism *in most cases* occurs, not because of newly discovered resources which *permit* year-round residence in a single location, but rather because of the decline of resources associated with other parts of the traditional annual cycle, or because of territorial impingement by other groups.
>
> (1977: 83; original emphases)

The advance of flora and fauna from the Epipalaeolithic in the Near East argues for resource plenty and not pressure, even with a rising human population; and even to Cohen himself (1977) after 281 pages:

> It is clear, however, that the explanation which has been offered is not yet adequate to account for the *particular* sequences of local events in which the more general pattern is played out nor for the regional irregularities [sic] in agricultural origins. I cannot yet explain satisfactorily why, given the overall build-up of population pressure, agriculture began slightly [sic] earlier in some regions

than in others, nor why it was developed independently in some regions and diffused to others.

(ibid.; original emphasis)

In his own words, then, even were 'population-pressure' to be empirically present, its explanatory power is very limited. Part of the problem lies in the assumption that there is any one single prime-mover in social evolution, and that this engine drives all the rest as if they were inert within the system which is society.

A corollary of this is that one can postulate a single cause as sufficient across such distances of time and space as Cohen does: he works on continental proportions and a millennial scale. But surely this is a totally mistaken level of analysis. For: from such a 'macro'-conspectus nothing can be said about generative mechanisms, since nothing of substance can be discerned about the micro-relations of small groups of people to their immediate environment. To have any integrative value the overview would need to be derived from substantive micro-knowledge; a process vitiated by picking an 'explanatory' hypothesis, making some sweeping assertions involving human nature and evolutionary process, then trying to fit some actual data to it.

However, Keeley (1988) has not done this, and that is why his argument for demographic pressure must be taken seriously. In a rigorous cross-cultural analysis of ninety-four carefully chosen and coded hunter-gatherer societies, he looked for correlations between *population pressure* – defined (in one measure: LNX) as the 'population density relative to the productive potential and the resource diversity of a group's territory' (op. cit.: 385) – and socio-cultural *complexity*, defined as the presence of sedentism, dependence on storage, social inequality and the use of a medium of exchange (ibid.: 387). Only hunter-gatherer groups for whom there was good ethnographic information were included in the ninety-four, while those whose economy was involved with other types of economy were excluded.

Employing a range of tests, he is able to show (cf. 1988: 394, Table 4) that

the demographic variables are highly correlated with the socio-economic ones, especially sedentism and storage dependence. It is clear from the correlations . . . that *only those groups whose population densities are high relative to the productivity of the environment are complex.*

(ibid.: 393; his emphasis)

Especially valuable in Keeley's methodology is his attempt to derive measures for intrinsic environmental productivity, so that high population numbers responding to high natural productivity are not simply read as 'population pressure'. And he concludes that

> Whatever the cause of socioeconomic complexity in hunter-gatherers, demographic pressure on resources must be considered a crucial component of any causal models. To ignore or dismiss the role of demographic pressure means not only ignoring the empirical correlations determined here but also the simple, and therefore robust, hypotheses that argue that complexity and demography *must* be related.
>
> (1988: 396–7; original emphasis)

Indeed they must: the question is 'how'? Being statistically sophisticated, Keeley himself stated at the beginning of his essay, that

> even if all of these implications were confirmed by reliable data, it would not necessarily strengthen the case for demographic pressure being an independent cause, *or even a cause* of complexity.
>
> (1988: 377; my emphasis)

The point surely is about mechanism and process. The (time-based) process may well be that population rises in both absolute and relative (to the areal resources exploited) terms; the mechanism is what determines whether there is 'pressure' or not. In other words, it is well known that hunter-gatherer populations operate a 'satisficer' strategy, whereby security, in which there is a cultural premium, is provided by maintaining mobile and small populations relative to the territory exploited. By contrast, more complex societies employing both sedentism and storage are exploiting their environment more intensively, and thus able to provide for a larger population by operating more of an 'optimizer' strategy. Whether this last strategy is more or less stable is another, and empirical question, which basically turns on how variable are the variables, and the efficiency of the organizational means (such as storage) used to provide for a population extracting more from its environment. In the next chapter we shall see how Pre-Pottery Neolithic populations in the Levant coped or failed to.

But whether 'population pressure' exists depends on the specific evolutionary trajectory of the society which is being studied in the ethnographic present (i.e. by social anthropologists), or which is being reconstructed from its material remains by archaeologists. In other words, what are the *actual* operative chains of cause and effect present in a determinate society at a particular point in time (say, over the three coeval generations)? We know that Epipalaeolithic hunter-gatherers in the Near East were responding to conditions of expanding opportunity by exploiting newly available resources, storing them, and reducing their mobility until they were sedentary. This process *allowed population to rise and enabled it to be sustained*! (cf. Maisels 1990: Chapter 4, section 6, 'Demography in the pristine Neolithic'.) By contrast the histories of the societies Keeley employs are barely known, but since they were studied only in the past few generations we do know that their history embodies around ten millennia of adaptation to the Holocene, so on their own they can tell us relatively little about the earliest adaptive transitions. And since neither Keeley nor anyone else can demonstrate *mechanism* by the correlation of traits, their presumed implications for transformative *process* must fail.

As it happens, we are better placed to elucidate process – chains of cause and effect – from the material record of the prehistoric Near East. Put at its simplest, sedentism lifted some of the previous constraints on population, particularly those imposed by the need for mobility. Birth spacings could then be closer, with the consequence that

> if, in a Neolithic village of 100 persons, one woman in a decade allowed one infant to live, which she previously would have killed, the village would grow by one person every ten years. And an increase of one person every ten years in a village of 100, is equivalent to an average annual rate of growth of 0.1 of 1 per cent.
>
> (Carneiro 1981: 79)

This is the sort of rate of population growth reckoned (cf. Maisels 1990: 124–5) to characterize the early Holocene in the Near East. Even if the reduction or elimination of infanticide was not the mechanism, or not the only mechanism involved, this estimation nonetheless shows that a relatively small effect derived from the 'settling-down' process is sufficient to account for all the population growth archaeologically manifest. In sum, it shows that demographic increase is consequence and not cause. Of course, consequences are in turn causes of subsequent events, but in this case we can see that an ongoing pressure of population increase cannot function as the prime mover.

## A MODEL OF DE-MOBILIZATION

Patterns of mobility and landuse in the process of sedentarization are shown in the model (Figure 4.1), the start conditions of which in the late (Geometric) Kebaran, are of mobile hunter-gatherer groups moving round their 'estate' in a seasonal rhythm, but forming larger, merged camps with other bands in times of seasonal abundance, say late summer. Thus Kaufman (1986, 1989) has cogently argued for annual 'in-gatherings' of the otherwise mobile Geometric Kebaran groups, to form fairly large temporary settlements, this pattern, well-known from ethnography, serving as prototype for the Natufian settlements, as indeed do Geometric Kebaran burial patterns. He argues (1989: 278–9) that the sites

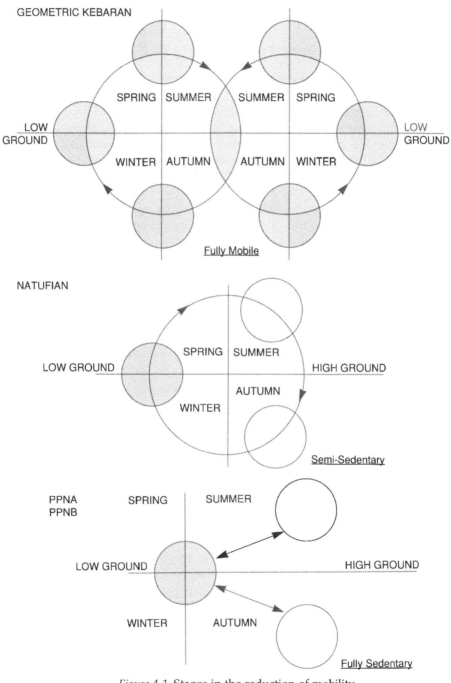

*Figure 4.1* Stages in the reduction of mobility.

of Neve David, extending over 1000 m², and Hefziba, covering about 1500 m² represent 'regional macrobands which gathered for economic and/or social reasons'. Accordingly, the basic pattern is shown in panel A, where the formation of larger, longer-stay sites like Neve David and Hefziba is obvious.

Panel B represents the Natufian situation, in which an all-purpose site is occupied for most if not all of the year, with moves of all or just some of the inhabitants to short-stay sites for seasonal activities/benefits. If gathering and small-game hunting was by family units, then the most intensive use could be made of a relatively small area. As will be suggested below, actual group moves need not be very far, and as Henry's (1989: 184) illustration shows, vertical zonation meant that Natufian groups did not have to move long distances in order to access qualitatively different resources. Indeed, all of this may well be true of Geometric Kebaran groups in more favoured zones, making the differences between conditions A and B more one of degree (and statistical incidence) than kind.

Panel C represents the position after the onset of the Holocene proper, with permanent villages established at locations offering both a permanent water supply, and (optimally) where standing water-bodies or seasonal water-courses provided permanently moist soils for agriculture, with the opportunities to hunt fowl and other animals coming to drink or feed (the earliest Neolithic still relied heavily on hunting).

Thus

> Each of the Neolithic settlements in which cultivation was practised (whether wild or domesticated species) was located on or near alluvial soils. This situation enabled them, during a few generations, to till the land that was often renewed by an additional veneer of sediment which accumulated seasonally. On the whole it seems that the regime of annual precipitation [i.e. deposition] contributed considerably to the success of early farming communities.
>
> (Bar Yosef 1989: 60)

(A success which was, however, only relative, as discussed in the next chapter.) The detached circles in summer and autumn thus represent special-purpose encampments, such as those in summer pastures for the deployment of shepherds with their flocks (PPNB [Pre-Pottery Neolithic B] and later); or, in the autumn perhaps, to particularly favourable hunting or collecting sites.

In the Zagros[5] even today farmers of northwestern Luristan rotate four times annually between no less than three types of habitation (Edelberg 1966–7: 382). These types are the *zemga*, or 'boulder-built village' occupied in December, January and February; the *siah cador*, or black tent occupied in April and May, some of which are pitched in the mountains with the sheep, goats and cattle and some by the barley fields; the *kula*, 'booths' or 'bowers' constructed at the end of May of posts with leafy branches for roofing and having rush mats for walls, and corresponding in ground-plan almost exactly to the tents (ibid.: 386–7). Later in the autumn (October and November) the villagers move back into tents, then into stone-built houses with the onset of winter (December).

Although the actual distances moved are not great, perhaps only a few kilometres, moving even short distances effects considerable changes in topography in the Zagros, and greatly assists in providing pasturage for animals, failing which many fewer could be kept. Not to be overlooked also, such seasonal moves conduce to human well-being, making living conditions more congenial by taking account of the weather, and also more hygienic by 'resting' locations. How cereal and animal husbandry is combined with changes of habitation can best be seen in the *Lur Calendar* recorded by Edelberg (op. cit.: 381).

This slow settling-down process, extending over millennia, shows that hunter-gatherers did not 'adopt' agriculture. It was indeed impossible for them to do so, since they would have needed a pre-formed conception of what it was! Neither was it 'invented' as a set of practices; although once the practices had been established, only one or two human generations would have been required for domesticated grain to appear (Hillman and Davies 1990: 212–14).

Instead, as with all evolutionary processes, an *incremental-cumulative* process took place whereby the next step depended on present conditions which were themselves the cumulative result of previous steps. Thus the Epipalaeolithic hunter-gatherers embarked unwittingly on the path to agriculture by actually extending their *gathering* activities through accumulating the readily available wild grains. Harlan (1967: 197–201) found from experimental work in southern Turkey that 'a family group . . . could easily harvest wild-cereals over a three-week span or more and, without even working particularly hard, could gather more grain than the family could possibly consume in a year' (ibid.: 198). This amount of grain requires dry, secure storage if it is to be consumed over a twelve-month period; this is an inducement to staying put, and requires facilities which are perhaps best managed from permanent architecture.

Katherine Wright (1991), in a thorough discussion of the origins and development of ground stone assemblages in the Late Pleistocene (= Upper Palaeolithic to Earliest Neolithic), concludes that while such mortars, etc. were multi-functional, they were also used for dehusking wild grains. Thus 'In the Early Natufian 49 per cent of the known sites contain ground stone assemblages and many sites with ground stone occur in a north–south belt in or near the Jordan Valley', and further, 'the presence of ground stone in Early Natufian sites is associated with architecture' (1991: 38–9). As dehusking is a labour-intensive activity, she goes on to suggest that heavy reliance upon cereals is more likely to be a result of stress, possibly climatic, than choice (ibid.). Nonetheless, the use of grains may be more a matter of social than environmental pressures and she states that 'social acceptance of labour intensive foods as staples may have been more critical to the eventual adoption of agriculture than any climate or environmental variables alone' (op. cit.: 39).

The sedentary lifestyle thus established allows population to increase, for a number of related dietary and reproductive-physiological reasons discussed in Maisels (1990: 121–30). Those include reduced birth spacings (since babies no longer have to be carried long distances), the shift to a carbohydrate-based diet (which, *inter alia*, by reducing breast-feeding reduces its fertility-inhibiting effects), lowered energy demands and higher fat-to-body-weight ratios, thought to be important in sustaining fecundity. Henry (1989: 43) provides this summary (see Table 4.1): that is, 'A comparison of mobile and sedentary foraging strategies in regard to various factors that influence female fecundity. Note that "energy drain" and "diet" are both likely to affect the "fat : body-weight ratio".'

*Table 4.1*   Mobile and sedentary foraging

|  | *Mobile foraging* | *Sedentary foraging* |
| --- | --- | --- |
| Lactation | Longer, more intense | Shorter, less intense |
| Fat : body-weight ratio | Lower | Higher |
| Energy drain | High | Low |
| Diet | High protein–low carbohydrate | Low protein–high carbohydrate |

Note also that it is still two types of *foraging* that are being compared; that is, those population-expanding effects would be seen as early as the Natufian.

At first new households are simply added. When the immediate vicinity can no longer sustain the increasing population, especially in its demands for meat (i.e. game), then new hamlets are established at some distance. When the process has repeated itself a number of times, there are no longer 'free' fields of wild grain to be harvested. Then grain must be sown in order to be reaped, and the land chosen will be that adjoining water-bodies and water-courses where a population would want to site a village for other reasons. This gives them the benefit of permanently wetted and alluvial soils of fine structure requiring a minimum of tillage. There are, however, not very many such sites in the Levant as compared with the potential of Mesopotamia and the upper Euphrates. Accordingly once it was necessary to construct such optimal conditions by means of irrigation, it was natural that the Levant should experience something of a hiatus between the Neolithic and the Bronze Age, while Mesopotamia became the 'Heartland of Cities' as early as the fourth millennium, a distinction it maintained well into the second millennium.

# 5

# HARBINGERS IN THE LEVANT

In this chapter I want to show how Epipalaeolithic hunter-gatherers became Neolithic farmers despite themselves. That is, they became farmers as a consequence of developing their gathering regime. Thus, they became caught up in a sequence of changes, the outcome of which was settled village agriculture and this process of cause and effect become the cause of another effect and so on, can best be expressed in the form of a flowchart (Figure 5.1).

The start-condition is 'plenitude of resources' following on from 'a short abrupt climatic crisis around 13,000–12,500 BP' (Bar-Yosef and Belfer-Cohen 1989: 486–7) in which loss of Mediterranean littoral may be implicated, marking the transition from Geometric Kebaran complex foraging to the Natufian. 'Plenitude of resources' simply means that there are plenty of subsistence resources relative to the demands the population is making on them. Epipalaeolithic populations in the Near East were highly selective as to where they lived and what they ate. Indeed, to Moore (1989: 624),

> It seems that occupation during the critical phases before and immediately after the adoption of agriculture was confined to the Levant and the Zagros with its western foothills. There appears to have been little penetration of Anatolia and remarkably sparse use of the northern Jazireh eastward to the Zagros. Within the in-habited areas there were certain locations that were highly favoured for settlement, presumably because they offered a par-ticular set of desired resources. These were the Jordan Valley, the Damascus Basin, and the Middle Euphrates in the west, the Deh Luran plain and certain valleys of the Zagros from Rowanduz to Kermanshah in the east'.[1]

Further, although most sites (like Abu Hureyra, a very large site on the mid-Euphrates, or Nahal Oren on the seaboard) had several desirable species of ungulate available in their vicinity (e.g. onager at Abu Hureyra, fallow-deer, caprines and cattle at Nahal Oren), the former

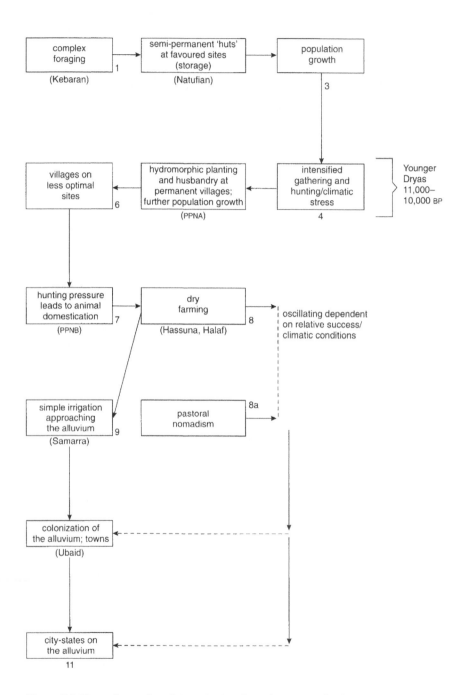

*Figure 5.1* Flow chart of social evolution from hunter-gathering to city-states in the Near East.

concentrated on gazelle for some 80 per cent of their mammal kills, as did the inhabitants of Nahal Oren, both largely ignoring the wild pigs which were locally plentiful. Such selectivity leads Moore (1989: 627) to conclude that 'this evidence strongly supports the view that the inhabitants of Epipalaeolithic sites chose a few animals to exploit intensively and that this trend became more marked through time'; which hardly suggests anything other than conditions of plenty, especially after 10,500 BP. Rather than go through the steps of the flowchart point by point, it is better to get to grips with the sites that have given rise to the model, beginning with the Natufian as the culture which shows the earliest approach to permanent, year-round settlement.[2] The chart opposite draws upon the Levantine experience until step 7 (PPNB). At the hiatus between Pre- and Pottery Neolithic, the focus shifts to Mesopotamia. Early urbanization is not a Levantine feature. As late as the second millenium BC, it is not extensive and does not render the society urban (cf. Falconer and Savage 1995).

## THE NATUFIAN

Nahal Oren, on the western face of Mt Carmel, some 10 km south of Haifa on the old Tel Aviv–Haifa road, lies in the Natufian heartlands, and is therefore taken to be representative. Stekelis and Yizraeli (1963: 1), in their preliminary report, describe the site as

> located on the right bank of a valley [the Wadi Fallah] near the opening of a cave on the slope of a large terrace, about 45–55 m above sea level. At one time this valley had a small stream which wound through sands and emptied into the Mediterranean. There are also three springs at a distance of about 500 m from the excavation. One of the reasons why this site was chosen by prehistoric man for settlement was undoubtedly its copious supply of water.

Four prehistoric cultures are represented at the site: what Stekelis and Yizraeli (ibid.) call Upper Palaeolithic VI ('the Kebaran') located in a gravel deposit, followed by a Natufian assemblage, which was followed by a stratum from the subsequent Pre-Pottery Neolithic A (PPNA) period, plus PPNB also.

The Natufian material found on the terrace was a product of two periods. In the lower phase Stekelis and Yizraeli (1963: 11) discovered

> an interesting stone-walled camp site, 7 to 10 m in diameter. It was surrounded by a solidly constructed wall built of dry stone blocks and large mortars which at that time were no longer used for domestic or ritual purposes. . . . Inside the camp site abundant

evidence of flint, stone, and bone industries was found, as well as hearths and silos.

Near the campsite a graveyard was found, which it seemed was levelled before each interment (ibid.). A particular hearth built of smooth flat stones encircling a half metre thick layer of ash, suggested to Stekelis and Yizraeli (op. cit.) that it formed part of Natufian burial rites; as also apparently did limestone mortars, about 70 cm high and pierced through the bottom (often a consequence of sustained wear) found standing in most of the burial pits from which they protruded about 20 cm.

The excavators suggest (op. cit.: 12) that the mortars served both as tombstones and had considerable ritual importance, indicated by their piercing right through. Likewise their numbers in the perimeter wall indicate their considerable utilitarian basis, which poses a great problem. From their later excavations at Nahal Oren, Noy, Legge and Higgs (1973: 96), concluded that 'The site territory was not of exceptional productivity such as would automatically encourage primitive sedentary occupation.' Indeed, 'the unsuitable nature of the site territory for grain agriculture, suggests that grain-growing was not an important aspect of the economy. The grinding tools are not necessarily indicative of the grinding of grain.' From the site catchment analysis conducted (i.e. a detailed landuse evaluation of the territory in a radius of 5 km from the site) it was estimated that presently only about 8 per cent of the area was arable land, while no less than 58 per cent was rough grazing, 7 per cent good grazing and 27 per cent seasonal marsh, the remaining 8 per cent being sand dune (ibid.: 95). No wonder Eric Higgs concluded that 'the site economic potential was low and was likely to have been even lower prior to the twentieth century when as in earlier times extensive areas were drained'. However, with a lower sea level the catchment potentials would have been rather different, given Wadi Fallah's proximity to the coast (D. Baird, pers. comm.). In other words, some of the best land might now be drowned.

Despite pioneering work in recovering floral remains through flotation washing devices, not many individual items were recovered, nor were many taxa represented at Nahal Oren (Noy, Legge and Higgs 1973: 92), possibly a consequence of a destructive depositional environment. In the Natufian no instances of *Triticum dicoccum* (emmer) or *Hordeum sp.* (barley) are found, in contrast to remains of pig (3.9 per cent), roe (0.7 per cent), fallow (2.6 per cent) and red deer (0.1 per cent), cattle (9.2 per cent) and goat (0.2 per cent), all dwarfed by the 83.3 per cent of gazelle remains found in the Natufian. Accordingly, when taken with the site catchment analysis, the presumption must be that the site was favoured because it was an excellent one from which to hunt for gazelle. The proportion of gazelle remains in the Kebaran is 77.4 per cent, 83.3 per cent in the Natufian, even rising to an amazing 87.9 per cent in the PPNA, before declining somewhat to 76.4 per cent during the PPNB. This still represents over three-quarters of all animal remains, none of which were even then, in the PPNB, domesticated (although Legge 1972 has argued from the death patterns in which the largest proportion are of immature animals, that this represents a form of domestication of gazelle). Only during the PPNB, Legge (1973: 91) argues, does the proportion of goat (presumably domesticated) rise significantly (to 13.9 per cent) and the ratio of immature gazelles killed fall below 50 per cent, to 39.1 per cent (though animals killed earlier in the year will comprise a higher proportion of immature individuals).

Accordingly, Eric Higgs concludes (1973: 96), against the opinion of Stekelis and Yizraeli (1963: 12), that the Natufian occupation of Nahal Oren was not year-round, but undertaken in conjunction with an inland/upland site with complementary resources (such as Rakefet). This despite the fact that Stekelis and Yizraeli (1963: 11) found 'In the upper phases of the Natufian layer, remains of an oval-shaped house', whose walls were 'from 20 to 50 cm high and built of undressed stone taken from the eroded slopes of Mt Carmel. In the house, small installations such as silos were found.' Nonetheless, in stratum II of the Pre-Pottery Neolithic period, no less than fourteen houses, each covering an area of between 9 $m^2$ and 15 $m^2$ were uncovered, laid out on four terraces, with common walls serving contiguous houses on different levels (Stekelis and Yizraeli 1963: 5). Yet despite such ingenuity, the plan and section, with suggested reconstruction provided, shows a very compact house whose major permanent feature is its low walls of approximately sitting height, covered over by support poles reminiscent of a tepee frame, eminently (re)movable.

Similar shelters of perhaps fifty structures (in three successive levels) covering some 2000 $m^2$, and containing round storage pits 80 cm deep, occur at 'Ain Mallaha (Eynan), north of Lake Tiberias (Perrot 1966). Notwithstanding a material culture which at Nahal Oren is summarized by Stekelis and Yizraeli (1963: 12) as including, in addition to bone harpoons and awls: 'many sickle blades, knives, bladelets, burins, microburins, crescents, gorgets, and sickle hafts' (the latter with a deep groove running down one or both edges), Jean Perrot, the excavator of 'Ain Mallaha, is of the opinion that the Natufian regime was still mobile (or semi-nomadic), and that this indeed accounts for the presence of both primary and secondary (re)burial, whereby the bones of those who died when away from the base-camp were brought 'home' to their final resting place.

Only a decade separates the publications of Stekelis and Yizraeli (Stekelis having originally worked at Nahal Oren in 1941 under the auspices of the British School of Archaeology in Jerusalem), from that of Noy, Legge and Higgs. Although that of Stekelis and Yizraeli is only a fairly brief preliminary report, its traditional approach shows in its concentration upon lithic artefacts and architectural remains. Very little is said of the floral resources exploited in any period. No doubt any recognizable bones found would have been recorded and eventually identified as to species; however, vegetal remains are not so visible, especially when seeds are involved.

Thus, despite the fact that the excavations of Noy, Legge and Higgs covered a much smaller area than those reported ten years before (being confined to three rectangles of only 2.5 × 2.5 m, one (R100) at the top of the slope, one (R300) in the centre and one (R400) at the foot of the slope, with subsequent extensions (Rectangles 500 and 600) linking 100 and 300 into an L shape beyond the northern limits of the previous excavation), materials for reconstruction of the economy are relatively plentiful in the later account. It greatly benefited from the methods (such as wet sieving and site-catchment analysis) developed by the British Academy's Major Research Project, the History of Early Agriculture, in which Legge and Higgs were involved, the latter in a directoral role. The point was to apply the exact methods of the natural sciences to the humanistic discipline of archaeology so that, amongst other matters, economic prehistory could be advanced on a solid basis (Clark 1972: viii).

Accordingly, at Nahal Oren

Each rectangle was subdivided in north, south or north, south and centre subsections. Deposits were removed layer by layer and each layer excavated in 10 cm depth units taken from an arbitrary datum. Finds of exceptional interest were recorded in three dimensions.

Recovery tests based on 1060 litres of deposits which contained 28,677 artefacts showed that, with careful excavation by experienced operators, only 25–30 per cent of the small microliths were recovered if the deposits were not sieved and washed. From this volume of soil, 388 microlithic tools were recovered, 43 per cent by dry and 52 per cent by wet sieving. Ninety-five per cent of the smaller bones were collected by wet sieving, which also increased greatly the percentage of immature animal bones recovered. Eight thousand bones of the larger mammals identifiable to genera or species were obtained and 400 identifiable plant species.

(Noy, Legge and Higgs 1973: 75–6)

Even then the plant remains are disappointing, with only 2–8 seeds recovered per cubic metre of spoil processed. Only *Graminae*, *Viciae* and *Vicia sp.* occur in all levels from Kebaran to PPNB (ibid.: 92). However, an important caveat must be entered here: even in a relatively small site there is no sure way of knowing how representative the results from selective excavation really are.

Nevertheless, thanks to the fine-grained resolution possible by such rigorous methods even in limited exposures, Noy, Legge and Higgs (1973: 86) record layer IV as

> a small layer between the Natufian and the 'Pre-Pottery Neolithic A' levels. The small arrowheads with a hollow base may indicate that this is Late Natufian [*vide* Perrot 1952a]. Such small arrowheads were found at el Khiam phase IV and Poleg 18M [Burian and Friedman 1965].
>
> (1973: 86)

Those sorts of arrowheads are now called *Khiam points* (see Figure 5.2) and appear in Levantine assemblages towards the end of the eleventh and the first half of the tenth millennium BP. The Khiamian, which is also characterized by asphalt-hafted sickle blades, marks the transition of Natufian communities to very early farming practices just as the Holocene was commencing. It is contemporary with the last part of the Harifian (an adaptation of other Natufian communities to the desert conditions of the Negev and Sinai), Mureybet 1B and, in the Jordan Valley is succeeded by the PPNA Sultanian.

The notched Khiam arrowheads displace lunates and other geometric microliths in the lithic inventory. Is this merely technological evolution or does it represent the need for extra stopping power? Probably the greatest change from the Natufian to the Khiamian lithic assemblage, however, is the increase in borers from zero or a few per cent to around 20 per cent of the total. Bueller's (1989) microwear studies of PPNA borers from Netiv Hagdud in the Jordan Valley (with radiocarbon dates RT 502C and RT 502A of 8,230 ± 300 BC and 7,840 ± 380 BC), indicates that the tools were hafted in bone and their tips used to bore small holes in dry hide. He convincingly suggests (op. cit.: 26) that this was done to produce clothing, and that the skin most suitable would be gazelle. This helps explain the heavy concentration on gazelle hunting in the Pre-Pottery Neolithic. As the Neolithic advanced woven clothing would be used, but the intriguing question then arises as to what the Natufians wore?

In a meticulously detailed and reasoned work, Henry (1989) argues for a two-stage process in the emergence of farming culture in the Levant consequent upon rising world temperatures (perhaps 6–8°C) and heightened biotic activity after 13,000 BP. In Henry's model, the Natufian is definitely not a farming culture but a culture of complex, specialized hunter-gatherers, exploiting the conditions of opportunity presented with the spread of trees and cereal grasses around 12,500 years ago, at

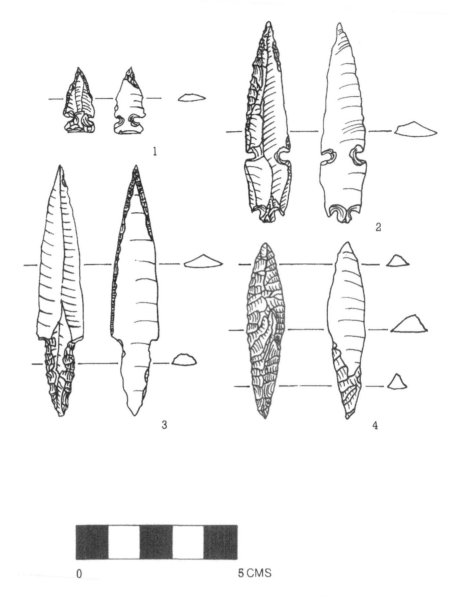

*Figure 5.2* Khiam, Byblos and other characteristic projectile points. Levantine Neolithic projectile point types from Azraq project sites in the Wadi el-Jilat, eastern Jordan, arranged chronologically, in order of their original appearance. (1) Khiam point, (2) Helwan point, (3) Byblos point, (4) Amuq point.

which time the cereals colonize the uplands (to 1200 m above sea level) from their former refuges near sea-level (ibid.: 35). Accordingly:

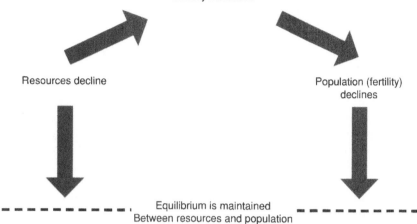

*Figure 5.3* Mobility as stabilizer of hunter-gatherer resources (Henry 1989: 44).

Natufian hamlets were restricted to the Mediterranean environmental zone and they followed a specific pattern relative to the
local setting. Hamlet sites are consistently found at the foot of
slopes that divide hill and mountain regions from broad valleys or
coastal plains. These topographic divides also form boundaries
between the Mediterranean woodlands and open grassland.
Hamlets established along this divide had access to the wild cereals
and nuts of the uplands in addition to the gazelle herds occupying
the open grassland. Furthermore, the hamlets were closely tied to
the abundant water sources, represented by springs or rivers, that
are concentrated along the edge of the hill and mountain zone. In
contrast Geometric Kebaran and Mushabian sites display a much
wider environmental distribution, and local site settings vary
greatly. Though found in the Mediterranean zone, settlement also
extended into steppe and perhaps even desert zones. Local site
settings vary from coastal lowlands to mountain with no specific
pattern emerging.

(Henry 1989: 48)

Henry (op. cit.: 44) provides this elegant illustration of how stability in
the relationships between the resources and population of simple
hunter-gatherers is maintained by mobility (see Figure 5.3). This because the Geometric Kebaran which preceded, and the Mushabian
culture which was perhaps coeval with the Natufian, were generalized
('simple') hunter-gatherers, while the Natufians were complex hunter-
gatherers, with a specialized subsistence repertoire focusing on the

79

hunting of gazelle, plus the collecting and storing of cereals and nuts (pistachio, almond and acorns), those sequenced gathering activities demanding sedentism with its storage facilities and domestic architecture (Henry 1989: 34–5). Natufian sites average in excess of 1000 m², while their predecessors, the Geometric Kebarans average only 200 m², with only the very largest exceeding 600 m²; excepting of course the likes of Kharaneh IV, whose 21,672 m² encompasses Ancient, Classic, Geometric and Final Geometric Kebaran phases (Muheisen 1988: 353–67), which may or may not be related to the 'in-gathering' sites seasonally occupied (or just expanded?) when a number of groups come together for heightened social interaction in the season of plenty (shown as the first panel in Figure 4.1). Indeed, Douglas Baird (pers. comm.) is strongly of the opinion that the differences between Geometric and Final Geometric Kebaran and Natufian land-use patterns are ones of degree and not kind.

Thus while the basic Geometric Kebaran would on Henry's (1989: 39) reckoning have had a population of around twenty-two persons (i.e. that of a typical foraging band), Natufian hamlets would have contained about 150 persons. This because sedentism induced by the exploitation of newly abundant resources mitigates some of the population-inhibiting mechanisms intrinsic to mobile hunting and gathering, which range from the problems of child-transport through the absence of mothers' milk substitutes and the fertility-suppressing effects of continued suckling, to the variability of subsistence resources themselves (cf. Maisels 1990: 24–31 for a fuller discussion of various factors).

However, the resulting growth in a population dependent on the co-occurrence of a few critical resources – gazelle, grains, nuts and water – resulted in an even denser 'packing' of Natufian hamlets, which were unable to increase their resource base so long as they remained complex hunter-gatherers. This is clearly illustrated by Henry (1989: 4) as their inability, despite sophistication in collecting, storing and processing, to permanently lift available resources to a higher ceiling by food production (see Figure 5.4). In sum, the resource ceiling can only be permanently raised by agriculture. Sustained intensification of foraging only serves to *lower* the resource ceiling; that is, the sum of available resources actually diminishes. Natufian settlements, remaining hunter-gatherers, thus turned in on themselves with the development of strong boundary definition to secure resources, probably underpinned by matriliny,[4] matrilocal residence[5] and endogamy,[6] for which last there is particularly strong evidence based on third molar agenesis at Hayonim Cave; plus intra-group ranking indicated by the differential presence of grave goods, where its association with children is held to be strong evidence of inherited rank. Evidence of dietary stress (which occurs at a similar stage two millennia later in the Zagros), can be found in the

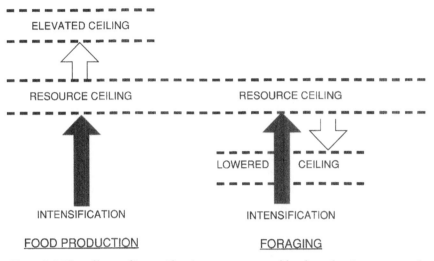

*Figure 5.4* The effects of intensification on systems of food production compared with foraging (Henry 1990: 4).

increased frequency of (tooth) enamel hypoplasia from Early to Late Natufian (Henry 1989: Table 2.5); and also in evidence of female infanticide from the distribution of Natufian skeletal populations by sex, all of which exceed the 56 per cent (44 per cent) threshold of a normal distribution (i.e. 128 : 100, males : females), seen in Table 5.1, also from Henry (op. cit.: 45).

*Table 5.1* Distribution of Natufian skeletal populations by sex. Note that all of the samples are skewed in favour of males and that all exceed the 56 per cent threshold of a normal distribution (Henry 1989: 45)

| Site | Male | | Female | | Source |
|------|------|------|--------|------|--------|
| | N | % | N | % | |
| Ein Mallaha | 9 | 75.0 | 3 | 25.0 | (Ferembach, 1977) |
| Hayonim | 11 | 68.7 | 5 | 31.3 | (Bar-Yosef & Goren, 1973) |
| Nahal Oren | 11 | 61.0 | 7 | 39.9 | (Crognier & Dupouy-Madre, 1974) |
| El Wad | 8 | 57.1 | 6 | 42.9 | (Garrod & Bate, 1937) |
| Combined mean/ percentage | 39 | 65.0 | 21 | 35.0 | |

Since intra-group ranking and inter-group rivalry aggravate the situation by consuming yet more resources, the Natufian was a culture that could not continue in the face of additional pressures. This was provided by the progressive drying process as the rain-supplying winter storm tracks receded northwards (with the high-pressure air masses) from a latitude around 31°N at 13,000 BP, moving toward their modern

positions at 35–36°N (i.e. along the Syrian coastline) around 11,000 BP
(Henry 1989: 65). Consequently, by the end of the Natufian culture – i.e.
around 10,500 years ago, about the time modern, Holocene, conditions
became established in the Levant – the Mediterranean woodlands which
had caused the Geometric Kebarans (as seen at the lowland sites of Neve
David, Hefsibah and Ein Gev I) to adopt what became the Natufian
lifestyle and which lasted some 2000 years, had shrunk to about half its
original area (Henry 1989: 47).

Thus,

> Within 500 years after the onset of drier conditions, all but five of
> the 23 major Natufian hamlets had been abandoned. By this time
> the Natufian adaptive system had failed and the society was
> undergoing major changes. The Natufian population replaced
> complex foraging with divergent strategies: incipient horticulture
> in what remained of the Mediterranean woodlands and simple
> foraging in the expanded steppe zone.
>
> (ibid.: 52)

This latter, sharing artefact inventories with the Natufian and still occupying large base camps at higher elevations during the wet season, was
the Harifian; while by contrast, 'the PPNA adaptive strategy followed that
of the Natufian in being based on intensified exploitation and strategic
placement of settlements' (ibid.: 54), to pursue where they could the
Natufian strategy in reduced circumstances. Davis (1989: 47) suggests
that 'During the PPNA, population levels may have passed a certain
critical threshold, so that the gazelle came under intense culling pressure' leading to domestication of goat (at least) during the PPNB. But it
may not have been population levels that grew in the PPNA, it could
rather be that the quantity of resources shrank with diminished rainfall.

The PPNA itself consists of two facies: the Khiamian, whose Natufian
microlithic technology is seen in lunates and sickle-blades, for example,
and whose sites, at 1000 m$^2$ to 3000 m$^2$ are quite large. They are, however,
confined to locations with permanent water sources in the core
Mediterranean woodlands, and thus are restricted to low elevations
(Henry 1989: 224–5).

The other facies is the Sultanian, best known from the Jordan Valley
and Jericho, which has connections with but may be somewhat later
than the Khiamian, though the Sultanian lacks the other's strong microlithic features (ibid.: 225). However, Sultanian settlements which, at 1–3
hectares, seem larger by an order of magnitude, are like the Khiamian
confined to permanent water sources, and thus none is higher than
300 m above sea level (ibid.: 226). The locus classicus of such a site is of
course Jericho, and if population estimates seem generally over-inflated,

PPNA levels there do appear to show domesticated emmer, two-row barley and possibly einkorn (Hopf 1969). Such processes may explain the difference in average site size between Khiamian and Sultanian (if indeed there is any real difference between the two).

Unger-Hamilton's (1989: 101) microwear studies of (polish and striations in) sickle-blades, indicate that only at the beginning of the PPNB (c. 7000 BC) was ripe or dry grain being harvested when previously the grain had been cut wet or green. This suggests that only by PPNB times had the wild-form brittle rachis which shatters on contact been replaced by the domesticated tough rachis, in which the seed remains attached during harvesting and has later to be separated from the ear by threshing. She therefore concludes (ibid.) that 'It was therefore probably only the beginning of this period [c. 7000 BC] that saw the transition to full-scale agriculture in the southern Levant.' However, despite Davis's (1989: 45) well-supported suggestion that goat-herding in the Levant 'began in the seventh millennium BC, sometime during the PPNB', it seems that this was a rather long drawn-out transition to 'full-scale agriculture' where domesticates had to be the chief support, in contrast to a few sites well-favoured edaphically and in terms of supplementary resources, such as the early emmer-wheat and pulse farming settlement of Aswad in the Damascus basin (cf. Maisels 1990: 74–5). There, during the PPNA (at least), local game, including gazelle, boar, water-fowl and fish, was abundant thanks to its lakeside location (De Contenson 1989: 260). Figure 5.5 shows the location of Aswad (from Van Zeist and Bakker-Heeres 1979: 161), which then as now receives too little rain for farming without irrigation.

If, as the flowchart suggests, by the Late Natufian/Earliest Neolithic, the best sites already had hamlets on them, and if the population in them expanded in this period enlarging those optimally-sited hamlets into villages and causing new ones to appear in less optimal situations during the PPNB, then it would not take much in the way of environmental deterioration (climatic or edaphic) to cause a fully-stretched extractive system to collapse. Perhaps due to the very precocity of Levantine conditions, social and environmental, populations may have been making demands on the environment that only the full (i.e. later and better managed/integrated) suite of plant and animal domesticates could answer.

## EXPERIMENTAL NEOLITHICS

Even at this period there is considerable variability in what 'farming' involves! Garfinkel (1987), who did some of the rescue archaeology at the seventh millennium Neolithic village of Yiftahel in Lower Galilee, concluded that

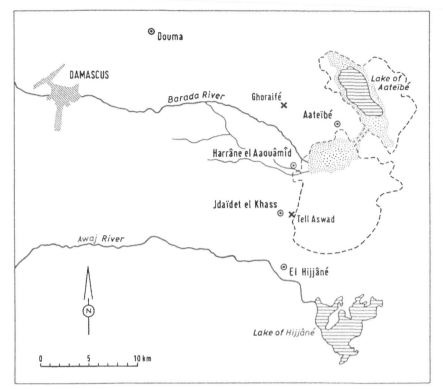

*Figure 5.5* The location of Aswad in the Damascus Basin (Van Zeist and Bakker-Heeres 1979: 16).

In the Neolithic villages of the Levant in the seventh millennium BC, there is a high degree of unity in the material culture: rectangular architecture, plaster floors, lithic technology, and typology of flint artefacts. From the economic point of view, however, there is great variability between different sites. *It appears that the diffusion and exploitation of domesticated plants and animals was not uniform in the Neolithic communities of the Mediterranean Levant.*

(ibid.: 212; my emphasis)

Neolithic Yiftahel is a village covering about 15,000 m² at an elevation of 145 m above sea level, some 8 km west of Nazareth. The climate is 'typically Mediterranean', there are *terra rossa* soils in the vicinity, and the local climax association is *Quercus ithaburensis/Styrax officinalis* park woodland (Garfinkel 1987: 200). Indeed a topographical transect – an invaluable tool taught in school Geography but too often noticeable by its absence from Archaeology (a non-school subject) – indicates that the village site is located just where oak-covered hillsides rise from the valley floor of the Nahal Yiftahel, which in little more than a kilometre joins with the valley of the Nahal Sepphoris. Basically this is an ideal site for early farmers, and indeed Garfinkel (op. cit.: 203) estimates the village to consist of about fifty houses, with a guesstimated population of around 250. 'The tool inventory is typical of the PPNB and includes arrowheads, sickle-blades and axes as well as burins, scrapers, and other implements' (ibid.). Radiocarbon dates of carbonized pulses from the major structure 700 (stratigraphic layer 2) range between 8890 ± 120 BP (lentil seeds) and 8570 ± 130 BP (horsebean).

Area C excavated by Garfinkel was dominated by a tripartite domestic structure composed of a rectangular covered central area, flanked by two rectangular courtyards. Three such houses were uncovered at PPNB Jericho. Called Structure 700, Garfinkel (1987: 209) states that

> The central unit was used for storage; in the southern courtyard grinding and milling activities were performed; and the northern courtyard served as a workshop. Unlike other Neolithic sites such as Beisamoun and Ain Ghazal, hearths are lacking inside the house. Those found in the area north of the structure were used for cooking, but lime production and greenstone-working were also carried out here.

The size of the covered area is 30 m$^2$, the size of the roofed areas in Early Bronze Age Arad and also, as Garfinkel (1987: 209–10) remarks, the area of roofed living-space characteristic of single-family houses in early villages both in the Near East and in Mesoamerica. Though hearths, no doubt for safety reasons, did not occur in the covered area, a silo 40 cm deep and at least 3 m$^2$ in area, providing at least 1.2 m$^3$ of storage, was found built on top of the plaster floor in the northeast corner of the room. Constructed of clay with straw and stones, it contained not grain but no less than 2000 carbonized horsebean seeds (*Vicia faba*), the oldest certain identification of that legume. In the northern half of the room, in a location where they must have been stored in perishable containers such as baskets, were found embedded in sediment 1,400,000 lentil seeds (*Lens culinaris*) with a weight of 7.375 kg. In PPNB Jericho only 640 lentil seeds were found. On the basis of the contents of the silo, which has a storage potential of some 1.5 tonnes, Garfinkel was able to make some very illuminating calculations:

> As the rate of energy of legumes is 3300 calories per kg, this storage space could potentially have held five million calories. On the basis of a daily intake per person of 2200 calories, the food stored in this silo could support six persons all year round, without any other source of nutrition. As it is likely that legumes constituted no more than 60–70% of the diet, and probably less, this silo may serve as

evidence of surplus production that could have been exchanged for other items, such as greenstone. Another thing that may be calculated from the potential storage space of the silo is the area cultivated in order to fill the silo. If 50 households lived simultaneously in the Neolithic village of Yiftahel, then about 150 ha of cultivated land was necessary to support the entire community. Suitable soils are to be found in the alluvial valleys of Nahal Yiftahel and Nahal Sepphoris within a 2 km radius of the site.

(1987: 210)

One hundred and fifty hectares represents one good-sized farm, although no doubt the 150 ha was farmed in different patches or fields by individual families.

Further, scattered throughout layers 1–4, that is, during the whole lifetime of the site, many lentils were found, indicating that this was another staple, possibly in association with roasted or boiled acorns from the Tabor-oak forests then surrounding the site (ibid.: 210).

However, the villagers did not live by pulses alone, with or without acorns. From stratigraphic units 1 and 2 alone, 1000 identifiable bones were recovered, found to consist of approximately 75 per cent gazelle bones. Some fish was also consumed, but this concentration upon a single species is remarkable for a 'farming' community. Although we have seen a figure of 76.4 per cent gazelle bones at PPNB Nahal Oren, other PPNB sites give much lower percentages: Jericho 14.1 per cent, Beisamoun 14.5 per cent, Abu Gosh 13.3 per cent and Munhatta layer 5–6, 34.1 per cent (Garfinkel 1987: 210). Accordingly, to Garfinkel (ibid.: 212), 'It appears that the Neolithic community of Yiftahel lived on legume-farming and gazelle hunting.' This makes one wonder yet again about local preservation conditions.

Thus, although the concentration upon pulses seems to be a local specialization (and indeed Lower Galilee may be the locale of the domestication of horsebean, called *ful* in Arabic), this combination of the cultivation of only a few species, combined with concentration on the hunting of a few wild species, seems to be the rule even as late as the PPNB; that is, during the seventh millennium. This becomes clearer if we look at another PPNB village right at the southern edge of their range, namely at Beidha south of the Dead Sea, 4.5 km north of Petra on the eastern flank of the Jordan Rift. This is a fairly arid interior environment but offering some local advantages, one of which may be proximity to the sources of greenstone (malachite and rosasite) worked into beads and other objects at Yiftahel and other PPNB sites, including Jericho. Certainly large chunks of malachite ($Cu_2CO_3(OH)_2$) occur at Beidha, excavated in seven campaigns (from 1958) by Diana Kirkbride, who thereby provided what is probably still the broadest exposure of any

Neolithic village in the Levant (Redman *et al*. 1978). And as Beidha is fortunately not a rescue archaeology site, there exists the prospect of yet further exposures, not least of the Natufian substrata noticed by Kirkbride.

Compensating for a southerly and interior location that presently receives less than 200 mm of rainfall annually (though the Jebel Shara to the east normally receives more than this amount),

> The site, at an elevation of about 1020 m [above sea level], is situated in an alluvial valley which is drained by the seasonally flowing Wadi el Ghurab. The wadi originates northeast of the site on the slopes of the Jebel Shara (maximum elevation 1700 m a.s.l.) which forms the beginnings of the Transjordan plateau. The wadi flows generally from northeast to southwest and near Beidha it runs along the sandstone cliffs on the south side of the valley. Two and a half kilometres further downstream it drops dramatically (over 400 m) before joining the Wadi Musa and flowing more gradually down into the Wadi Araba.
>
> (Byrd 1988: 176)

The people of Beidha used stone bowls, troughs and mortars, with baskets coated with bitumen and lime-plaster also serving as containers (Kirkbride 1968: 268). Indeed, if extensive bone-working characterizes the Natufian, then extensive use of lime-plaster, already noted at Yiftahel and found at PPNB period sites all the way up to Çatal Hüyük and Hacilar in Anatolia, characterises the Earliest Neolithic. Wood, however, seems to have been the preferred medium for food preparation, given the relative scarcity of stone bowls.

Though parching ovens have not been found (Kirkbride 1966: 16), wild barley (*Hordeum spontaneum*) was actually cultivated, according to Helbaek (1966: 62); as also, in his view (ibid.), was emmer wheat in a range of forms indicative of transition from the wild race (*Triticum turgidum subsp. dicoccoides*) to the domesticated. No less than five gallons of carbonized pistachio nuts were found (ibid.) in the fire-destroyed house that provided most of the site's floral information. Here acorns were used, together with other vegetable foods such as fieldpea, two kinds of wild lentil, large vetch (*Vicia narbonense*), medick (*medicago sp.*), cock's comb (*Onobrychis cristagalli*), plus other leguminous plants (ibid.: 63). Goat herding is said to coexist with hunting (Hecker 1982, actually speaks of 'cultural control' of goats), whereas hunting is characteristic of all Pre-Pottery Neolithic sites, putting herding at Beidha in some doubt. The bezoar, ancestral to the domesticated goat, occurred in the vicinity, as also the remains of aurochs, ibex, gazelle, boar, hare, jackal, hyrax and half-ass (*hemionus*), plus 'innumerable species of birds, including rock partridge and doves' (Kirkbride 1968: 264), with their predators and

87

raptors, so the present condition of the environment should not be read as the original one. Raikes (1966: 70) states that 'during the whole occupation of Beidha the high ridge to the east would have been wooded as it was in recent times', containing pistachio, and inhabited by both aurochs and boar.

The Natufian levels (IX–VIII), consisting of three superimposed living floors with post-holes and sunken hearths, indicate only seasonal occupation. Byrd (1988: 180) also exposed a number of hearths, but found no architectural features. He did, however, find samples suitable for radiocarbon dating by tandem accelerator mass spectrometry. Those University of Arizona results date the Natufian levels from the beginning to the end of the thirteenth millennium BP (Byrd 1988: 191).

For the level of the earliest permanent houses exposed (level VI), 'built with boulders from the mountains and wadi-beds', Kirkbride (1968: 266) obtained a carbon-14 date of 6990 BC (K-1086; note date is BC). Entry to the living-floors, some 50 cm below outside surface level, was by stone steps. Similar to Nahal Oren, the houses were

> arranged in separate clusters, like cells in a honeycomb, each individual building was roughly circular in plan, erected around an inner skeleton of posts and beams. Stout posts dug in round the perimeter of the floor at regular intervals, usually 30 or 50 cm, were united by beams to a strong central post; to this inner skeleton was added a wide stone wall with short, straight segments of its inner face built so closely to the posts that they still outline the original shape of the wood.
>
> (Kirkbride 1968: 266)

Walls and the vertical slits holding the posts were originally smoothed over with a fine, sandy lime plaster, as was the ceiling beneath the beams, on which were placed brush or reeds at right angles to support a thick clay roof surface (ibid.).

> Within a cluster the individual houses or rooms shared party walls along the converging arcs of their circular plans; they intercommunicated through anterooms and short corridors, while steps regulated the differing floor levels of the separate rooms. Each cluster of these post-houses seems to have been surrounded by its own strong encircling wall beyond which lay the courtyard. Here were the hearths and, in one case, a line of small post-holes, parallel to the wall and about a metre from it, which must have supported props to uphold awnings for shade. Small storerooms were squeezed into the space between the encircling wall and main dwelling rooms.
>
> (Kirkbride 1968: 266)

Being full of wood, since in principle the houses are wood and brush huts made permanent with stone footings and walls, the majority of level VI houses were destroyed by fire, providing good conservation of the vegetal materials.

By level V some of the houses were becoming 'detached' and a considerable variety of house-forms were being used. Some employed the traditional 'post-house' technique while others used various curvilinear forms, from the circular to one even approaching the rectangular, but free from posts. Those are the ones that did not burn.

> The material culture continued without interruption into and through level IV, which also seems to have been built at about the same time all over the site. An unbroken evolution is still to be seen in the architecture. On one hand there was a fine house with its plan a practically perfect circle, while in others the walls straighten out, retaining a very gentle curve and sometimes rounded corners to betray their ancestry.
>
> (ibid.: 269)

Also in this level (IV), perhaps 200 years after level VI, a series of large fine houses, about 5 × 6 m appear, disposed along two sides of an open area like a plaza. Floors and walls were plastered containing large hearths with raised and plastered sills. Stone bowls were set into the plaster near the hearths. The excavator saw the large houses on the body of the tell, from which the smaller ones were 'respectfully removed' toward the perimeter, as a 'hint of the presence of a privileged and not so privileged class' (Kirkbride 1967: 8). Nonetheless, the smaller houses are described (1968: 270) as 'beautifully built, rectangular in plan with plastered floors and walls and some with small hearths with raised sills'. Any differences that existed were obviously still only matters of degree, not kind.

Between levels IV and III there is a discontinuity, after which the whole village was rebuilt simultaneously, perhaps as a result of earthquake damage to the now more vulnerable stone buildings, when previously fire had been the abiding danger (1967: 9), or perhaps just after a break in occupation. For the first time, truly rectangular buildings appear (formerly they were curvilinear or rectangular with rounded ends), integrated into a gridplan layout for the whole village. Constructional similarities of the large (9 × 7 m) house in level II, disposed around which were a series of long rectangular buildings, to the techniques employed in level IV are so strong that cultural continuity is suggested (Kirkbride 1968: 270). As in level IV, the level II house had its walls and floor covered by highly burnished white plaster, with a metre-wide strip of red paint running along the floor parallel to the walls, and impinging upon them. A similar red band highlighted the hearth and other important fittings: a circular stone-lined pit (at the bottom of which was large stone), and a highly polished stone seat or table situated against the wall just inside the door (ibid.: 270–1).

However, the level II village seems to have been smaller than its predecessors, and after the end of this level the new village was smaller still (1968: 272). This will be discussed below. Indeed, the architecture of this latest phase is also 'reversionary' to level IV: 'the small rectangular buildings with gently curving walls, floor and walls plastered, and the presence of an interior hearth with raised sills are all reminiscent' (ibid.).

Summarizing the architecture, Kirkbride (1966: 22) observes a sequence 'beginning with polygonal houses (VI) continuing through round houses (V) and the subrectangular houses with gently curving walls (IV) to the highly complex layout of corridor buildings and large houses of III and II'. Those levels manifested a high degree of craft activity for the size of the village, seen in rectangular 'corridor buildings' consisting of three pairs of cubicles $1 \times 1.5$ m, disposed along a corridor 1 m wide by 6 m long, and full of the raw materials: bone, wood, stone and ochre. As those cubicles were separated by stone baulks, some wider than the cubicles themselves, it appears that the cubicles were basement storerooms to the actual workshops on a floor above (Kirkbride 1968: 271). Querns were abundant and, as in earlier levels and in other sites, when worn out were used in construction. Fine bone tools included what may be weaving implements made from aurochs' ribs (ibid.).

> From all the finds in levels II and III it can be said that the flint assemblage was not essentially different, although a development can be shown, from that of earlier levels. The notched arrowheads became rare and borers were the most prolific class. More sickle-blades were used but scrapers and burins remained scarce. Most noticeable was the greatly increased numbers of chipped-stone axe-heads, some polished others not. This was in contrast to the earlier levels where only two such axe-heads, one polished, were found.
>
> (Kirkbride 1968: 272)

Many skeletons were recovered – adults decapitated to release their spirits and remove their power to affect the living – infants and young children intact. As the remains of nine babies were found in a single level II workshop, this suggests to the excavator (ibid.) a high infant mortality.

About 45 m east of the village, and apparently linked to it by a wall and path, lies a special quarter which includes three adjacent buildings, curvilinear in plan and with sunken floors (1968: 272). Though their stratigraphy is not directly connected to that of the village, they seem to be coexistent with most of its history, as different building levels are manifest. The earliest (T2) approximately circular, with a door toward the east and a floor of large flagstones, 'carefully laid and unlike any other at the site. Outside the southern wall was a large, flat, roundish slab of white sandstone' (1968: 272). The latest building (T3), was unremarkable, but the intermediate one (T1) certainly was. An oval of 6 × 3.5 m, floored with small, angular pieces of stone expressly broken for this purpose, it was the largest and the most elaborate of the three. It was also very clean except for a scatter of shell beads, one of the items made in the workshops.

> In the centre was a standing stone: a big flat block of sandstone (1.00 × 0.75m ) set on edge, its narrow ends facing N–S and the broad flat sides E–W. Against the south wall, just west of the monolith, another very large flat stone (1.60 × 0.75 m) was let in flush with the floor. In the SE corner another large thin slab (1.50 × 1.00 m) stood on a small foundation of boulders that would have brought it to about the original ground level, and with a small wall or parapet built just round its edges. Outside the NW corner and adjacent also to T2, was still another of these great slabs, on the original ground level and also with its own small wall built along the edges. In addition to all this, outside the south wall and attached to it in part, lying again at the original ground level, was a huge, shallow, roughly subtriangular basin fashioned from a single slab of sandstone measuring 3.80 × 2.65 × 0.25 m. A few stone survivals show this too had a parapet built round the edges. This astonishing complex had the same kind of fill as T2, again containing a burnt patch and the remains of a meal halfway up.
>
> (Kirkbride 1968: 273)

There can be no doubt that this was a religious complex, and indeed that it manifested continuity parallel to that of the village. The ritual meals seem to have marked the deliberate filling of the previous building when replaced. For the argument to come, it is probably significant that the last of those (T3) is the least distinguished.

'Ain Ghazal in Jordan is one of the largest sites other than Jericho to contain PPNB occupation, though the Late PPNB sites of Basta and Baga in the Greater Petra area of Jordan range between 10 and 14 ha (Gebel *et al.* 1988: 107; Starck 1988: 137)! But the value of 'Ain Ghazal consists not only in the fact that it was already a substantial site of 4–5 ha when the PPNB commenced around 7250 BC, but that after the ending of the PPNB at about 6000 BC, occupation continued into subsequent periods, namely the PPNC and the Yarmoukian. The PPNB consisted of a minimum of nine occupational phases on the site, which around 6500 BC peaked at no less than 12.5 ha (31 acres) straddling the Zarqa River (Rollefson *et al.* 1985: 71). In fact the principal occupation lies at 700–740 m above sea level on the gently rising (approximately 10 per cent) slope of the west bank of the Zarqa, near the spring of 'Ain Ghazal, one of the springs that fed the Zarqa and made its flow permanent, not a wadi (Rollefson and Simmons 1988: 393). And this may explain the site's longevity.

But this too is rescue archaeology, for the site has been damaged by highway and commercial development, and indeed 17.5 acres (*c.* 7 ha) are due to be lost to commercial and residential uses, with only about three acres kept as an 'open air museum' (Rollefson, Kafafi and Simmons 1991: 114–15). Accordingly, the vicinity of the car park is where the first four seasons' (and subsequent) work has been concentrated, initially exposing the PPNB over an area of around 200 m$^2$, the PPNC in 45 m$^2$ only, and the Yarmoukian in approximately 60 m$^2$ (ibid.). Although those exposures represent only around 1 per cent of the site area, 'Ain Ghazal amongst other things, offers a particularly thorough sample of the fauna of Jordan in the seventh and sixth millennia.

No complete building was recovered in the first four seasons, but the rectangular houses on hillside terraces seem to consist of large rooms ranging from around 10–25 m$^2$, whose uses were varied by continuous relocation of walls and doorways, as houses were expanded, contracted and remodelled (Rollefson and Simmons 1988: 396). The 1988 season added a further 280 m$^2$ of excavation by the digging of sixteen trenches, all but one adjacent to those of the previous seasons, upon which the account below is largely based. The further areas added in 1988 tended to confirm the reality of a distinct Pre-Pottery Neolithic 'C' stage, followed *in situ* by an early pottery Neolithic, the Yarmoukian. They also provided further architectural information.

Also the white-ware, first produced in the Middle PPNB, is seen to continue into the Yarmoukian. But while Rollefson, Kafafi and Simmons (1991: 104) characterize Yarmoukian pottery as excellent, geometric objects of clay and plaster which were so prominent in the Middle PPNB become very rare in the later occupations. The 1988 season revealed, in the South Field, more details of PPNC buildings (and there are others in the Central Field):

The PPNC structure, exposed in its entirety, is a small, compact 'corridor building' approximately 3.5 m on a side, with a doorway facing east (downslope). Exterior and interior walls averaged about 50 cm thick. The interior space was divided into three long rooms, each approximately 2.5 m (east–west) by 1.0 m (north–south), with central doorways in the cross-walls forming a corridor that connected all three rooms and subdivided them into northern and

southern chambers. Although the floors of the rooms were plastered, the small size of each room suggests that they did not serve
as the normal living and sleeping areas, but as 'basement' storage
and work areas beneath an upper floor.

(Rollefson, Kafafi and Simmons 1991: 106)

A substantial Yarmoukian structure was also found in the South Field,
which had stone walls and beaten earth floors. It consists of a minimum
of two rooms (the westernmost wall was destroyed by later Yarmoukian
pit-digging), divided by a north–south cross wall in which there is a
connecting door 1.25 m wide (ibid.: 107). The east room has minimum
dimensions of 3.5 m (east–west) by 5.0 m, (north–south), while the
western room's preserved dimensions are about 2.5 × 5.0 m (ibid.). At
0.5 m, the interior and exterior walls are simililar in width to the PPNC
structure. Rollefson, Kafafi and Simmons (op. cit.: 107) conclude that
'The size of this substantial building indicates that the earliest
Yarmoukian inhabitants of 'Ain Ghazal maintained a permanent occupation of the settlement, although the latest phases of Yarmoukian
presence probably had changed to temporary, perhaps seasonal
occupation.'

In PPNB 'Ain Ghazal, as at Beidha and the other PPNB settlements, walls
and floors were plastered, even burnished, and coated with red pig-
ment. Also found were what at Beidha were taken to be weaving
implements in bone. Here there is direct evidence of weaving in the
discovery of the powdery and charred remains of a woven mat of spun
fibres (ibid.: 408), showing that true weaving, not just basketry, was
taking place; as indeed were experiments in pottery ceramics. Following
on from earlier sun-dried examples, over twenty fired sherds from
securely dated mid-seventh millennium locations were found in the first
four seasons. More representative, however, are 'white-ware vessels'
(containers made from carved chalk or moulded plaster), deriving from
early and mid-PPNB layers (Rollefson and Simmons 1988: 408). Typical
also is the treatment of the dead, with adults buried individually (and
here intramurally) and decapitated; the infants of a year old or less,
buried intact or simply discarded, indicating that as they were not yet
full human beings their spirits were not a threat. The 1988 season
recovered, from a pit datable to c. 6800 BC, an adult male skull with
plaster features, which Rollefson, Kafafi and Simmons (1991: 113) say is,
in its rendition, unlike any of the plastered skulls from Jericho,
Beisamun or Tell Ramad.

Thanks to its location on the 250 mm isohyet at the borderline of
Mediterranean scrub and Indo-Turanian steppe phytogeographical
zones, with Mediterranean oak and pine forest as well as desert, half to
one day's walk from the site, 'Ain Ghazal had access to no fewer

than four environmental zones (Kohler-Rollefson, Gillespie and Metzger 1988: 423). With half a million bone fragments already recovered, belonging to more than fifty vertebrate taxa alone, no wonder Kohler-Rollefson *et al.* speak of 'the inordinate variety of faunal remains recovered' (ibid.). Of the approximately 10 per cent that are identifiable, *c.* 20,000 fragments belong to the PPNB levels (7250–6000 BC), with only very small samples from the PPNC (6000–5500 BC) and the Yarmoukian periods (5500–5000 BC).

Of the number of identified specimens (NISP) goats compose 53 per cent in the PPNB, and as much as 70 per cent in the Yarmoukian, though the latter is known from as yet small exposures. Gazelles (*Gazella sp.*) at 13.4 per cent are the next most important during the PPNB, falling to only 6.4 per cent in the Yarmoukian (Kohler-Rollefson *et al.*, 1988: 423); with, unusually, *Bos sp.* comprising as much as 12 per cent in the PPNB, and 6 per cent in the Yarmoukian. Pig, hare and other small mammals were also consumed, including, more surprisingly, many predators/ scavengers such as wolf and fox, though their pelts may have been their principal attraction (ibid.: 424). Gamebirds are represented – quail, partridge and rockdove, and corvids also – as at Beidha.

The rather poor state of health of many of the goats at 'Ain Ghazal, combined with the high proportion of immature animals killed (though as ever, possible seasonal predation on wild nursery herds is a complicating factor) suggests that we are witnessing the early stages of domestication of this species. Since their horncores are not yet twisted or laterally compressed, it is apparent that they have not undergone full domestication (ibid.: 425), by which time their management and health should have been improved. Cattle were not husbanded, but from the number of cattle figurines and incised metapodials found the excavators assume they possessed cultic significance (ibid.), no doubt as incarnations of concentrated (male) power. That bulls are represented is unmistakable, in contrast to the less numerous and more ambiguous representations of goats, equids and pigs. Remarkable caches of human statues from early and mid-seventh millennium contexts have also been found (Rollefson and Simmons 1988: 412). They consist of figures about 35 cm in height ('dumpies') and others approximately 90 cm high ('figures') 'made of lime plaster modelled on a reed/rush core which served as an armature for them' (Tubb 1985: 117). The eyes are particularly clearly modelled and striking, but mouths and ears are also modelled, as are other anatomical details (such as toenails!) on the 'figures', though not on the 'dumpies', which are busts only (ibid.: 123). The statuettes are quite different from the usual pregnant woman fecundity blobs, usually headless and legless, found in so many Neolithic contexts. Those too are represented at 'Ain Ghazal where they bear a sort of linear tattoo (Rollefson and Simmons 1988: 410). Whereas 'pregnant women' represent fecundity in general, the statuary seems to represent ancestral continuity in permanently occupied sites. The presence of both appears to be a recognition on the part of the villagers that without continued fecundity of people and land, the settlement could not be sustained; and that ancestors, the very embodiments of continuity, were the ones in the best position to secure it by their watchfulness (eyes), and in turn by their descendants' attentiveness to them.

By the PPNC only twelve species are represented by identifiable bones, falling even further to nine species in the Yarmoukian. The excavators (ibid.: 426) attribute this to 'a dramatic decrease in the exploitation of smaller animals'. However, the consistently smaller size of the goat, cattle and pig bones belonging to those periods indicates their domestication, and the post-PPNB regime is similar to that of the rest of Jordan, consisting overwhelmingly of goat and sheep, with small numbers of cattle and pig, but little evidence of hunting (Kohler-Rollefson, Gillespie and Metzger 1988: 426).

Floral analysis was by flotation samples from a variety of provenances. Of 95 samples (in Donaldson 1985), 37 representing 35 distinct provenances, no less than 23 (65.7 per cent) showed carbonized remains of barley, including the domesticated two-row hulled form, *Hordeum distichon* (ibid.: 97). As barley is particularly well adapted to semi-arid and even saline conditions, it not surprisingly also occurs in this domesticated form at Tell Aswad, Hacilar, Abu Hureyra, Tepe Ali Kosh and the PPNA plus PPNB levels of Jericho (ibid.). Wheat resembling emmer (*Triticum dicoccum*) was found in only 15 (42.85 per cent) of the samples (ibid.: 98).

However, legume seeds occurred nearly as frequently as the cereals, with peas, probably the field pea (*Pisum sativum var. arvense*) found in 15 (42.8 per cent) samples (ibid.: 100); while lentils (*Lens nigriscans*) were rather less numerous. Chickpeas (*Cicer arietinum*) occurred in 3 samples (8.6 per cent), and are also found in low proportions at PPNB Jericho and Abu Hureyra. Signally absent, however, is the horsebean (*Vicia faba*), so prominent at Yiftahel, and pistachio (*Pistacia atlantica Desf.*), found, for example, at Beidha. However, at 24 (68.9 per cent) of the samples, the most frequently encountered of the plant remains derived from another tree, the fig (*Ficus cf. caria L.*), whose pips, sometimes in the fruit matrix, were recovered by the thousand (ibid.: 100). While some fig seeds occur at Jericho, they are rare at other sites of this period.

Although 'Ain Ghazal (with Jericho) is the only site so far known to possess PPNC and Yarmoukian phases, we have seen that the size of the village and its quality declined later in the PPNB. This, it seems, is indicative of deep-seated problems which this site alone survived, *since all known PPNB villages in Jordan and Palestine were abandoned at the end of the seventh millennium* (Kohler-Rollefson 1988: 91), including Beidha and

Yiftahel, which may even have been abandoned earlier. While it may be overstating the case to say that every single known PPNB village in Jordan and Palestine was abandoned, something serious was affecting them.

If we dismiss for lack of evidence the traditional favourite of destructive invaders, we are left with environmental/ecological stress as the only explanation. Kohler-Rollefson (1988: 88) contends that the stage of the Neolithic represented by the PPNB was dangerously unbalanced, in that while it allowed larger populations to be supported, 'the one-sided propagation of a few plant and animal species at the expense of the rest of the faunal and floral spectrum also represented an enormous and consequential interference with the eco-system'. After a millennium of degradation the farming system collapsed in the comparatively marginal areas where rainfall (at *c.* 250–300 mm) was just sufficient to support mixed farming *in the conditions obtaining at the onset of the farming regime.*

In the first place the replacement of perennials by annual grasses and even legumes was highly deleterious, leaving the soil bare for much of the year. The nitrogen-restoring effects of legumes when used in rotation are of no help under those circumstances, as

> the absence of plant cover and soil-binding roots during extended parts of the year increased the susceptibility of the surface soil to erosion, accelerating the loss of fertile topsoil. Decrease of the vegetational cover also affected the 'effective precipitation', i.e., the amount of rainfall that actually enters the ground to be retained by plants. Because of diminished plant cover, more than 50% of the annual rainfall could have been lost, effectively transforming, for instance, a 300 mm rainfall zone into a 150 mm rainfall zone with the concomitant changes in vegetational composition.
>
> (Kohler-Rollefson 1988: 89)

But actual precipitation as well as effective rainfall, soil loss and leaching, were also affected by other aspects of the farming regime, notably the destruction of trees, particularly oak, the climax species (the most massive that an environment can support). Not only have climax species the greatest depth and spread of roots, but their floral and faunal associates are also of the greatest extent. Loss of climax species is not merely loss of one item in the landscape, but the loss of its very backbone.

We have seen how much use PPNB villagers made of lime plaster, covering and re-covering floors and walls with it. However, the fuel demands of such lime production

> were especially exorbitant and have been calculated to consist of over 40,000 oak trees during the 1500 years of preceramic 'Ain Ghazal. An additional 14,000 trees were estimated to be necessary

for building construction at the same site during the PPNB. Pressure on the arboreal resources is evidenced by the consistently decreasing size of postholes over the whole length of the PPNB period and by a change in the 'PPNC' to a construction pattern that required much less structural timber.

(Kohler-Rollefson 1988: 90)

And all of this destruction additional to the daily demands for cooking fuel, great chunks of charcoal being found in PPNB deposits. (Indeed, the last firm date for the PPNB there – 6215 BC – is from a charred log at the base of a 15-m architectural complex.) Charcoal disappears from PPNC levels (ibid.) and Kohler-Rollefson sees in this the move to animal dung for fuel, as in subsequent and fuel-deficient Levantine history. This of course does nothing for soil structure, fertility or organic content. While their dung was being thus consumed, the goats continued to feed on young trees and shrubs, the younger the more desirable to goats and the more easily destroyed. Whereas sheep, as ground-surface feeders, can be grazed on the likes of field-stubble, goats are hard to keep away from green leaves and shoots. In a landscape already highly dissected by natural erosion, the removal of all the climax and most of the perennial shrub vegetation in the vicinity of a settlement, presumably sited there in the first place because it was the most fertile location, can readily be seen to make for an 'inevitable' disaster. When it is realized that oak in such areas does not form a closed canopy (i.e. is fairly well spread out) then the amount of territory devastated by the loss of 'only' the 54,000-tree minimum (not including saplings of course), can be imagined.

Thus while, alone of all known sites, 'Ain Ghazal continues beyond the end of the seventh millennium into the PPNC, this is only at the price of a different regime. Accordingly,

The 'PPNC' phase, although still aceramic, differs from the PPNB in many important aspects: most crucial maybe is the almost total reliance on domestic animals which compose over 90% of faunal remains. Other changes include architectural constructions which utilize only negligible amounts of timber, different burial practices, modifications in the stone tool kit with a very low frequency of sickle blades, and the absence of charcoal.

(Kohler-Rollefson 1988: 91)

The low frequency of sickle-blades would mean that, previous fields having blown/washed away, baked hard or lost most structure and fertility, only catch crops were sown (e.g. in wadi beds) or residual wild stands reaped. The almost total reliance on domestic animals in place of the former wealth of wild animals killed would mean that their habitat was no longer extant. Thus while new village sites could probably have been found to undertake the sort of limited agriculture practised, the main animal protein element of the PPNB regime – hunted animals – were probably no longer available in sufficient numbers to balance the diet. This seems to be confirmed by the preliminary results of the 1988 season: Rollefson, Kafafi and Simmons (1991: 27) certainly maintain that 'the broad spectrum of wild animal species that characterized the Middle PPNB period [7250–6500 BC] collapsed to a fraction of that in the PPNC and Yarmoukian periods'.

At least the later part of the Yarmoukian, then, is characterized by semi-subterranean huts 'evocative of the remains of Bedouin tent sites' (Kohler-Rollefson 1988: 91). Plant-processing utensils, such as sickle-blades and grinding-stones, also increase relative to the PPNC and there is increased reliance upon domestic animals (ibid.). This indicates that, like the bedouin, animals have to be taken on annual circuits to avoid overgrazing one particular area, such as seems to have afflicted the vicinity of PPNB villages. Therefore, it is maintained, the residence pattern can only be one of seasonal occupation in the Yarmoukian (e.g. by water sources in summer), in contrast to the 'fluctuating' occupation in the PPNC, where part of the village had to decamp with the herds of goats when the first autumn rains began, not to return until the harvest (ibid.). (This, however, could be a function of the location of 'Ain Ghazal on the edge of the steppe and not common to all Yarmoukian sites.) In two contemporary examples studied by Kohler-Rollefson in southern Jordan at Al Qurein and at Suweimra, village population fluctuated in the former between 3000 in the summer and 400 in the rainy season at Al Qurein, and between 800 and 250 at Suweimra.

Kohler-Rollefson (op. cit.: 92) therefore concludes that 'To cope with the legacy of PPNB environmental destruction the southern Levantine population had to develop another set of far-reaching adaptations which included realignments in social interaction and settlement patterns as well as economic specialization', becoming pastoralists in steppic areas and agriculturalists in hydromorphic zones. Accordingly, 'The formation of these adjustments undoubtedly required time and effort, and it is possible that the archaeological hiatus between the southern Levantine pre-ceramic and ceramic Neolithic represents such a trial-and-error phase' (ibid.).

If, as Bar-Yosef and Belfer-Cohen (1989: 483–4) state, early farming communities were originally located within the limits of the Mediterranean vegetation belt, and if this boundary were to move westward with increased aridification during the seventh millennium (as it had done in the eleventh millennium, when the boundary had moved north and west) then this could only make the effects of man's ecological degradation more widespread and permanent. Bar-Yosef and Kislev (1989: 635) make the point that PPNB sites such as Beisamoun, Tell

'Eli, Munhatta, Yiftahel, 'Ain Ghazal and Beidha were located on alluvial terraces, that is, on soils which are most easily worked and highly productive if plenty of water is available (optimally from groundwater where the water table is high). Where reliance is on rainfall, however, alluvial soils, being relatively structureless, porous and often deep are a liability compared to forest-derived soils, which have good structure, and thus potentially high water- and humus-retention capabilities. This property of forest-derived soils is particularly important in the Near East where water is quickly lost and organic matter is so quickly burned off top horizons by the sun.

Paradoxically, support for a progressive aridification is found not in the Pottery Neolithic A, but in the Pre-Pottery Neolithic A and comes from the PPNA site of Gilgal, located on the western edge of the Jordan Valley Basin about 15 km north of Jericho. Covering around 10 dunams (*c.* 1 ha), Gilgal is situated on a low flint ridge, 230–40 m below sea level, between Wadi el-Baqar to the north and Wadi Salibiya to the south (Noy, Schuldrein and Tchernov 1980: 63).

The architecture is very similar to PPNA Nahal Oren, comprising walls only 40 cm high (possibly the original maximum), consisting of small-sized stones forming semi-oval structures (Noy, Schuldrein and Tchernov 1980: 64). It is suggested by the excavator (ibid.: 65) that those walls served as the base for huts or tents. Again, querns and flat stones with cup-holes occur, finding a secondary re-use in the walls (ibid.). The querns were made of limestone, while pestles were made either of limestone or basalt, as were the polished axes, showing the mixed geology of the area. Lime-coated floors also occur, as do cup-holes made of limestone and flat stones set into the floors, as at Nahal Oren, where each house additionally contained a hearth. Hearths do not occur inside the Gilgal houses however. Interestingly, arrowheads, small and well-formed on coloured flint, are mostly Khiam Points. Lithic utensils are plentiful, in comparison with bone tools, of which the majority are points (ibid.: 68). And while obsidian is entirely absent, blue and green stone was manufactured into beads, as was the ubiquitous dentalium shell. Noy, Schuldrein and Tchernov (1980: 68) state that the source of blue and green stone was the Judean Hills.

Given the topography and geology, Gilgal I is situated where it is to exploit faunal, not floral resources, the overwhelming majority of animals killed being vertebrates, the only invertebrates being representatives of the phyla *Mollusca* and *Athropoda* (Noy, Schuldrein and Tchernov 1980: 73). Aurochs, boar and Mesopotamian fallow deer were hunted, but the main food source for the site was the mountain gazelle, *Gazella pallas* (gazelles at Jericho in the same period and Beidha, were the desert gazelle (*G. dorcas*)) plus ducks and geese from the freshwater marshes then present in the vicinity (ibid.: 78–9). Not only do the majority of species found at Gilgal (i.e. all the aquatic and woodland and many of the grassland dwellers) not occur today in the lower Jordan Valley, but some of them have retreated northwards right out of Israel altogether. Accordingly, Tchernov concludes that

> In order to sustain so great a variety of aquatic elements, such as *Arvicola terrestris* (water vole), ducks, water plants, freshwater molluscs and crabs, or woodland and grassland dwellers such as *Dama mesopotamica*, *Bos primigenius* and *Sus scrofa*, environmental conditions must have been basically different from the barren land of today which can support only typical desert animals. It is not yet possible to ascertain exactly when the drastic deterioration began, but it could have severely affected human behaviour and culture, even towards the Pottery Neolithic period.
>
> (op. cit.: 79–80)

This is just what our review of PPNB sites indicates: increasing aridification exacerbating ecological degradation by human agency becoming critical towards the end of the PPNB, and producing in the PPNC and Yarmoukian, adaptations to those new, difficult conditions.

The type-site for the Yarmoukian (i.e. Pottery Neolithic A), namely Sha'ar Hagolan on the River Yarmouk in the central Jordan Valley, is situated upon sandy clays over river gravels. Of course, the location of the settlement, which is described as consisting of 'circular huts . . . half sunk below ground level . . . the roofs made of organic matter, the floors of *terre pise'* into which were sunk circular hearths (Stekelis 1972: 42), says little about the surrounding terrain, which in this case was kept moist by the presence of the river, here near its junction with the Jordan. And although no grain samples were found, Stekelis finds clear evidence for agriculture in 'picks for planting; adzes and hoes for digging and loosening the soil; flat stones with biconical holes as weights for digging sticks, used to loosen the soil and for planting; and sickle blades and knives for harvesting'. On hand along the river were excellent lithic raw materials – flint, basalt, limestone and clay – and with those, in addition to pottery, a range of innovations occur which include new types of arrowhead, spearhead, denticulated sickle-blades, grinding-stones and whetstones 'and an increasing porportion of axes, adzes and chisels. Fragments of stone spindle whorls are evidence of weaving' (Stekelis op. cit.: 42). We now know that of those items only the heavily denticulated sickle-blades are an innovation (4–6 in a sickle, representing nearly 15 per cent of all lithics) but taken with the coarse chaff-tempered pottery (mostly red-slipped and incised with herring-bone designs) the material culture does represent a new configuration.

At the even better watered Yarmoukian site of Abu Thawwab to the immediate south, on the perennial Wadi er-Rumman (and in the vicinity of several springs) rectilinear structures occur in addition to the rounded ones with hearths seen at Sha'ar Hagolan (Kafafi 1988: 455). Deep round pits with debris (flints, sherds and plant remains) are also present (ibid.). Though denticulated sickle-blades are plentiful, so too are arrowheads, showing the continued importance of hunting, despite the presence of domesticated sheep and goat amounting (in the small sample of 125 animal bones) to no less than 68 per cent, while gazelle were 15.2 per cent of the sample, *Bos sp.* 12.8 per cent, *Equus sp.* 2.4 per cent, with one each of pig and dog (ibid.: 466). The cattle and pig in particular underscore the water-resources around the site. Predominant crops were lentil (*Lens culinaris*) and emmer (*Triticum dicoccum*) with two-row barley also (*Hordeum distichum*) and field pea (*Pisum sativum*). In addition, it appears that pistachio fruits and almond were gathered (idem). The low-fired pottery was, not unexpectedly, similar to that of Sha'ar Hagolan, but the range of forms is quite wide, including cups, simple and deep bowls, simple jars, holemouth jars and globular jars, with a variety of handles and flat, rounded and flat-ring bases (ibid.: 455). As at Sha'ar Hagolan too, there is a striking range of human, animal and symbolic figurines in clay, with a heavy stress on the sexual-reproductive aspect.[7]

Discussing site location in his overview of the PPNA, Bar-Yosef states that

> The environmental situation of Early Neolithic sites conveys a clear idea of the preferred localities, especially those selected by cultivators. Proximity to permanent water sources was crucial for a large community even if they have spent only part of the year in place. The Jordan Valley and the coastal plain sites are situated near springs although those of Netiv Hagdud and Gilgal have long disappeared, possibly the result of seismic activity. Tell Aswad in the Damascus basin was on a lake shore, Mureybet on the bank of the Euphrates river and Nemrik 9 and Qermez Dere were in somewhat similar situations. All these sites were never as far from open forests or woodland as they are today. Proximity to the rivers or large wadis assured the supplies of firewood and building materials from the gallery forests.
>
> Each of the Neolithic settlements in which civilisation was practized (whether wild or domesticated species) was located on or near alluvial soils. This situation enabled them , during a few generations, to till the land that was often renewed by an additional veneer of sediment which accumulated seasonally. On the whole it seems that the regime of annual precipitation [deposition] contributed considerably to the success of the early farming communities.
>
> (Bar-Yosef 1989: 60)

Permanently wetted alluvial soils, especially those with significant annual rainfall, are relatively scarce in the Levant, as are potentially wettable soils, given that the Levant has no major rivers and not so many minor ones either. But there is an area of the Near East where very extensive alluvial soils are found in association with either naturally high groundwater or where water can be supplied by irrigation from rivers. This area is of course Mesopotamia, and it is to this area, which saw no hiatus like that following the PPNB,[8] that we now turn.

In the following lengthy chapter, detailed site evidence is given for the development of, and relationships between, the earliest village-farming cultures, namely the Hassuna, Samarra and Halaf. If this proves to be too much of the nitty-gritty of excavation for some then they can move directly on to Chapter 7 ('The Ubaidian Inheritance') without losing the thread of the argument, the controversial parts of which are:

(a) that there is a direct line of succession from Samarra to Ubaid;
(b) that if there were not, then Ubaidian settlements would not have colonized the alluvium as speedily and successfully as they did;
(c) that having done so there was a Ubaidian reflux from the south of the alluvium up and out from the central alluvium to the rainfed north, there incorporating or displacing Halaf settlements;
(d) central to Ubaidian success in farming rain-deficient zones was social organization based upon the omnicompetent, augmented and stratified household (the *oikos*) whose prototypes can be found, for example, in Samarran Tell es-Sawwan; and finally
(e) that the *oikos* had a formative influence in Sumerian proto- and early-historic social structure; that is, during the Uruk and Jemdet Nasr periods spanning the fourth millennium and the first few centuries of the third.

# 6

# THE LAND THAT TWO RIVERS MADE

Not all of Mesopotamia is alluvium, however. The alluvium proper is contained in the state of Iraq, and appropriately – for the term *al Iraq* means 'the shore' or 'the cliff' in Arabic – extends from the head of the Gulf to (and beyond) Samarra on the Tigris and Hit on the Euphrates; rivers whose depositional activities have been largely responsible for filling this sunkland between the Arabian and Persian plates. This because only a small proportion of their alluvium reaches the sea, the rest deposited in the deltaic valley to a depth of at least 6 mm per annum (Brice 1966: 239). The weight of material causes continual sinking of the fill, so that at Nasiriyah, over 160 km from the Gulf, the surface of the Euphrates is only some 2.4 m above sea level (Brice 1966: 242), indicating the dangers inherent (waterlogging, salination) in irrigation agriculture.

The intrusive wedge of land between Hit and Samarra is the southernmost tip of *al Jazira*, 'the island' (between the rivers), or 'Mesopotamia' as it was known originally to Strabo and Ptolemy, while the alluvial region to the south is known as 'Babylonia', where the cities were concentrated. Consisting of crystalline rocks overlain by Cretaceous and Eocene limestones, interspersed with bands of slate and gypsum, the whole tilted from 450 m at the foot of the Turkish escarpment to about 76 m above sea level where it meets the alluvial delta. The Jazira thus extends from the Zagros foothills below Amadia and Rowanduz, across the Euphrates (which here, like the Tigris, is deeply incised into the tableland) to the stony desert of the Hamad (Brice 1966: 229–30).

The Hamad is the true desert stretching westwards to the Jordan Valley and southwards into peninsular Arabia. The northern Hamad, in the rain-shadow of the Anti-Lebanon mountains, receives only 125 mm of rainfall per annum (an amount similar to that received by the alluvium), but this can double in the Jazira (in the north of which Hassuna village farming flourished), while in the interrupted ranges of hills across the north rainfall can easily exceed 500 mm (Brice 1966: 230).

It is only east of the Tigris and north of Samarra that rainfall agricul-

ture can be presently secure, and this is clearly seen in the ac-
companying land-use map (Map 6.1) (from Fisher 1978: 377). Centred
around the confluence of the Great Zab river with the Tigris (with Mosul
to the north and ancient Assur to the south) these are the Assyrian
plains, actually a gently rolling piedmont zone of between 228 m and
380 m above sea level, receiving from 305–510 mm of rainfall annually
(Brice 1966: 234). Nonetheless, even here a supply of irrigation water is
desirable for the bad years, and the plain of Erbil receives water through
*karez* tunnels from the outer foothills. This foothill zone, rising from
380 m to 914 m, receives from 510–760 mm of rain in an average year,
and while the piedmont plains are grassy but treeless, vestiges of former
piedmont woods remain: oleander in the valleys and oak on the ridges
(ibid.). This is the zone that Braidwood and Howe (1960: 9) expressly
refer to as 'the characteristic "hilly flanks of the Fertile Crescent"'.

Beyond the foothills rise the high (Kurdish) Zagros, reaching 3350 m in
Iraq and receiving around 1000 mm rainfall. In the Zagros Mountains
proper, only limited agriculture is possible and they are accordingly largely
given over to sheep and goat pastoralism, with only some supplementary
agriculture. Here there are remains of the original oak, pine and juniper
cover. The Euphrates receives no tributaries in Iraq, but from Iraqi
Kurdistan the Tigris is supplemented by major flows from the Great and
Little Zabs and the Diyala (themselves augmented by intermontane-valley
streams), which break through successive ridges to join the Tigris at the
lower edge of the piedmont (Braidwood and Howe 1960: 12).

For a summary statement of the broad setting, the opening account in
Braidwood and Howe's seminal report cannot be bettered:

> The geographical locale of the great culture-historical sequence
> leading to full civilization in western Asia may be likened to an
> enormous amphitheatre with its stage toward the south. On the
> west, the tiers rise to the Judean, anti-Lebanon, and Lebanon
> mountains which border the Mediterranean Sea. To the north and
> east, they rise to the high ranges of Anatolia and Persia. The
> amphitheatre serves as a basin for the Euphrates–Tigris drainage
> system. These rivers cut down from the high tiers on the north and
> run in roughly parallel courses through the vast orchestra pit of the
> Syrian desert to flow onto extreme left stage in classic southern
> Mesopotamia at the head of the Persian Gulf. On extreme right
> stage lies Palestine, and Egypt beyond it to the southwest. In
> centre stage are the desert wastes of Arabia. . . . The mountains,
> especially the Anatolian flanks and the Zagros on the north, north-
> east, and east, build up in a series of ridges which are concentric
> about the orchestra pit;
>
> (1960: 9)

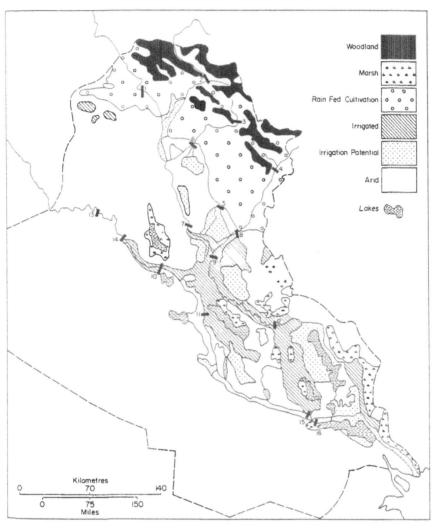

*Map 6.1* Land-use map of present-day Mesopotamia (Fisher 1978: 377).

which, however, they neither shut in nor shut off.

## THE EVOLUTION OF THE NEOLITHIC

From late in the nineteenth century it was clear that civilization had first arisen in the Near East, somewhere in this amphitheatre which was taken to include the Nile Valley. Indeed, for the Diffusionists (W.H.R. Rivers, H.J. Massingham and W.J. Perry), disciples of the anatomist Grafton Elliot Smith, who had developed his ideas while Professor of

Anatomy at Cairo, divine kingship, civilization and indeed the original 'discovery' of agriculture by the 'accidental' harvesting of wild barley and millet was held to have occurred, and could only have occurred in the unique Nile environment. Those attributes of civilization were then 'diffused' to all other regions later manifesting them (even in the Americas!) through the agency of Egyptian merchants seeking *materia medica* to prolong life. Smith was much interested in mummification.

Such views were enunciated in opposition to the theories of independent (if coincident) social evolution assumed by the 'founding fathers' of anthropology – such as Tylor, McLennan and Morgan – for whom such evolution was implicitly 'natural' or even inevitable. However, Diffusionist views had a popular and literary following, an outstanding example being the famous Scottish novelist James Leslie Mitchell, who wrote (*inter alia* the *Sunset Song* trilogy) under the name Lewis Grassic Gibbon. He had served with the army in Egypt, Palestine and Mesopotamia, between 1919 and 1923 (Young 1973: 7), and therefore the effect on him of W.J. Perry's evocative major works, *The Children of the Sun* (1923) and *The Growth of Civilization* (1924) were particularly powerful, as were the Diffusionists' Rousseauesque notions of an original Golden Age before the advent of civilization (originated by uniquely unlucky contingencies) so clearly set out in Massingham's *The Golden Age* (1927). Indeed by 1930 Mitchell was in correspondence with Elliot Smith, and he wrote a flattering introduction to Mitchell's *The Conquest of the Maya* (Young 1973: 7). However, the body of professional archaeologists and anthropologists did not subscribe to such constructs, and neither did the narrow geographical limits of the Nile Valley, nor what was already known of high and early civilization in southwest Asia, encourage them to look elsewhere than in the Levant and Mesopotamia for seminal origins. One of the great assets of the evolutionist approach was that it could admit of the early and independent developments in the Nile Valley without seeking its transference from elsewhere. However, in contrast to diffusionist dogma that complex innovations occur only once and thus get diffused from a source, so denying independent invention/evolution, evolutionists do not deny the possibility of diffusion, only requiring some tangible evidence for it.

Accordingly, by the mid-1930s the great archaeological theorist V. Gordon Childe's much read *Man Makes Himself* (1936) delineated specific concepts of linked Neolithic and Urban Revolutions, and localized these in southwest Asia, treating developments in Egypt separately. In the Preface to the third edition, Childe even took account of Braidwood's recent discovery at Jarmo in Iraqi Kurdistan of a 'genuinely Neolithic village' without pottery, the presence of which he had hitherto assumed to be a Neolithic characteristic, and he further recognized the same at Jericho. Jarmo is a Pre-Pottery village of the seventh millennium, paralleling developments in the Levant.

The first full account of Jarmo is contained in the 1960 report of the Iraq–Jarmo Project of the Oriental Institute of the University of Chicago, led by Robert Braidwood and Bruce Howe, and entitled *Prehistoric Investigations in Iraqi Kurdistan*. Initiated not long after the end of the Second World War, this was probably the first specifically 'problem-oriented' archaeological fieldwork, something that only became orthodox with the advent of the 'New (i.e. processual) Archaeology' in the late 1960s. Concerning the 'problematic' which was largely concerned with the transition from hunting and gathering to farming in the Neolithic of southwest Asia, Braidwood and Howe (1960: 3) wrote that

> our thinking was strongly influenced by the writings of Childe [e.g. 1934: 'New Light on the Most Ancient East'] and by discussion with our colleagues in both the Department of Anthropology and the Oriental Institute. Moreover, it seemed increasingly clear that there was a high degree of facile assumption and some inconsistency in the generalizations about the transitions which were being made by most cultural and natural historians. Some of these assumptions came from purely chance finds of prehistoric or protohistoric materials in areas which now appear to have been peripheral, and some stemmed from archaeologically baseless speculations of the earlier natural historians. On the other hand, we had no reason to suspect from the evidence available that traces of the transition should be sought outside western Asia. There were clearly traces of human occupation in western Asia well back into the Pleistocene, for example in the cave of Zarzi. In caves of southern Lebanon and Palestine the sequence of stone-age archaeology seemed fairly complete, ending in the apparent cultural richness of the levels called 'Natufian'. True, we could not see signs of a direct transition from the level of culture suggested by the Natufian catalogue to that of the then available basal layers of Jericho or other such minute village exposures. Nevertheless, all indications suggested that such traces of early village-farming communities as had been found in western Asia were the earliest available anywhere in the world. We were quite prepared to see independent beginnings of food-production, based on other plants and sometimes animals, in other parts of the world, . . . but we reasoned that these were later experiments than the Near Eastern instance.

So the stage of 'incipience' of agriculture was sought by finding sites that would not be buried at great depths under later settlement (as at Jericho, amongst many others), but which might stand alone as representatives of this earliest transition, free from later overbuilding owing to the possibility that sites suitable to early husbandry might not be those best suited to later expanded settlement. This said, it was not too difficult to determine where to look, for

> There were just enough present-day field observations by natural-ists and historical clues – from either written documents or artistic representations – to point to the 'hilly flanks of the Fertile Crescent' as a natural 'nuclear' area. It was reasonable to suspect that the transition took place there. Within the hilly flanks zone occur in nature (or, in the case of some of the larger animals, occurred until recently) a remarkable constellation of the very plants and animals which became the basis for the food-producing pattern of the Western cultural tradition. Nowhere else in the world were the wild wheats and barley, the wild sheep, goats, pigs, cattle, and horses to be found together in a single environment. Such is still the case (save for the extinct wild cattle and horses) in the range of elevations and rainfall concentrations which the hilly-flanks zone represents. The coincidence of the distribution of such early village sites as were known within the hilly-flanks zone itself was striking when mapped.
>
> (Braidwood and Howe 1960: 3)

Thus although cities, sites and monuments had been undergoing (often suffering!) excavation for a century previously, it is remarkable that it was not until 1933, one year before Leonard Woolley wound up his twelve years' excavations at Ur (on which he had at one time employed as many as 400 men, but painstakingly recovered the justly famous Early Dynastic Royal Tombs), that the very 'first conscious and knowledge-able selection of a small and easily excavable village site in southwestern Asia was made' – in the words of Braidwood and Howe (1960: 5) – on the strengths of its prehistoric potential, by Mallowan and Rose (1935). This was the site of Tell Arpachiyah, just east of Mosul, which although only excavated during a six-week season, still remains one of only two Halaf sites extensively excavated. Mallowan had earlier cut a (very deep) sounding trench to prehistoric levels in excavations at nearby Nineveh, under the direction of Campbell-Thomson, the first modern excavator of Eridu and Ur (and the last to dig the Kuyunjik mound at Nineveh) and thus the first archaeologist on the southern alluvium. However, R. Campbell-Thomson's main interest, as an accomplished epigraphist, was in tablets, and Mallowan in his *Memoirs* (1977: 77) describes the work at Nineveh as 'a glorified tablet-hunt', while recognizing its contri-bution to epigraphy. However, this, like the previous 'art-historical' mode of rummaging for artefacts, is the wrong sort of 'problem-oriented' excavation, since it loses so many other sorts of information en route.

## JARMO AND THE PROTO-NEOLITHIC

The second earliest excavation of an early village site, based on 'deliberate and informed choice' was that of Seton Lloyd and Fuad Safar (1945) at Tell Hassuna, south of Mosul. This too remains a fundamental piece of work, which reveals a village-farming culture even earlier than the Halaf, for it straddles the seventh–sixth millennium boundary, while the Halaf is recognizable from late in the sixth millennium.

To see the antecedents of Hassunan villages we have to look at Jarmo itself to examine the proto-Neolithic period prior to that of the developed farming village, but following the Zawi Chemi/Karim Shahirian semi-sedentary hunting-and-gathering stage in the Zagros.

Qalat Jarmo lies on the crest of an 800 m hill overlooking and eroded by a deep wadi in the intermontane valley of Chemchemal, some 48 km east of Kirkuk. The site extends over 1.3 ha (3.2 acres), but a third of its original extent has been eroded away by the Cham-Gawra wadi. Nonetheless, of what remains only about 10 per cent has been excavated, and some of this to only one metre or less although the depth of occupation material can be eight times this in parts. Radiocarbon dates from Jarmo have always been what Braidwood himself (1983b: 537) calls 'whimsical', but he is convinced that the village flourished for about 300 years in the mid-seventh millennium. Braidwood and Howe (1960: 183) describe Jarmo as

> a permanent village establishment with perhaps 20 or more houses and of rather long duration. Its people possessed at least the domestic goat, two kinds of wheat and a barley, and a variety of artefacts adapted to the cultivation, storage and processing of vegetable foods. Compared to what preceded it the Jarmo assemblage was elaborate, but it retained elements in its flint-working tradition which were at least as early as the Zarzian in ancestry.

In contrast to Karim Shahir, however, obsidian occurs at Jarmo.

The wheats were both wild and domesticated emmer and einkorn, plus what seems, from the tough rachis, to be two-row barley in the process of domestication (Watson 1983b: 501). Wild emmer (*Triticum dicoccoides*) still grows in the area. Sickles are certainly present, but non-cereal gathering was still very important, as seen in remains of pistachio nuts and great quantities of snails, particularly the large land snail, *Helix solomonica* (Braidwood 1983c: 542). The transitional nature of Jarmo is further indicated by the remains in lower levels of wild, and thus hunted, animals, which include red deer (*Cervus elaphus*), cattle (*Bos primigenius*), onager (*Equus hemionus*) and gazelle (*Gazella subgutturosa*). At 49 per cent of the osteological remains (Stampfli 1983: Table 26), they are equal in importance to sheep and goats. However, of those domesticated animals goats outnumbered sheep by three or four to one (ibid.). But even in later levels which included pigs amongst the domesticates (though not cattle), of the identified mammal bones only 60 per cent were from domestic animals (op. cit.).

Braidwood and Howe (1960: 43) estimate the human population at not more than 150 in a maximum of twenty-five houses of rectilinear form, constructed in all levels of *tauf*; that is, pressed mud packed, not poured, into courses to form the wall. Those walls in later levels were raised on fieldstone (i.e. unworked stone) foundations. Early levels are aceramic, but employ stone vessels instead, such that,

> although the making of stone vessels was a normal concomitant of early village life throughout the Near East, there was at Jarmo a rare cultural emphasis on this industry that found expression not only in volume but also in quality of output. Many of the wide variety of shapes that are present are aesthetically very fine, and the regularity of form, the high polish, and the extreme thinness that were frequently achieved reflect a high degree of craftsmanship.
>
> (Adams 1983: 209)

The materials used include limestone, marble and, to a lesser degree, sandstone, all locally occurring. Pottery tended to selectively supplement the highly developed stoneware at Jarmo, where it seems to be introduced as a technique from without. Indeed, Adams makes the most interesting suggestion connecting the obsidian present, the availability of which increased over time with the introduction of pottery; namely that 'its early practitioners at Jarmo may have been women from some distant village, perhaps brought back as wives by men trading for obsidian' (Adams 1983: 223), in exchange for fine stoneware perhaps. Certainly, when pottery appears it does so as an accomplished practice and not as 'the fumbling beginnings of a new craft' (Braidwood and Howe 1960: 43). This pottery is hand- and not wheel-made, 'vegetable tempered, buff to orange in colour, and frequently exhibits a darkened unoxidized core on a clean break' (ibid.).

Very striking are the thousands of lightly fired clay figurines, realistic and impressionistic, representing both animals and humans, or, more literally their parts, notably pregnant torsos and phalluses, the latter also occurring in stone (Moholy-Nagy 1983: 300). Morales surmises that

> the figurines were probably used for daily or regular sympathetic magic of a more or less individual nature. . . . The more realistic

forms appear to be 'personal wishes', with the 'desire' expressed in the *act* of modelling the form. The figure was then dried, fired and kept until the wish was fulfilled, or it was discarded immediately after manufacture.

(1983: 392–3; original emphasis)

This is a useful corrective to the all-too-common assumption that cultic artefacts are (a) expressions of group or corporate wishes, and (b) that some specific ritual needs to be done in employing them.

Morales's view of the essentially individualistic and 'automatist' use of the figurines, receives support from Mallowan's reflections upon the Halafian clay (with a few in stone) 'mother goddesses' he found at Arpachiyah:

Although we called these figurines 'Mother Goddesses' they may not have represented the Mother Goddess in person, but were perhaps dedicated to her by women in the expectation of the favour of the goddess during childbirth. Some were women of a certain age, others maidens. . . . It is also odd that many were simple pieces of plastic mud, only just recognizable as women, but the breasts and the female markings were always clear; particularly prominent were the steatopygous buttocks, primitively associated with successful child-bearing. Several figures were represented as squatting, the natural position in primitive childbirth and although these figurines had been variously interpreted, the most reasonable explanation is that they were for the most part intended to hasten parturition by sympathetic magic and that they also served as charms to bring fruitfulness to barren women. The vulvar region was often, but not always emphasized, and this together with the protuberant navel suggested the imminence of delivery.

(1976: 92–3)

This was no doubt a much-sought-after state if Adams's hypothesis is correct, and if current Near Eastern and Asian norms of acceptance for married-in women also obtained in the early stages of peasant society.

More recently a Russian expedition has found a site, Tell Maghzalia, in the Sinjar Valley piedmont zone, just 1 km north of the junction of the uplands with the plains, which parallels the early, aceramic levels at Jarmo. Located on the Abra river, west of Mosul, 4500 m$^2$ remain of a settlement originally covering 1 ha (Merpert, Munchaev and Bader 1981: 29). The deposit derives from rectangular clay-walled structures on stone foundations, and is 8.2 m deep. Indeed, there are fifteen clear structural layers, with an average depth of 50–60 cm. Walls were of tauf and the floors paved with stone slabs which were plastered with clay and covered with alabaster (ibid.: 30). A cylinder-shaped grain bin and a rectangular oven were found, the latter having stone foundations like house walls and built in the same tauf technique as employed at Hassuna sites later. A defensive wall, whose footing consists of edgewise limestone blocks up to 1.5 m thick and which incorporates at least one tower, runs along the western slope of the tell closing off the settlement, which is essentially unicultural throughout, and so 'can be treated as a single archaeological complex' (Merpert and Munchaev 1984: 50–1).

But in contrast to Jarmo (and Shimshara) many arrowheads were found at Maghzalia, all of flint and both tanged and leaf-shaped. The obsidian which is very common at all levels is used also to make sickle reaping knives, which exist in great variety, many of them in flint. Rubbing-stones, pestles and querns are also common. Some of the querns, which are generally small, flat and rectangular, have a few shallow holes drilled in their working surfaces, and so could have been employed for grinding stone and bone tools such as awls, needles and spatulas (Bader, Merpert and Munchaev 1981: 62). A hammered copper 'awl' (from its description a chisel: a cold-forged 'rod square in its section with distinct facets. One of its ends is cut off flatly, while the other is tapered by forging and, probably, flattened'; Munchaev, Merpert and Bader 1984: 52) was found on the floor of one of the houses (square E8, 23 cm below the reference point) 'the stratigraphic conditions of the find being indisputable' (ibid.).

Tell Maghzalia was aceramic, though a baked clay statuette was found in addition to other anthropomorphic figurines in clay and stone. The Soviet excavators relate it to the aceramic levels of Jarmo and Shimshara on the basis of similar traditions of flint-working, while all three employ large quantities of obsidian. However, Bader, Merpert and Munchaev (1981: 62) discern a more marked similarity between Maghzalia and sites in Syria and Turkey, such as Mureybet, Abu Hureyra, and Çayönü Tepesi.

Merpert, Munchaev and Bader (1981: 31) conclude that

> the assemblage of Tell Maghzalia suggests a culture with a developed flint industry and a developed house-building technique, but still pre-pottery or almost [sic] aceramic. The economy was built on hunting and on well-developed gathering which, in all probability, was turning into farming. A greater number of tanged arrowheads on blades and animal bones, apparently wild bulls, indicate hunting activity. At the same time the permanent character of the habitation, the numerous querns, sickle knives, grain bins and other finds suggest that farming predominated;

or rather was assuming prominence, indicated by the hundreds of grains found of wild and domesticated barley and emmer wheat, namely *Triticum monococcum L.*, *T. dicoccum Schrank*, *T. compactum Host.*, *T. spelta L.*; *Hordeum distichum L.* and *H. vulgare var. nudum* and flax (*Linum usitatissimum*), perhaps indicating connections with the contemporary PPNB sites of the Levant. However, the first actual farming villages on the Mesopotamian lowlands, employing pottery and deriving the majority of their subsistence from domesticated resources, are those of the Hassuna ceramic tradition which commences around 6000 BC.

The greatest concentration of Hassuna villages occurs in the northern Jazira plains on either side of the Jebels Sinjar and Ishkaft which, running west–east, divide the plains into a northerly and southerly section. The plains are also traversed in a basically east–west direction (from the Nineveh/Mosul area) by important routeways, particularly the prehistoric 'hollow-way routes' which trend northwest from the southeast (Wilkinson 1990b: 51). In the 475 km$^2$ of the northern area around the site of Tell al-Hawa (which seems to have occupied more than 15 ha by the Ubaidian period) surveyed by the British rescue team on the North Jazira Irrigation Project, no less than thirty-nine 'minor or significant occupations' occur (Wilkinson 1990b: 55). Rainfall in this (narrowly defined) project area averages between 300 and 400 mm annually, which is what makes 'dry' farming possible here. Towards the south, that is south of Tell 'Afar in the gap between Jebels Sasan and Ibrahim, rainfall is somewhat less, but is compensated by greater groundwater and wadi resources, with many springs issuing from the southern edge of the hills behind Tell 'Afar (Wilkinson 1990b: 51). 'The plains to the north and south of the Sinjar/Ishkaft ranges thus comprise respectively: a higher rainfall, lower runoff/springfed zone, and a lower rainfall, higher runoff/springfed zone' (ibid.). However, since the period of Hassunan occupation may have lasted a thousand years, with much movement between sites, density of settlement may only have been one site every 13–15 km. Accordingly,

> although a number of these earliest settlements are sited on wadis or relict wadis, by no means all are, and it seems that during this stage, settlements had already started to move away from areas of potential perennial water supply towards areas where wells or waterholes could have formed the only sources of supply.
>
> (ibid.: 55)

One such, site 174 (which is 22 km east of Tell al-Hawa), is illustrated (Figure 6.1; from Wilkinson 1990b: 53):

In general villages seem to have ranged between 0.75 and 2 ha in extent, and, if the preliminary faunal evidence from the late Ubaidian site of Khanijdal is representative of earlier periods, what is suggested is 'mixed animal husbandry dominated by pig (35%) and cattle (35%)

113

*Figure 6.1* A multi-mounded Hassuna-period site (from Wilkinson 1990b: 53).

with sheep/goat forming only 25% of the identifiable bone fragments' (Wilkinson 1990b: 60, citing Alan Pipe). However, by the late Uruk, as sampled at Tell Hilwa, a more 'modern' situation had developed, where sheep/goat overwhelmingly predominate (71 per cent), pig has fallen to 18 per cent and cattle form only 8 per cent of the identified bone assemblage (ibid.).

## THE CLASSIC NEOLITHIC: HASSUNA, SAMARRA AND HALAF

Above, Braidwood is cited as stating that prior to his expeditions, only two village farming sites were known in Mesopotamia: Mallowan and Rose (1935; Halafian Arpachiyah), and Lloyd and Safar (1945; Hassuna). The full title of this latter article, which Braidwood himself edited, and to which he contributed prefatory remarks is 'Tell Hassuna: Excavations by the Iraq Government Directorate General of Antiquities in 1943 and 1944'. As Braidwood remarks, it is to their eternal credit that they kept excavating during the Second World War. This key site is only 200 × 150 m, and lies at the confluence of three wadis which unite to form a tributary of Wadi Qasab, 35 km due south of Mosul.

Hassuna is the site which established the modern periodization of Mesopotamian prehistory, which is superbly summarized in Lloyd and Safar's chart (1945: 257), reproduced here (Figure 6.2). As can be seen, in

114

| Levels | Stratigraphy and Architecture | Details |
|--------|-------------------------------|---------|
| XV | | Disturbed materials, which include sherds of Assyrian, Ubaid, and Halaf type |
| XIV | | |
| XII | | |
| XI | This range of floors appeared only in the small sounding, 2, on the crest of the mound, and in a connecting trench; total depth – *ca.* 4.5 m. No architecture is presented; little was encountered | Appearance of Ubaid type of pottery |
| X | | |
| IX | | Main range of Halaf pottery. A few specimens of earlier pottery persist, especially in the lower levels (cf. Fig. 5) |
| VIII | | |
| VII | | |
| VI | Called the "Hassuna levels," this range of floors is characterized by adobe architecture throughout; total depth – *ca.* 4.2 m. The structures are all of domestic type; they indicate several roomed buildings of a definitely permanent character | This range includes three pottery wares: the "Hassuna archaic," the "Hassuna standard," and the Samarran. The first seems to be restricted to the lower levels, the third to Level III and above. The first two wares are divided into groups, based on significant decorative treatments (cf. Fig. 5), and the wares themselves are directly comparable to those of Ninevite I. Various small object industries in clay, stone, and bone are well represented. While no grain is described (cf. p. 268), the sustenance pattern is indicated by sickle blades, silos, and the bones of sheep and/or goats, cattle, and some wild or probably wild forms. Burials appeared, but studies of the human physical types are not yet complete* |
| V | | |
| IV | | |
| III | | |
| II | | |
| Ic | | |
| Ib | | |
| Ia | Third camp site <br> Second camp site <br> First camp site | Classified as "neolithic," a sequence of hearths and, presumably, tent sites. Pottery either coarse or burnished ware; a significant series of chipped and ground stone tools. The sustenance pattern said to be that of herdsmen and hunters |
| | Virgin soil | |

* It might be considered whether the adjective form of the site name, "Hassunan," should be used to denote this assemblage. Such a usage could be convenient, but would depend on general agreement as to what a "Hassunan assemblage" included; cf. the points raised below.

*Figure 6.2* The classic Mesopotamian sequence from the stratigraphy of Tell Hassuna.

7 m of occupation debris there are fifteen levels from virgin soil (the result of two soundings), spanning the whole spectrum from pioneering early neolithic 'campsites'to the Ubaid period:

> The two clearest lines of demarcation are between Levels Ia and Ib and at Level VI. These, in fact, mark respectively, the beginning and end of the local Hassuna culture. From Level VII upward (occupations of course represented in sounding 2 only) it has been entirely replaced by Halaf material, while in Level Ia, directly upon virgin soil, none of the elements by which it is characterized had yet appeared. The whole of the material from Level 1a has, in fact, to be treated as a separate assemblage. Apart from the eight fragments of burnished bowls, one bearing a trace of paint, the pottery, which is plentiful, consists entirely of a very coarse straw-tempered ware with a dark core. Combined with the flint and stone polishing industries, this suggests that there need be no hesitation in applying to Level Ia the designation 'neolithic', regardless of which current definition of the word is to be accepted.
>
> Equal in importance to the technological results in the ceramic sphere is the social picture produced by the excavations of the earliest settled community yet found in Mesopotamia. There is abundant evidence of the beginnings of agriculture.
>
> (Lloyd and Safar 1945: 262)

This was inferred from the presence of large 'hand-axes' which did not function as such, but were attached with bitumen to wooden hafts to function as hoes; in Lloyd and Safar's words 'the only evidence to show they sowed as well as reaped' (ibid.), since at the time of the excavation and even for two decades after, systematic recovery of floral remains by sieving was not standard practice. No trace of architecture was encountered in this Ia phase, hence the 'campsite' inference. Hearths consisting of wood-ash on a foundation of sherd and pebbles set in some kind of cement were found, as were obsidian lanceheads, sling ammunition, implements for skin dressing, and a great quantity of animal bones, suggesting that what drew the colonizers south of Mosul were the hunting opportunities.

The next phases, Ib and Ic, indicate that the agricultural opportunities have been fully realized, for they

> manifest a series of innovations which constitute an important first step in the evolution of an agricultural society. The settlers now live in adobe [i.e. tauf] shelters. Again they break the ground with stone-headed hoes, but their flint-toothed sickles also are found almost intact. There are corrugated terracotta trays, which seem to

116

us to have been used for 'husking' wheat or barley, and sunk beneath the floors of the houses are great spherical grain bins built of clay, coated outside with bitumen and sometimes lined with gypsum plaster. Flour is ground between two flat-sided basalt rubbing-stones, and bread is baked in clay ovens only slightly different from the modern Arab *tanour*. Furthermore, the potters' art has improved immeasurably. Comparatively finely made vessels are now decorated with paint or point-scratched designs, and the main elements of the Hassuna standard style are already in evidence. There are even crude attempts to combine the two forms of ornament.

(Lloyd and Safar 1945: 262)

Level Ib is the first to contain permanent architecture, which consists of an 'adobe'-built single room, rebuilt with additions in level Ic into a building of at least three rooms, in one of which (no. 6) a complete, contracted human skeleton was found without grave goods 40 cm beneath the floor (Lloyd and Safar 1945: 272). Sections of other walls also occurred in Ic, varying between 20 cm and 45 cm in thickness, and either rectilinear or curvilinear (ibid.). At least three houses or units seem to be represented here, in one of which 'the rooms were grouped around a recognizable courtyard' (ibid.).

The third building unit in Level Ic (No. 11) was unique in Hassuna architecture in that it was circular. The compartments into which it was divided, however, with their pottery, bread ovens, and heavy deposit of wood ash, gave it an unmistakably domestic character. The principle of construction must have been a sound one, since it survived into the period represented by Level II.

(Lloyd and Safar 1945: 272)

In level II the clay was finer and the wall remains longer, although the layout is not clear (ibid.: 273). Two multi-room houses seem to be represented, one of which had five rooms (one containing an oven) and a courtyard; while external(?) to the other group was found

an astonishingly large accumulation of domestic objects. They included at least six complete incised jars and fragments of others; two large coarse-ware jars, one with saucer-shaped cover; a large group of flint nodules with a dozen worked flints and chips; several flint blades set in bitumen, and an almost complete sickle; at least five bone awls; a pounding stone, two spherical polished stone balls, and miscellaneous stones; the horn of a sheep or goat and bones of small animals; numerous 'sling-pellets'; lumps of ochrous paint and other minerals; and knuckle bones. In the northwestern corner of the excavated area we found an infant burial in a tall-sided standard incised jar accompanied by two vessels for food and water. The bones appeared to be those of twins, and among them was a tiny pottery cup for drinking. East of this burial were the remains of the circular building founded in Level Ic.

(Lloyd and Safar 1945: 273)

Level III walls, by contrast, did reveal an intelligible plan. Here a large house composed of rooms around a courtyard was separated from another by a narrow passage (ibid.). Room no. 10 contained two grain bins sunk into the floor, in one of which two skeletons, one headless, were found.

In the northwest corner of the sounding we found a clay platform with a grain bin on one side and a square recess on the other. Lying upon it was an almost complete sickle composed of flint blades set in bitumen, with traces of wooden backing which presumably was attached to a handle. A 30 cm deposit of trodden earth and ashes in the houses of this level suggested a long period of security.

(ibid.)

Notable here, in contrast to PPNB structures, is that floors at all levels consisted of tamped earth and ashes, not a surface of plaster. Instead gypsum was used as a 'cement' in the walls to hold together the clay lumps (with fine straw or pounded scrub) of which they were composed.

By level IV, however, a mixture of clay with chopped straw, about 3 cm thick, was being used to improve floor surfaces (Lloyd and Safar op. cit.: 275). Level IV is the one with the best preserved architecture, the well-built and straight 'adobe' walls being about 45 cm thick and still standing to a height of about one metre (ibid.). Two house-groupings or farmsteads were found, the more complete comprising eight rooms grouped round a courtyard (see Figure 6.4, p. 135).

Five of these (Rooms 3–6 and 15) compose a single almost symmetrical unit which is worth observing carefully. If one assumes that climatic conditions in North Iraq in antiquity were approximately the same as today and that the materials available for roofing have not changed, one is probably safe in imagining that low-pitched roofs of branches and mud such as are today the universal rule in every village from Sherqat northward and Hassuna eastward have been so for an immensely long time. Furthermore the unit mentioned above is exactly adapted to this form of roof, since the pairs of rooms (3 and 4 and 6 and 15) are separated by walls which, if linked by a short beam across Room 5, would support the ridge. It is in this way that we have recon-

118

structed the building, assuming at the same time that the wall extending between Rooms 1 and 17, on the cross-axis, has the same function.

(Lloyd and Safar op .cit.: 274)

Levels III–IV were the ones which saw the advent of Samarran pottery, and rooms 6 and 15 of level IV contained the best examples of both indigenous and Samarran ware; the latter a highly valued import, often repaired.

Level V was even more densely built-up over the area excavated, the buildings still divided into two distinct groups of dwellings (Lloyd and Safar 1945: 275). The northern group consisted of no less than nine rooms clustered around a central court, rooms 7–9 producing a fine collection of Hassuna standard pottery (ibid.), while room 1 of the southern group, in addition to a grain bin and large milk jar with knob handles, produced a fragmentary 'mother-goddess' (ibid.). In complete contrast, level VI contained no architecture and little but the remains of a small kiln, its walls only a few centimetres high, oval in shape, roughly paved with stone (Lloyd and Safar 1945: 275).

In the second sounding, a pit into the centre of the mound in 1943 and a trench dug in 1944 to link this pit to sounding 1, little by way of architecture was found. However, it did continue the stratification down to Ubaidian times, largely by recognition of the pottery recovered. In level V, Hassuna and Samarra pottery is represented in almost equal amounts (Plate II), but 'among the Samarran finds was the remarkable painted jar neck with a representation of a human face, partly in relief' (op. cit.: 276).

Plate II Examples of Samarra pottery, hand-made.

119

*Plate III* A Halaf oval-topped jar from Arpachiyah.

From level VI, however, Halafian pottery increasingly preponderated (Plate III), through to levels VIII–X, in which classically fine fragments of polychrome ware occurs (ibid.). However, the remains of adobe walls that occur in various levels form an 'unexplained round structure' in level VII (ibid.).

Level XII marks a significant change: not only does it contain Ubaid pottery (Plate IV), but the rectangular sun-dried bricks (*libn*) that were to become ubiquitous in Sumerian building, first occur here at 30 × 30 × 15 cm (Lloyd and Safar op. cit.: 276). From level XIV the stratification was unreliable, owing to the proximity of the surface, but pottery indicated some kind of Assyrian occupation (ibid.).

Does this Mesopotamian succession – Hassuna, Samarra, Halaf,

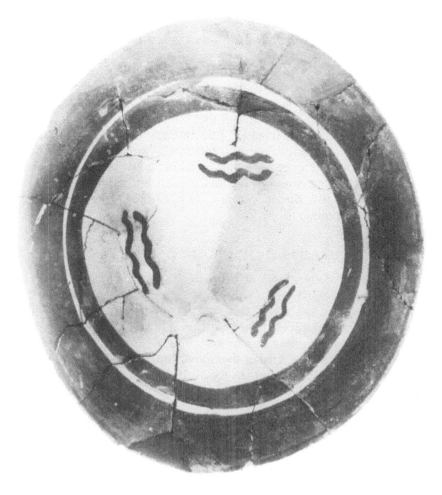

*Plate IV* A dish from Tell al-Ubaid.

Ubaid – mean that Hassuna culture developed into the others ? As I read it, while the Hassunans are confirmed as the earliest plains-dwelling village agriculturalists, the (somewhat later) Samarra culture led, once on the alluvium proper, to the Ubaidian which, expanding back north from the alluvium, displaced or incorporated the Halaf. The Hassuna, Samarra and Halaf 'classic trio' represent zonal specializations in different parts of northern Mesopotamia (the Ubaidian being the first truly 'alluvial' culture). Hassuna culture is the earliest on the plains, commencing with the sixth millennium, while the Samarran is apparent in the first half of the sixth millennium, Halaf in the latter part of the millennium. Directly ancestral to Hassuna is the 'Sotto' period or phase.

This is the period between the Jarmo early and the Hassuna developed Neolithic, that is, between the middle and end of the seventh millennium. Indeed, 'both Caldwell and Matson stress the commonality of the potting tradition of the later Jarmo pottery [e.g. jar profiles] with that of Ali Agha and basal Tell Hassunah' (Braidwood and Howe 1960: 44). Thus while Samarran culture, specializing in rain-deficit farming may derive from the Hassunan, it is too early to be sure that the Samarran does not derive from earlier phases that both have in common. On the other hand, no 'Sotto-Samarran Transitional' (or the like) is as yet known or even suspected. Further, the time-lapse between the emergence of recognizably Hassunan and Samarran settlements is quite sufficient to permit the evolution of the latter from the former, while no evidence of easterly influences upon, or derivations of the Samarran, has been forthcoming.

## PRECURSORS OF HASSUNA ON THE PLAINS

The term 'Sotto' derives from a site on the plain of Sinjar, west of Mosul, discovered by a Russian team which has been working in the area since 1969, focusing on the 'classic trio' and their antecedents. Sotto levels have also been recognized at Kul Tepe, Telul eth-Thalathat XV & XVI, Umm Dabaghiya, Hassuna Ia, and in strata 1 and 2 of Yarim Tepe 1, the latter one of a cluster of sites of that name situated 10 km southwest of Tell Afar on the plain of Sinjar. As the Yarim Tepe material is the fullest, this will be used to illustrate the early stages of developments represented by the Halaf.

The Sinjar plain, which has always been a major highway linking northern Mesopotamia to the Mediterranean, runs westward from Mosul, to the south of the Jebel Sinjar, hills rising to about 1250 m. Soils are good, rainfall is high, and so 'a number of small perennial streams flow from the hills into the soft alluvial soils of the plain, which are extremely fertile and favour the construction of simple irrigation systems' (Merpert and Munchaev 1973: 93).

> Yarim Tepe I is the easternmost tell within a group of tells of the same name situated by the Wadi Ibra, here known as the Joubara Diariasi. The original settlement occupied nearly two hectares, but the modern tell is only 100 m in diameter, its surface having been eroded by years of ploughing. The total thickness of its archaeological deposits is over 6 m, 1.5 of which lie below present plain level. The modern surface yielded only Hassuna sherds.
>
> (Merpert and Munchaev 1987: 2)

This site has, for once, seen decent-sized exposures. In addition to the usual trenches (here for stratigraphic purposes on the southern and northern slopes), the upper levels have been excavated over 1660 m$^2$, the lower levels down to virgin soil over 400 m$^2$ (ibid.). This revealed no less than twelve Hassunan building levels, with each one occupied for a considerable length of time, manifested by rebuildings within levels. The six upper levels (in which the 'standard' Hassuna ceramics predominate), though badly damaged, seem generally to reproduce the layout of the buildings immediately below, while the fifth and best preserved level is composed of eleven complexes totalling over 150 rooms grouped around an open central square (ibid.). Lower levels are characterized by 'archaic' painted pottery 'which is plentiful from the 12th level upwards. In this earliest level it is found together with "coarse" ceramics of Hassuna Ia–c type' (ibid.). The five earliest levels correspond to Hassuna Ia–c of Lloyd and Safar.

As could be inferred from the presence of pottery in the lowest levels, permanent house-building techniques were already well established. 'From the very beginning we encounter multi-room structures with substantial plastered walls. These force us to reconsider the premise according to which the Hassuna house-building tradition started from primitive single-roomed structures'; (i.e. Hassuna Ib, with no building activity attested by Lloyd and Safar in Hassuna Ia).

> We can now assert not only that the building tradition was already rather developed at the time, having been in existence since the pre-Hassuna culture of Tell Sotto, but also that the structures were themselves diverse. The residential area [squares 37,47,57] is characterized by multi-roomed houses with rectangular rooms. By contrast, no such complexes have been discovered in the northern area excavated [square 27]; the structures there are small and, together with the rectangular ones, some round buildings of tholos type have been found. The latter are known *not* to be typical of the Hassuna culture; only one other such building has been found, at Tell Hassuna itself [level Ic], where it was described as a dwelling. By contrast, the round structures from the lowest level of Yarim Tepe I cannot be classed as dwellings either by their size, form or contents . . . but they are undoubtedly connected with burial practices.
> (Merpert and Munchaev 1987: 4–5: my emphasis: present but *not* typical)

Accordingly, the very earliest levels at Hassuna, Ia and Ib, though they undoubtedly represent a settling-in period during which the houses actually had to be built and a settlement established, do not represent the 'primitive beginnings' of Lloyd and Safar's 'herders and hunters' learning *in situ* to become settled agriculturalists. Pisé clay slabs are used for construction in all levels, with both sides of the walls being plastered from level 12 upwards. Indeed such plastering occurred on the walls of all three original building complexes (ibid.: 6). Further, from the earliest levels the buttresses so characteristic of later Sumerian architecture are found. Also found from level 12 onward are sophisticated ovens, round or rectangular in plan, and with side or top openings, coexisting with primitive hearths (ibid.).

The full repertoire of domesticates is also present at Yarim Tepe I. In evidence at level 12 are the wheats *Triticum monococcum L.*, *T. dicoccum Schrank*, *T. aestivum L.*, (bread-wheat), *T. compactum Host.* (club-wheat), *T. spelta L.* (spelt wheat), and *Hordeum vulgare var. nudum* (naked barley), plus the pulses *Lens esculenta L.*, *Pisum sp.*, and wild members of the *Gramineae* and *Leguminosae* (ibid.: 19). The near identity of this suite to that occurring at Tell Maghzalia will be apparent. Further, no less than 82 per cent of the bones recovered are from domesticated animals, with domestic cattle (*Bos taurus*) of especial importance. Alongside the domesticated forms, wild sheep, goat and pig seem to be hunted along with onager, gazelle (*subgutturosa*) and deer (*Dama mesopotamica*).

Remarkably, metal was very common,

encountered 26 times in the settlement as a whole, with 21 examples coming from the lower levels discussed here; 17 pieces of copper ore (two from Level 7, four from Level 8, three from Level 10, and four from Level 12), which suggest the smelting of metal in the settlement itself, and four copper artefacts: a copper sheet bead (Level 7), a copper ring (Level 10), a ring-shaped pendant made of a copper plait (Level 11) and, perhaps most important, a lead bracelet (Level 12). The latter lay on virgin soil under the corner of room 345, the earliest in the central section of the excavations. It seems to have been buried there as a sacrifice when construction began.

(Merpert and Munchaev 1987: 17)

Though only two copper beads occur at Tell Sotto and two pieces of copper ore or malachite, plus the copper chisel ('awl') in the earlier, preceramic settlement of Tell Maghzalia; in association with the ceramic continuities linking those settlements to the Hassuna, Merpert and Munchaev nonetheless declare that while the earliest levels of Yarim Tepe I are comparable to Hassuna Ia (and doubtless would be more so with bigger exposures), 'its genetic connection with the earlier Tell Sotto culture is unquestionable' (op. cit.: 17).

## THE HALAF

Across the Wadi Joubara Diariasi, 250 m away, lies the eroded 'half-mound' of Yarim Tepe II, the characteristic which has given its name to

*Plate V* A jar from Arpachiyah.

the whole cluster of mounds on both banks, though this particular mound contains some of the best *Halaf* material so far exposed. In Yarim Tepe II excavation started in the centre of the surviving tell over an area of 600 m² at the surface, 500 m² at the lowest of nine building levels. Since 'In all the Yarim Tepe II levels the main house form was a single-roomed domed tholos, 3–5 m in diameter' (Merpert and Munchaev 1987: 20), we immediately know this to be a Halaf settlement, for the tholos is the defining characteristic of Halaf culture, in addition to its particularly fine ceramics: painted (Early and Middle) and the magnificent polychrome (Late). See Plate V (above), from Mallowan/Arpachiyah.

Although mud-brick was known to the villagers it was rarely used, the standard building material being clay slabs of different sizes and 5–6 cm thick on average but reaching 10 cm. In the earliest levels three narrow rectangular, multi-room structures oriented along the north–south axis were found in the northern section (Merpert and Munchaev 1987: 21). Those three rectangular structures, which the excavators think were granaries, were built at the same time of clay slabs (85–87 × 22–24 × 8–10 cm) and fell out of use more or less together, all within this earliest level (ibid.).

To the west of this 'industrial area' as Merpert and Munchaev call it, 'stood several dwellings, including the remains of six houses of the tholos type' (ibid.). Of those, four have been excavated almost completely and their walls, made of overplastered clay slabs like the rectangular building, still stand a metre high in places. Another rectangular structure occurs in the southern corner of the excavations. Belonging to the earliest period of the settlement, this was built at the same time as a potter's kiln and both are earlier than tholoi LXVII and LXXV, which are in turn earlier than tholoi LXI and LXVI (ibid.: 23). From the sophistication of the kiln we can see how the fine wares were achieved:

> Only the inner platform of the kiln (dia. 1.85 to 1.98 m), with six flues some 15 cm in diameter, and the lower part of the fire chamber have survived. In the centre of the platform was a larger hole (dia. 35 to 40 cm) . . . the fire chamber was connected to the upper kiln oven not only by the six smaller channels, up to one metre deep, but by the larger central hole as well. The entrance to the kiln, on the south, was oval (40 × 40 × 18 cm).
>
> (ibid.: 23)

Cooking, 'tanour' ovens also occur, along with ordinary hearths. Both of those occur in a tholos LXI, which had a flat roof (ibid.: 22).

In this same early period, the largest tholos (LXVII) has a diameter of 5.3 m, and is reinforced by additional walls, interior and exterior, on its eastern side.

> The walls of this tholos rested on a specially prepared clay platform. Beneath the floor plaster was a small depression containing fragments of an intentionally broken painted vessel with a corrugated surface, and three microlithic obsidian tools, covered with the ash of a fire. In addition, animal bones, fragments of vessels, five clay and two stone spindle whorls, a pendant of grey stone with circular ornament, a pierced flat stone pendant, a fragment of a clay figurine and a unique, triangular, copper seal-pendant were found under the floor just north of the depression. It seems possible that these items were placed under the foundations when the house was built, and that they have some ritual significance.
>
> (ibid.: 23)

What they do not signify is that tholoi were religious structures as their unusual shape has suggested to some. Intramural burials and cult in domestic structures are standard in the early Neolithic. Indeed, the very largest structure at Yarim Tepe II stands at the centre of the settlement. It was uncovered in level 6, and consists of a cruciform building complex with a tholos (XXXI) at its centre. This tholos, with massive walls 60–70 cm thick, and an inner diameter of 2.60 m, was divided in two with the southern half the smaller, while the northern part was subdivided yet further by two transverse walls into three compartments measuring 0.5 × 1.0 m, 1.5 × 0.7 m and 1.4 × 0.65 m.

> On the inside of the central compartment there have survived two flat alabaster slabs, and it seems probable that the upper part of the inner walls of the tholos was also finished with similar stone slabs. On its northern and southern sides the tholos was directly ad-joined by rectangular structures; on the eastern and western sides, there was a corridor (0.5–0.9 m wide) between the tholos and its ancillary rooms. The tholos was further enclosed by rectangular multi-roomed structures, comprising some 22 rooms in all.
>
> (Merpert and Munchaev 1987: 21)

By its scale and complexity this seems a perfect candidate for a 'temple', and yet its very complexity speaks against this. Likewise the small size of rooms makes the structure impossible as a housing complex, some-thing confirmed by the lack of pottery and other domestic debris (ibid.). Also against the religious nature of the complex is the fact that it was built 'on a site previously occupied by ordinary structures, and that after its destruction, it was built over once again with ordinary buildings' (ibid.). The excavators therefore conclude that the building was a large public storehouse. In proto- and prehistoric Mesopotamian practice as in the historical period, ground was sanctified by levelling and purification so that a 'pure house of the god (N)' could be erected on it. Once done, the site remained consecrated and so only further religious structures could be (and for millennia were) erected there.

'The Yarim Tepe Halaf pottery finds its closest parallels at Arpachiyah', according to Merpert and Munchaev (1987: 3). Ismail Hijara (cf. 1980), then a research student at London's Institute of Archaeology, dug a trench in an eight-week season at Arpachiyah in 1976 in order to re-examine the key stratigraphy of Mallowan and Rose. Although the trench did not produce enough exposure to expand knowledge of architectural phases, it did produce important floral and faunal remains (the former analysed by R.L.N. Hubbard, the latter, vertebrates, by J.P.N. Watson), with three large bulk soil samples col-lected for macrobotanical investigation. That this is now the developed Neolithic can be seen from the presence of emmer, hulled and six-row barley, and also two-row hulled barley (Hubbard 1980: 154). Present, though not common, was einkorn, as also was the hexaploid wheat *Triticum compactum*, and, in one sample, lentils (ibid.). From a compari-son of those findings with what Helbaek (1972: 35–48) reported from the Samarran site of Choga Mami, Hubbard (ibid.: 154) concludes that 'it seems doubtful whether the differences between the carbonized seeds found at Arpachiyah and Choga Mami reflect any real difference be-tween Halafian and Samarran agriculture'; except of course that the

Samarrans were 'incipient irrigationists'. The presence of peas and flax at Choga Mami and the relative rarity of hulled barleys there might reflect this emerging Samarran practice, or it may just be a product of the excavation or preservation conditions at Arpachiyah. There domestic cattle, sheep and goats (sheep being three to four times as common as goats) domestic pigs and dogs were kept, the importance of cattle and pig increasing over time (Watson 1980: 152–3).

At the Yarim Tepe sites the evolutionary order of Hussuna, Samarra and Halaf is confirmed. The Hassuna settlement of Yarim Tepe I was founded on a previously unoccupied site, while the five upper levels contain Samarran material (Merpert and Munchaev 1987: 17). Seven-metre-thick Halafian deposits at Yarim Tepe II overlay a small Hassuna settlement there which comprises both early and late phase materials. The Halaf village graveyard was in fact located on Yarim Tepe I, which by that time was clearly abandoned (ibid.).

This periodization is confirmed by radiocarbon dates reproduced in Hijara (1980: 151), excepting only a dating (W-660) from Tell Hassuna level V, which has a large uncertainty range (± 200 BP) and is probably unsound:

*Samarran*
Tell es-Sawwan   P-855   7456 ± 37 BP, 5506 BC level I floor
Tell es-Sawwan   P-856   7299 ± 86 BP, 5349 BC level III
Tell es-Sawwan   P-857   6806 ± 82 BP, 4858 BC level III

At Tell Hassuna the Halaf pottery begins with level VI. There is a radiocarbon dating (W-660) from level V (with, however a large uncertainty range):

Tell Hassuna   W-660   7040 ± 200 BP, 5090 BC level V

Halaf dates from a variety of sites span the 5th millennium:

Banahilk        P-1501   4359 ± 79   BC D II 1.3 m down
Banahilk        P-1502   4801 ± 85   BC D I floor 6 feature 1
Banahilk        P-1503   4904 ± 72   BC D I floor 6 feature 1
Girikihaciyan            4515 ± 100 BC
Chagar Bazar    P-1487   4715 ± 77   BC levels 11–12

Chagar Bazar is another site of importance that we owe to Mallowan's incredibly productive campaigns of the mid-late 1930s, when he dug one site after another in successive seasons, until stopped by the Second World War. Chagar Bazar lies in the centre, and the Halaf type-site at Ras el 'Ain just within the western margins, of the 'Habur headwaters' triangle, the southern apex of which is at the modern town of Hasseke. Mallowan describes it as that wonderful triangle of territory bounded on the west by the Upper Habur from Ras el 'Ain to Hasaka, on the east by a small river with the improbable name of the Jaghjagha, and on the north by the railway line which demarcates the frontier between Syria and Turkey. In this area, hundreds of ancient mounds, an archaeological paradise clutter the plain: the majority contain remains of agricultural settlements which flourished in the fifth millennium BC and lived on the fat of the land. This triangular area is intersected by numerous wadis. The wadi Waj contains the mounds of Tell Saiqar and Tell Baindar; the wadis Khanzir and Dara contain Tell Mozan and Tell Chagar Bazar; the Jaghjagha contains the mounds of Tell Hamidi and Tell Brak;

(Mallowan 1977: 108)

the last also known through Mallowan's enterprise.

Tell Brak on the Jaghjagha river astride the route to the Ergami Maden copper mines in eastern Anatolia, at 40 ha in extent and 43 m high (Oates 1982: 62), is the largest site known in the Habur triangle, reflecting settlement there reaching back to the sixth millennium at least. The Late Uruk period occupation was marked by eleven small sites within a 1.6 km radius of Brak, where there is the famous 'Eye Temple' that Mallowan excavated and which, with its 'tripartite plan, buttressed exterior façade, and bent-axis approach is of unmistakable southern derivation in spite of its unique eastern wing' (Algaze 1989: 578). Indeed David Oates goes further, remarking that

the temple plan, its contents, the cone mosaic decoration and indeed the method of construction, on a high platform enclosing the remains of earlier versions of the shrine, can be precisely paralleled in the south, for example at Uruk and Eridu.

(Oates 1982: 64)

The 'eye or spectacle idol' (Mallowan 1965: 47) which sits on an altar or plinth, also occurs at Ur, Mari and Lagash; and at Brak thousands of fragments (300 intact) of amulet-sized (c. 2–11 cm) versions in alabaster – some in the form of 'twins' or 'triplets', some with conical heads, some terminating just above the 'eyebrows', some with one set of eyes above another – were found with the four older buildings incorporated into the platform supporting the Eye Temple. But the temples are late, southern and urban in inspiration, while the Halaf, though widespread, was only ever a northern phenomenon.

It is entirely appropriate that the type-site of Halaf, only a few kilometres from the town of Ras el 'Ain ('spring head'), was recognized through the enterprise of Dr Baron Max von Oppenheim (with Sir Aurel Stein (1862–1943) who ranged over much of central and southern as well as west Asia) amongst the last of the explorer–archaeologists. Having already ranged over most of the region, from 1896 onward, Oppenheim worked out of the German diplomatic mission in Egypt as their principal intelligence agent in the Near East. Thus in 1899 he began a journey across northern Mesopotamia, just south of the Kurdi Mountains, in order to survey a route for the railway to be built between Aleppo and Mosul with finance by the Deutsche Bank. (Oppenheim's own wealth came from membership of a banking family.) That railway thus runs by Ras el 'Ain and Tell Halaf, reached by the railway builders in 1913; the latter a site to which Oppenheim had been alerted in 1899 by reports of villagers having dug up, and promptly reburied, statues of animals with human heads. In only three days' work Oppenheim's party exposed 'the great principal face of a temple-palace' plus basalt statues, one of which was a particularly striking veiled goddess (Oppenheim 1931: 8). Not having proper staff or equipment he reburied those finds to return when resources were available. This occurred in 1911 when he was able to engage the services of the architect Felix Langenegger, who had assisted Koldewey in the work on Babylon and Assur. Oppenheim, like all the German expeditions, came very well equipped, but unlike the others he paid for it himself. 'Taken together nearly 1000 camels were used in our transport from Aleppo to Tell Halaf, and for safety's sake a road was used that needed almost twenty days for the journey' (Oppenheim 1931: 11). One thousand camels were needed, for in addition to the usual field supplies, digging and scientific equipment, he brought 'a field railway with twelve tip-waggons, and nearly all the materials for building the house of the expedition' (ibid.); a house that was no cottage. Excavation lasted until the end of 1913, was interrupted by the First World War and its aftermath, so that the second (effective) season was from 1927–9.

The first season (1911–13) had exposed palaces, reliefs and statuary, that, in 1927, required thirteen railway trucks to get the finds to Aleppo. Here he established a small museum for the Syrian government's share, while for the German government Oppenheim built a museum of his own in Berlin. The second season, lasting for six months in 1929, was designed to get below the palace levels dug in the earlier season, and accordingly

> Immediately under the palaces and temples, belonging to the twelfth century BC, and at other places also we found in deeper layers great quantities of painted pottery in the area of the citadel and town wherever we dug down to the living rock: baked clay vessels decorated with glaze and painted, or fragments of them, always together with flint and obsidian implements. Also the lower layer of painted pottery was mingled with coarse, self-

coloured earthenware, which at the very bottom appears also by itself without the painted sherds. The deepest layers of Tell Halaf are therefore Neolithic and belong to pre-history.

(Oppenheim 1931: 36)

He rightly identified this with similar painted pottery 'found at the deepest layers in other places in Syria and Asia Minor', and in Assyria too; but he was wrong about its occurrence in Lower Mesopotamia ('such as Ur and Kish'), and his estimate of 'the Painted Pottery period' as falling within the fourth and third millennia (op. cit.: 39), is several millennia too late. The disjunction between Oppenheim's chronological conceptions and those of Lloyd and Safar (1945) – which emerge from their work at Hassuna just over a decade later and are thoroughly modern (though pre-radiocarbon) – is quite remarkable (see above). The painted pottery at Halaf was certainly disturbed by subsequent filling and building on the tell, but it seems that Oppenheim's real interests (other than clandestine) were traditional; namely in monumental structures and works of art. This was not helped by the publication of his full report (Volume 1) in Berlin during the Second World War (Oppenheim and Schmidt 1943). Thus Halaf pottery became known largely from Woolley's work (with T.E. Lawrence) in 1912–13 at Jerablus/Carchemish on the Euphrates, at the border between Turkey and Syria. This report was published in 1934 in the first volume of *Iraq*. The next volume (1935) contained, *inter alia*, the results of the work of Mallowan and Rose at Arpachiyah. In the following year the report on Mallowan's excavations at Chagar Bazar with an archaeological survey of the Habur appeared there. Yet knowledge of actual Halaf villages has had to await the work at Yarim Tepe of Merpert, Munchaev and others of the Russian team, commencing in 1969.

The Habur, which is in Syria, is a tributary of the Euphrates, and is indeed the only permanently flowing tributary of the Euphrates in Mesopotamia. However, there is also a Khabur which joins the Tigris just where the borders of Iraq, Turkey and Syria meet, so to differentiate I shall spell each as here; namely the Tigris feeder with a K. I have chosen Habur for the Euphrates tributary because it is nearest to the Sumerian $hu_2$ $bur_3$, meaning 'waters of plenty'; there are so many springs in this area that the Habur has two origin streams and at Tell Halaf is already 27 m broad, even in summer (Oppenheim 1931: 33). Those gently rolling fertile plains, which were known to the Sumerians as *Subir* – 'the north' – have always been highly productive rain-fed farming lands. As Oppenheim explains:

The many springs and the volcanic character of the ground are the reason for the extraordinary fruitfulness of the Habur headwaters region, which furthermore owing to its geographical position, is an important junction for the roads leading from west to east in Upper

Mesopotamia. Thus the territory seems made, as it were, to hold a ruling position in the wide areas around it and to be the capital of a great kingdom.

(Oppenheim 1931: 34)

Even today virtually the whole of the Habur plains lies within the 300 mm rainfall isohyet required for reliable dry-farming in areas of marked inter-annual variability (here only 250 mm is required) and this amount rises to 500 mm toward the northeastern sector, north and east of Tell Leilan, which is located on the present 450 mm isohyet.

The Habur triangle lies just north of the Jebel Abd Al-Aziz and the Jebel Sinjar, with the Habur river flowing south between the two ranges to join the Euphrates. Of Yarim Tepe II, which with the other Yarim Tepe sites, lies on the Sinjar plains immediately to the south of the Jebel Sinjar, Merpert and Munchaev (1987: 36) regard it as significant that 'Yarim Tepe II occupies a geographically central place in the Halaf area and combines traits of both western and eastern groups of Halaf sites'. Indeed Halaf and Halaf-influenced sites are known as far west as Carchemish on the Euphrates, Banahilk in the east (cf. date above), Girikihaiiyan and Yilki Tepe in the north, and as far south as Tell es-Sawwan and Choga Mami. Indeed at Chagar Bazar the three lowest levels contained not only Halaf pottery, but sherds with Samarran motifs, along with sherds of a grey and black burnished ware which is contemporary with, and closely related to, Amuq B ware from western Syria. Conversely, Halaf influence extends beyond the limits mentioned to Palestine and even, it is said, into the Transcaucasus. The mechanism is explained in Maisels 1998.

Prior to the Ubaid which supplanted it, the Halaf was the most widespread and most influential developed Neolithic culture. As a rainfall-farming tradition that probably utilized cattle for ploughing on the good soils utilized, the Halaf most likely had its origins on the plains of the Habur triangle, originating from either a pre- or an early Hassuna culture. Certainly work by the team under Peter Akkermans in the valley of the Balikh, another tributary of the Euphrates to the immediate west of the Habur system, indicates an unbroken development of the Halaf *in situ* from a local Neolithic basis (Akkermans 1991: 124).

The Balikh itself is a perennial tributary of the Euphrates in Syria, although in summer part of the Balikh is dry (Akkermans 1989b: 14). With its source in the spring of 'Ain al-Arous near the Syrian–Turkish border, where the Balikh is widest, for most of its 100 km course the river is only about 6 m wide, and the average flow only 6 cubic metres per second (cumecs) (against 50 cumecs average flow for the Habur and 840 for the Euphrates). The river plain itself varies in width between 4 km and 6 km, except in the south, at the confluence of the old and the recent rivers; and in the north, around the site of Tell Sabi Abyad, excavated by the Balikh

Valley Prehistoric Project, which is yielding comprehensive knowledge of the Halaf and its Neolithic origins.

The Balikh Valley lies between the 200 mm and 300 mm isohyets, with the critical 250 mm isohyet required for successful dry-farming occurring around the confluence of the Balikh with its main tributary, the wadi Qaramokh (Akkermans 1989b: 14). Tell Abyad, which is just south of the border with Turkey, receives an average of 275 mm (while Raqqa on the Euphrates gets only 183 mm), making it highly suitable for rain-fed farming, though not as favoured as some of the northern locations in the Habur Triangle.

Tell Sabi Abyad is the largest (240 × 170 m, c. 4.1 ha) of a cluster of five mounds, and itself is formed from four small mounds which have fused over time (Akkermans 1989b: 11). So far the oldest remains occur on the north side of the tell, where Late Neolithic materials have been found immediately below the surface, while in the southeastern part of the mound Late Neolithic remains are overlain by no less than 3 m of Halafian material (ibid.). Unfortunately, the earliest Neolithic has not yet been reached, but radiocarbon dates now available from Sabi Abyad cluster towards the end of the sixth millennium and date the transition from the Altmonochrome-like Neolithic into the Halaf period around 5200/5150 BC, with the topmost Early Halaf placed about 5100–5000 BC (Akkermans 1991: 123). The architectural remains are particularly clear for the Halaf occupation, especially concerning the vexed question of the role of tholoi, or circular vis-à-vis rectangular plan buildings.

The 1986 season opened four 9 × 9 m squares on the southeastern part of the mound: O13, O14, P13, P14. However:

The most extensive traces of Halaf rectangular complexes were found in squares P13 and P14, strata 5 and 3 respectively, and in the topmost stratum (stratum 1) in squares P13, P14 and O14. The first mentioned complex yielded well-preserved traces of a central rectangular building extended by rectangular annexes and tholoi. The main building probably comprised the actual living quarters whereas the annexes and tholoi may have been used for storing and auxiliary purposes [see photograph of modern village house in Akkermans (1989b: 62), where the plan of the actual residence is rectangular, while the roofs and freestanding 'sheds' are 'tholoi']. The main building was constructed of thick mud-brick walls on a stone foundation. The northern and western faces of this building were white-plastered and also the interior wall faces showed traces of white plaster. Slightly south of the main building a number of tiny rooms appeared which were probably added to the main building at a later stage. . . .

133

*Figure 6.3* Domestic architecture at Sabi Abyad (Akkermans 1989b: 42).

In contrast to the main building, the added complex and the tholoi were built of small mud-bricks, simply founded on earth. Although incomplete, the present evidence suggests that the southeastern mound of Tell Sabi Abyad was largely covered by only one extended complex, housing only a limited number of people. Generally, the excavations give the impression of a rather open scatter of buildings. The site does not seem to have been densely built on.

(Akkermans 1989b: 67)

Halaf tholoi have a typical diameter of from 3–5 m, and at Tell Sabi Abyad have an average interior diameter of 3 m, producing an area of about 7 m² each (Akkermans 1989b: 63). They do not seem very suitable as domestic dwellings, not even to house polygynous 'kraal'-type dispersed households, as suggested by Flannery (1972) for the earliest permanent architecture in the Levant, a position criticized by Oates (1977: 465) (cf. Maisels 1990: 117–18).

As can be seen from the isometric reconstruction of remains in square P13, stratum 5, and the artistic reconstruction of it (Figure 6.3 – from Akkermans 1989b: 42), this (Late?) Halafian pattern is remarkably simi-

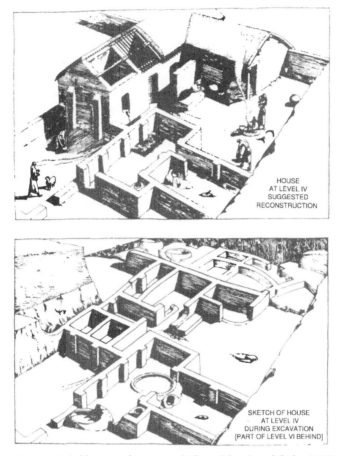

*Figure 6.4* A Hassuna homestead (from Lloyd and Safar 1945).

lar to domestic rural architecture in the Syrian Jezirah today, and it should be compared with a Hassunan example (Figure 6.4) from Lloyd and Safar (1945). The farmsteading at Tell Sabi Abyad consists essentially of a domestic dwelling unit, which is rectangular, with utilitarian outbuildings, the coolest and most efficient shape for storing grain above ground being the mud-brick domed tholos, a role further suggested by plastered and fired interiors. As they become older and less suitable, or if the amount to be stored shrinks, then tholoi can be used for other agricultural or domestic purposes, such as baking. Keyhole-shaped kilns are another characteristic of Halaf villages. Nonetheless, since the tholos is so efficient a shape for keeping the interior cool, tholoi would also be desirable for living in. A contemporary example would be Harran in south Turkey (picture in Brice 1966: plate 14) there described as a 'modern beehive village in ruins of ancient Sabaean city'.

135

Though osteological preservation was poor at Tell Sabi Abyad, evidence is good for the presence of domesticated cattle and pig, with sheep and goat dominant. Ovicaprids constitute between 60 per cent and 70 per cent of all domestic animal remains, and occur approximately in the ratio of 3 : 2 sheep/goat (Van Wijngaarden-Bakker 1989: 313). Gazelle and onager were occasionally hunted, but hunting equipment is conspicuous by its absence, and hunting seems to have been of minor importance (ibid.). More surprisingly, so too is plant collecting and fishing, though it is possible that this is an artefact of limited excavations as yet. However, the minimal finds of pistachio, almond and fig seeds probably indicate that the trees in the valley were riparian species: willow (*Salix*) and poplar (*Populus euphratica*); though ash (*Fraxinus*) occurred as a charcoal sample (Van Zeist and Waterbolk-van Rooijen 1989: 331).

Emmer and einkorn were grown, the former predominating over the latter and also over barley of the two-rowed form (*Hordeum vulgare ssp. distichum*). Pulses are represented, and that poorly, by lentil (*Lens culinaris*), certainly, and peas (*Pisum sativum*), one seed only. In contrast to, for example, the Halafian site at Girikihaciyan (on the upper Tigris in Turkey), there is no evidence at Tell Sabi Abyad for the growing of vetch (*Vicia ervilia*). The length of three flax seeds does, however, indicate domestication (Van Zeist and Waterbolk-van Rooijen 1989: 329). Today wheat and barley are the main crops in the north of the Balikh Valley; in the south, which has to be irrigated, cotton, vegetables and occasionally apricots are grown (Akkermans 1989b: 15).

Akkermans has been cited above as regarding Tell Sabi Abyad I as a rather dispersed complex of low density, housing only a limited number of people. If Tell es-Sawwan and Tell Abada are representative, this is in contrast to the Samarran-Ubaidian settlement pattern of large, extended (but centralized) households grouped with others into densely nucleated settlements. And this contrast affects not just settlement geography but the whole social fabric. Akkermans (1990: 297) argues that the heartland of Halaf society lay in the Syrian Jezirah between the Euphrates and the Khabur, only spreading from this area about 200 years after its initial appearance, but still confined to this northern belt where dry-farming was possible. He also (ibid.: 289) argues that overall population density was low, settlements were generally small and dispersed, that indicators of status were rare to absent, as were public monuments/institutions. He therefore concludes that 'Halaf social organization was mainly based upon small-scale "egalitarian" family or kin relationships . . .' and that notions of Halaf 'chiefdoms' are quite misplaced, all the indicators of which he examines and finds absent (ibid.: 290–3; cf. Maisels 1987).

However, precisely because settlements are both internally and externally egalitarian and basically autarkic, another set of relationships has to develop to knit them up into a coherent social whole, and all who have worked on the Halaf agree that their society was indeed a well-integrated one. Just such a mechanism has recently been postulated by Baird, Campbell and Watkins (1991, section 10) for whom the society is characterized by a two-tier settlement hierarchy of larger, longer-lived and more central villages engaged in a sustained web of exchanges with smaller and less long-lived villages, which are not necessarily pastoral ones. Whereas well-spaced (i.e. low-density), little rebuilt dwellings characterize the site of Kharabeh Shattani excavated by Baird, Campbell and Watkins (1991), and such features of relative impermanence are shared with Sabi Abyad, Shams ed-Din and Umm Qseir, they contrast this with Yarim Tepe II and III, Chagar Bazar and especially Arpachiyah, which are taken to be enduring nodal settlements. Those sites (but especially Arpachiyah and Chagar Bazar) house the specialists making the superb polychrome pottery produced at relatively few sites and sought after by most (Figure 6.5). Thus, the process is probably one in which sites with the potential for sustained subsistence productivity have the ability to support a comparatively large population in the longer term, a proportion of which can specialize in building the complex double-chamber kilns required (not found at smaller sites), acquiring suitable clays and pigments and generally developing the skills in painting and firing demanded for such fine ware (Baird, pers. comm.). The circulation of such 'valuables' (cf. Malinowski 1922, chapter 3) to sites like Kharabeh Shattani, where 'polychrome pottery is completely absent and bichrome occurs sporadically' (Baird *et al.* op. cit.) would thus serve, especially if it included other circuits with other items or people (exogamy), to knit-up dispersed autonomous units into a whole.

The famous 'burnt house', the largest and most central in level TT6 at Arpachiya (where the largest and finest corpus of polychrome pottery so far was found), seems to represent the archetypal production, storage and distribution centre for such goods. Mallowan and Rose (1935: 17) observe 'That the occupant was a potter and not merely a collector is proved by the discovery of a large lump of red ochre and of painters' palettes lying on the floor associated with the pottery'. Accordingly, their earlier statement (ibid.: 16) that 'This house, which alike by its situation and size was clearly the property of the headmen [*sic*] of the village . . .' seems an unwarranted intrusion of an 'obvious' sociological model to account for what may be a most interesting and rare situation: namely that of a society with (admittedly low-level) centres and specialists which is nonetheless not hierarchical or only minimally so. That the 'burnt house/potters' shop' is something peculiar to (and Mallowan says the culmination of) Halaf society, is shown by its disappearance in subsequent, Ubaidian, levels.

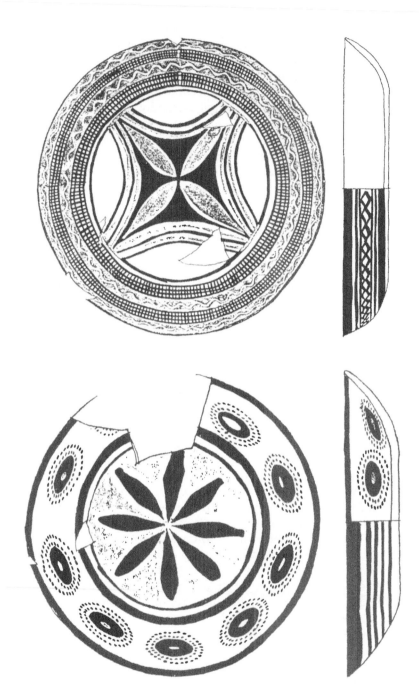

*Figure 6.5* Halaf polychrome pottery from Arpachiyah (Mallowan 1935: Plate XVII).

This is, then, the contrast between the rain-fed Halafian tradition and the Ubaidian, which had fully developed its irrigation technique on the alluvium from Samarran antecedents before, it seems, expanding outwards into the former Halafian provinces (*a fortiori* at Arpachiyah from where, Mallowan says (Mallowan and Rose 1935: 14), the Halafians were driven out).

At Yarim Tepe III and the lower levels of the corresponding Ubaidian layer at Tepe Gawra, 'in both cases the layers run directly over the final horizons of the Halaf culture and usher in the beginning of Ubaid culture in the northern variant of the latter' (Bader, Merpert and Munchaev 1981: 60).[1]

The Ubaid, accordingly, will be discussed in association with the Samarran, forming the subject of the next chapter. From Figure 6.6 (after Maisels 1990: 115) can be seen the interrelationships of the 'classic trio' – Hassuna, Samarra and Halaf – plus the Ubaid and proto-historic Uruk cultures.

Figure 6.6 is intended to illustrate simultaneity and succession of cultures. For cultures to be 'contemporary' they do not have to begin or end at the same time, merely to have a period of coevality. Now this can even mean that one culture is ending while another is beginning, since all that is logically required (or is likely to be visible in the archaeological record) is some overlap. But this *also* means that there *is* succession if one of the coeval cultures simply outlives the other(s); for example, if attributes of one culture are found stratified above another on a site formerly occupied by the other(s). But more complexly, if, for example, the Ubaid culture is an alluvial development of Samarran culture, this can mean that Ubaid 0 or 1 (say) exist in the south as cultural descendants of the originating Samarran culture, but also *are chronologically contemporary with* settlements of the Samarra culture still surviving/ thriving to the north.[2] Thus we have *both* succession *and* simultaneity for so long as Samarran settlements continue.

This is exactly the sort of situation that the Provisional chronology based on Tell Oueli represents – see Figure 6.7 (from Lebeau 1985–6: 106).

If this is true of 'ancestor' and 'descendant' then it is more obviously true of near contemporaries such as Halaf and Ubaid. Indeed Joan Oates (1983: 254) in a reconsideration of Ubaid Mesopotamia writes that:

It is quite clear that in the Hamrin at this time [Late Halaf/Ubaid 3] there were potters working in both the Halaf and Ubaid traditions, perhaps even side by side in the same villages [such as Kheit Qasim 3, Tell Hasan and Songor B]. Certainly, the contemporaneity of these two very distinctive ceramic styles cannot be in doubt. Such contemporaneity has always seemed a possible explanation

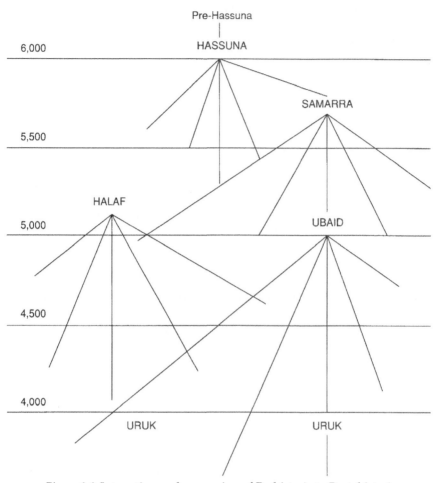

*Figure 6.6* Interaction and succession of Prehistoric to Protohistoric
cultures in Mesopotamia (Maisels 1990: 115).

of certain chronological anomalies (Oates 1968: 13; 1973: 176) and is
indeed the only explanation that makes sense of the Late Halaf
'intrusion' at Choga Mami, where the Samarran and early Ubaid
materials are very closely related. The modern situation may perhaps provide a relevant parallel, in that villages of Arabs, Kurds,
Lurs and Turcomans exist side by side, their inhabitants often
distinguishable by their dress and other cultural appurtenances. In
the Hamrin we have the first unequivocal evidence of such a
situation in Near Eastern prehistory, where previously we had
assumed a 'chest-of-drawers' sequence of cultures.

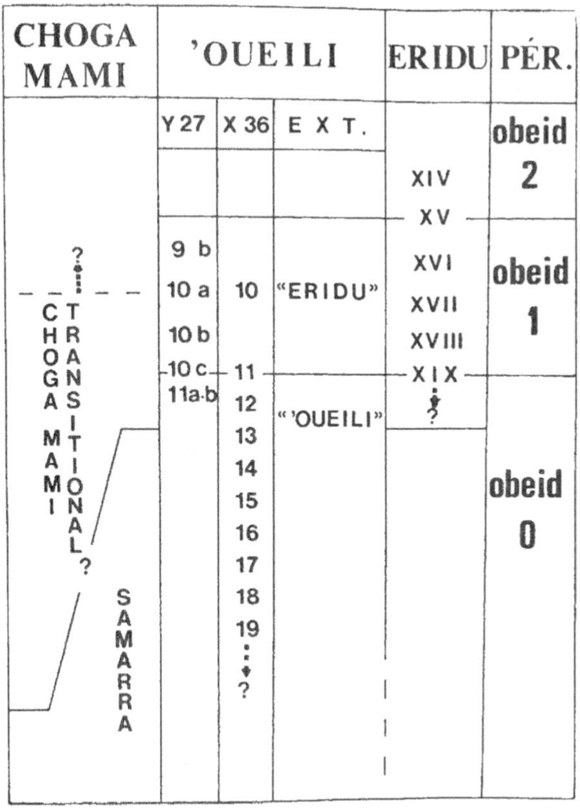

| CHOGA MAMI | 'OUEILI | | | ERIDU | PÉR. |
|---|---|---|---|---|---|
| | Y 27 | X 36 | E X T. | | obeid 2 |
| | | | | XIV | |
| | | | | XV | |
| ? | 9 b | | | XVI | obeid 1 |
| CHOGA MAMI | 10 a | 10 | "ERIDU" | XVII | |
| | 10 b | | | XVIII | |
| TRANSITIONAL? | 10 c | 11 | | XIX | |
| | 11a-b | 12 | "'OUEILI" | ? | |
| | | 13 | | | |
| | | 14 | | | obeid 0 |
| | | 15 | | | |
| | | 16 | | | |
| | | 17 | | | |
| SAMARRA | | 18 | | | |
| | | 19 | | | |
| | | ? | | | |

*Figure 6.7* Tell el-'Oueili: Provisional chronology (from Lebeau 1985–6: 1096).

Key parts of the model opposite (Figure 6.6) are reinforced by Mark Blackham's study (1996) of relationships between Hassuna, Samarra and Ubaid ceramic assemblages. Applying statistical analyses to paint styles and fabric at Tell 'Oueili (Tell 'Awayli), he concludes that 'it is likely that Ubaid 0 and Samarran wares were both manufactured locally and are not uniquely distinct except in design. The results support the argument that the Samarran and Ubaid wares are stylistic variants of a common ceramic tradition' (op. cit.: 13). The question is whether Early Ubaid potters of 'Oueili, as inheritors of the Samarran tradition, simply continued it, or whether Samarra is to be seen not as an actual culture but as a style of Ubaid ware. This latter view is contradicted by, among others, Tell es-Sawwan, Samarra/Ubaid transitional processes (best seen at Choga Mami), Yarim Tepe and the stratigraphy of Tell Hassuna (Figure 6.2), where levels IB–VII contain Hassuna archaic, Hassuna standard and the Samarran wares (level III and above), levels VII–VIII to X are Halaf, followed by Ubaid.

# 7

# THE UBAIDIAN INHERITANCE

Samarran culture, like Halaf and Ubaidian but in contrast to Hassuna, is not best seen at the site after which the culture was named, the historically well-known and continuously inhabited city of Samarra on the Tigris. Although work at Samarra had been undertaken by German excavators prior to the First World War, and indeed the mounds of Tell es-Sawwan 11 km downstream noted (Herzfeld 1930: 5), when operations commenced at Tell es-Sawwan in February 1964, Samarran culture was still 'represented by little more than pottery and graves', in the words of the Iraq Director of Archaeological Exploration, Benham Abu al-Soof (1968: 3). Their perspicacity in seeking to reveal 'a Samarran village community in all its material details, including its architecture' (el-Wailly and Abu es-Soof 1965: 17) was rewarded at

> The site known as Tell es-Sawwan ['Mound of the Flints'] . . . situated on the eastern bank of the Tigris some 11 km downstream of Samarra [lat. 34°80' N, long. 43°55 'E], where it stands on a cliff commanding an extensive view of the river. The site has a maximum height of 3.5 m above the level of the plain behind, and is roughly oval in shape, measuring approximately 230 m north–south by 110 m east–west; it is composed of three mounds . . . A, B and C, of which the highest (B) is partly separated from A and C, to its north and south respectively, by two seasonal watercourses.
>
> (ibid.)

The presence of watercourses is crucial, since the present level of precipitation is only 200 mm (Flannery and Wheeler 1967: 179). On the plain to the east there are some moist depressions suitable for 'dry' farming, but if the Tigris flowed, not as presently, at the foot of the vertical conglomerate bluff on which the village is located, but further out, then a substantial floodplain with an inherently high water table would have been available for 'hydromorphic' agriculture (Maisels 1990: 294–7). On the basis of three small samples of carbonized seeds and grains recovered in 1964 from the defensive moat, some two metres below its upper level (western end, northern side), Helbaek (1965: 45) recognized three barleys and three wheats, with the barleys the most important, and one of the wheats only possible. Those were: six-row naked barley (*Hordeum vulgare*), six-row and two-row hulled barley (*Horditum vulgare* and *Hordeum distichon*); emmer (*Triticum dicoccum*) possibly einkorn (which is not well adapted to alluvial situations), but certainly bread wheat (*Triticum aestivum*) though it is not too well adapted either; linseed (*Linum usitatissimum*), plus lots of wild caper seeds (*Capparis spinosa*) and shauk (*Prosopis stephaniana*). Kabar (caper) and shauk were also prominent at Ali Kosh and Tepe Sabz in the plain of Deh Luran, Khuzistan (cf. Maisels 1990: 100–7). Also akin to the Sabz and Khazineh phases at Tepe Sabz in Deh Luran, rather than the (later) position at Ras al Amiya and Eridu on the southern alluvium, are high frequencies of domestic sheep and goat relative to cattle (Flannery and Wheeler 1967: 182). The ready availability of large fish and plentiful mussels was exploited, as were fallow deer (*Dama mesopotamica*) and gazelle (*Gazella subgutturosa*) (ibid.: 180–1). With its riparian location at the junction between the Assyrian steppe and the alluvial plains, the inhabitants of Tell es-Sawwan would also be able to hunt wild boar (*Sus scrofa*) and onager (*Equus hemionus*).

Helbaek significantly concludes:

> Most probably agriculture was conducted on the basis of the seasonal flood of the river, spill pools were exploited, run-off checked in favourable spots by primitive damming – and generally the activities which we may visualize as the forerunners of later full-fledged canal irrigation.
>
> (Helbaek 1965: 47)

Five main building levels are known, with level I the earliest. A radiocarbon sample (P. 855) from a level I floor gives, on the Libby half-life, 5506 ± 73 BC (el-Wailly and Abu es-Soof 1965: 19). While levels I and II provided relatively little pottery, grave goods suggest that alabaster was more commonly used, but what there is closely resembles late archaic Hassuna Ib-II, though some may have yet earlier affinities in the opinion of el-Wailly and Abu es-Soof (op. cit.: 21). Pottery in levels I and II is coarse, being constructed of clay with large extraneous particles and poorly fired, producing a black unoxidized core. Surface colour is buff or light brown, decorated with a self-slip, and sometimes burnished. Fragments of very crude hemispherical bowls were found on a level I floor, and fragments of red-slipped and grey wares also occur in level II (ibid.).

In Level III the incised Hassuna ware becomes very popular and the crude archaic type disappears. Painted Samarra makes its

143

appearance in considerable quantities, and a few examples which were painted after firing are found. . . . In Level IV the incised Hassuna pottery appears for the last time, and the painted, and painted and incised, Samarra ware now predominates. Very little is left of Sawwan V, but it suffices to show continuity in pottery; Samarra wares are the only ceramic product of this level.

(ibid.)

The buildings of level I are not very un-Hassunan, despite their size and regularity of plan (see Figure 7.1 (from el-Wailly and Abu es-Soof 1965: Plate IX)):

Building I, to the west, has more than fourteen rooms and prob-ably more than one courtyard. . . . Building 2, further to the east, covers a greater area, but was designed with less regularity both inside and out. . . . The buttresses which are a notable feature of the external faces of both buildings normally occur at the junction of two walls, and have apparently the purely functional purpose of strengthening the outer walls. Both buildings, No. 1 at its north end and No. 2 at its west, contain unusual features which are probably to be understood as staircases leading to the roofs though they might be no more than platforms. Between the two buildings is a narrow lane.

(el-Wailly and Abu es-Soof 1965: 20)

Level II shows continuity and development from level I (see Figure 7.2 (from el-Wailly and Abu es-Soof 1965: Plate XIII)).

Level III is, however, entirely remarkable and unlike anything seen before anywhere, not because the building complexes have markedly changed, but because what now Sawwan comprises is a township consisting of freestanding individual housing complexes, which, front-ing onto the river, are enclosed on the other three sides by a mud-brick wall behind a ditch 3 m deep and 2.5 m wide cut in bedrock. Furthermore, those housing units reproduce in various forms a standard T-form groundplan. This does not mean that the size and layout of rooms is identical in each case, or that the configuration is symmetrical; it does mean that all have several large rooms or central halls flanked by subsidiary rooms and corridors (see Figure 7.3 for level IIIA (from Yasin 1970: Plate 1)). At Ubaidian sites like Abada, this later formalizes into major halls in the stem and across the top of the T, with rows of subsidiary rooms opening off them.

In 1978 appeared a collection with the signal title, 'Social archaeology – beyond subsistence and dating' (Redman *et al.*, eds). Chapter 7, by Patty Jo Watson, built on her ethnoarchaeological work in western Iran in 1959–60, and analysed 'Architectural differentiation in some Near

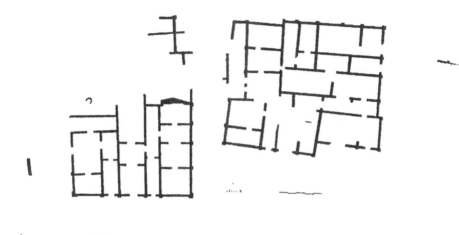

*Figure 7.1* Tell es-Sawwan, level I (el-Wailly and Abu es-Soof 1965: Plate IX).

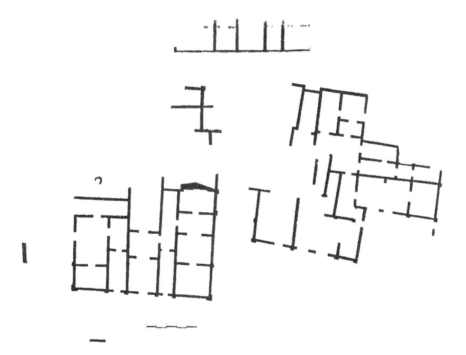

*Figure 7.2* Tell es-Sawwan, level II (el-Wailly and Abu es-Soof 1965: Plate XIII).

145

*Figure 7.3* Tell es-Sawwan, level III (Yasin 1970: Plate I).

146

*Table 7.1*  Summary table of house and room sizes for various prehistoric sites plus Hasanabad (Redman *et al.*, 1978: 155)

| Community | Number of houses | Mean area of houses (in $m^2$) | Average number of rooms per house | Average room size (in $m^2$) |
|---|---|---|---|---|
| Hassuna | 5 | 29.02 | 4.20 | 6.90 |
| Matarrah | 4 | 14.80 | 4.25 | 3.48 |
| Umm Dabag-hiyah | 2 | 39.64 | 6.50 | 6.10 |
| Sawwan | 7 | 44.65 | 11.29 | 3.97 |
| Choga Mami | 3 | 24.52 | 9.67 | 2.54 |
| Hacilar VI | 5 | 47.90 | 1.60 | 29.94 |
| Çatal Hüyük | 53 | 19.67 | 1.58 | 12.40 |
| Hasanabad | $-^a$ | $50.45^b$ | $3.80^b$ | $12.60^b$ |
|  |  | $62.30^c$ | $4.70^c$ | $12.46^c$ |

* The figures for mean area of houses and for average room size for Hasanabad are based on the dimensions of 60 rooms I was able to measure on the ground in the village (see Table 7.1). There are 41 households containing 193 rooms (counting surface stables: 156 rooms if stables are not included), so my sample of measured rooms is about 31 per cent of the total number of rooms in Hasanabad. The figures for average number of rooms per house, however, are based on counts made from the village plan. Room sizes derived from this plan are much less accurate than the figures for the 60 rooms just mentioned, hence the latter are presented here.

[b] Excluding surface stables; see note c.

[c] Including surface stables; subterranean stables are not included in any of the Hasanabad figures, although several are present in the village.

Eastern communities, prehistoric and contemporary', the latter a village referred to as 'Hasanabad'. Nine sites of the sixth millennium represented the prehistoric communities (Umm Dabaghiya, Hassuna I–II, Yarim Tepe I, Hassuna III–IV, Matarrah, Tell es-Sawwan, Choga Mami and Yarim Tepe II); with two in Anatolia: Hacilar and Çatal Hüyük.

Those analysed were selected on the basis of the availability of published architectural data, from which the 'Summary table of house and room sizes for various prehistoric sites plus Hasanabad' emerged (Redman *et al.* 1978: 155; Table 7.1).

Next to contemporary Hasanabad, it will be observed that Sawwan and Hacilar VI have the largest mean area per house. Watson remarks on the contrast between

> Sawwan and Hacilar with closely comparable house sizes of around 45 m$^2$ but with strikingly different patterns in subdivision of that space (see table): many small rooms at Sawwan versus one or two large rooms at Hacilar (the large rooms possibly subdivided by partitions but also possibly with a second storey). . . . At Hassuna, Matarrah, Hacilar, and Hasanabad the rooms making up a household are agglomerated around courts; at Sawwan and Choga Mami houses are separate or detached.

(ibid.)

Sawwan and Choga Mami are, of course, the two Samarran sites in the comparison; what makes those qualitatively different from the various others in their construction of domestic space? Given that the same materials (mud and wood) are available to all, the answer should be sought in the distinct social requirements the houses are intended to satisfy. Watson (1978: 156) concludes that, like Hasanabad, all of the prehistoric houses manifest 'social organization based on the nuclear family as primary residence unit, *and presumably primary economic unit as well* . . .' (my emphasis); but this ready equivalence does not explain either the architectural differences, or emergent economic ones.

Looking at the size and complexity of Tell es-Sawwan's houses (Figures 7.1, 7.2 and 7.3) and their existence as independent units, it seems clear that at least by level III the nuclear family *cannot* be the primary unit of residence or economic activity. On the contrary what the architecture represents is the *oikos*, a social unit of production, consumption and reproduction which is significantly augmented beyond its core family by the inclusion of non-core family members and other dependants or subordinates of more lowly status. Thus an *oikos* is a household that is *augmented and stratified*. The rationale for the *oikos* form of economic and social enterprise is to be found in the labour and management needs of irrigation agriculture, where a wide variety of labour-intensive tasks must be well integrated.

Samarran settlements such as Tell es-Sawwan pioneered this radical new departure whose socio-economic forms produced the cities of Sumer on the southern alluvium. First, however, irrigation farming settlements had to colonize that alluvium. In this learning/pioneering process Samarra became Ubaid (Figure 6.6), a transition which can be observed at the site of Choga Mami.

Choga Mami, a 5–6-ha site which is both topographically and culturally transitional, is crucial to an understanding of the trajectory. It was selected for excavation by Joan Oates after a survey in 1966 of the eastern margins of the alluvial plains where they slope down from the Zagros foothills. This area represents the 'borderlands' between the northern and southern cultural provinces of Mesopotamia, lying in an area of marginal rainfall, where rain-fed agriculture is just possible, and on an historic and prehistoric highway along the Zagros foothills between Khuzistan and northern Mesopotamia (Oates 1969: 115).

The mound of Choga Mami, only 6 m high at its highest point, and measuring 350 × 100 m, was the largest which (like Abu Salabikh) had no overlay of later occupation debris (Oates 1982: 22). Rather, on the surface were pottery materials very similar to early Ubaid types as found at Eridu, levels XVIII–XV; also many Samarran and a few Halaf sherds (ibid.). However, the later Ubaid and Uruk levels had been eroded, except, crucially at the northeast corner of the mound, where a guard-tower made of cigar-shaped mud-bricks (*libn*) in alternate courses of stretchers and headers, had originally protected the approach to the village along a cobbled path; and subsequently secured the survival of several post-Samarran levels, of which four phases were identified in the two main areas of excavation (Oates 1982: 24). Under the guard-tower, in addition to Samarran painted and incised wares, pottery associated with the earliest Ubaid levels of the south (Eridu levels XVIII–XVI) was found, as were (unsealed) materials of the next phase (i.e. Hajji Muhammad or Ubaid 2). The several levels postdating the classic Samarran levels were accordingly termed the Choga Mami Transitional, 'at the latest contemporary with an early phase of Al Ubaid 2' (Oates 1969: 120), and 'so designated because it displayed many characteristics in common both with the classical Samarran pottery that preceded it at the site and with the early Ubaid ceramic of the south' (Oates 1983: 256).

Of major significance are the finds in Samarran levels of terracotta figurines which included men and animals (mainly sheep/goat plus pig), but mostly were of women wearing bead necklaces, ear, nose and lip studs, overall body-decoration of painted stripes or (on the arms and torso), circles. They also bore three vertical incision lines on each cheek (as do many sub-Saharans today), and as is represented on the striking and justly famous 'face-pot' from Hassuna (which is presumably a Samarran import) and also on the face from Samarra and the pedestal foot from Tell es-Sawwan (Oates 1969: 130). These decorative representations, in particular of heads (including one of a pig) indicate a cultural tradition stretching possibly from Hassuna, through Samarra to Ubaid. At Choga Mami three different types of modelled clay heads were found (all detached). The first type is naturalistic, with 'Early Dynastic' hair-styles, though definitely Samarran. Those of the second type, with bird-like profiles and elongated headdresses, closely approach Ubaid examples (1969: 129); while two in particular 'bear a striking resemblance to one of the Ubaid figures from Ur' (1969: 130). The third type of head, which was found in a sealed fill above a Samarra ground surface between buildings in H7 and H8 (ibid.), is deliberately flattened, and has a pronounced aquiline nose and 'coffee-bean' eyes (ibid.). For its possible significance as the progenitor of Inanna, the goddess of fecundity in general and dates in particular, see Maisels (1990: Appendix B).

In this context the discovery of early irrigation systems assumes heightened importance. The earliest, on the north side of the mound, seems to consist of narrow meandering stream channels spreading out to form an irregular fan upon the alluvial fan created by the Gangir river as it issues, at 152 m elevation through its gorge (see Oates and Oates 1976: 129a). On the south slope of the site was a somewhat later Samarran canal, 6–8 m in width, and about 100 m further south, though on the same alignment, was another canal, of Ubaid 3 date (Oates 1982: 26). Then as now, the canals are fed by takeoffs from the River Gangir running to the east of Mandali; however, the system was improved and the area which could be irrigated extended during the sixth millennium, by the building of large lateral canals parallel to the line of the hills, the Jebel Kahnah Rig (here the outermost crest of the Zagros and the border between Iraq and Iran) which slope away northwest to the Upper Diyala Basin (Oates and Oates 1976: 128). To supply the fields, water is periodically drawn from the main canals into ditches. The dip of the plain between the 152 m elevation of the Gangir at entry, and the Ab-i-Naft at 91 m, makes flow easy and virtually eliminates the possibility of salination. And while 'the modern system is a fan of small channels, fed from the river [Gangir] at the mouth of the gorge, which waters the palm groves of Mandali itself and an area of cereal cultivation to the northwest and west . . .' (Oates and Oates 1976: 130), the modern settlement, 4 km to the south, is not entirely dependent on irrigation as it is an oasis lying on a spring-line.

As at Sawwan, emmer, bread-wheat, naked six-row barley and hulled two-row barley were grown, as was linseed. Of the legumes, lentil and a large seeded pea were grown, caper and *shauk* (*Prosopis*) collected, as also the ubiquitous pistachio. In the Samarran levels of Choga Mami sheep, goat, pig and dog have been recognized, as also domesticated cattle which are, however, rare (Oates 1969: 140). The proportion of goat to sheep declines from 92 per cent in the Samarran levels to 86 per cent in the Transitional phase, falling further to 76 per cent in the Ubaid well deposit and reaching virtual equality, at 58 per cent, in the small Early Dynastic sample (Oates 1973: 174). Cattle apparently assume greater significance on the southern alluvium, as at Ras al 'Amiya in the centre and, in the furthest south, at Eridu in the earliest 'hut sounding' level (ibid.).

Again like Sawwan, but in contrast to Hassuna, Yarim Tepe and Matarrah where construction is in *tauf* (packed mud), houses at Choga Mami are built from mud-bricks (*libn*), as in Sumerian practice (Oates 1973: 169). Indeed at Eridu the temple in the earliest level (XVI = Al Ubaid 1) is made of long prismatic mud-bricks, while that of the succeeding level (XV) bears a conspicuous row of double thumb imprints on the upper side of the brick, just as do the bricks of the Transitional Levels at Choga Mami (Oates 1973: 174–5). However, the houses at Choga Mami are not T-form but rectangular, divided into a large number of small square rooms. They are, however, buttressed at the corners and where the internal walls meet external ones, again foreshadowing later practice. And in their successive rebuildings within or upon the same walls, Oates (1973: 169) sees the presence of private property, something reinforced by the recovery of stamp seals at both Hassunan and Samarran sites (ibid.).

At Choga Mami, Joan Oates (1973: 169) also apparently detected larger buttressed walls which belonged to no particular structure but against which houses were backed. Accordingly, she interprets this as looking 'like the boundary walls of larger units, perhaps comparable with the modern Arab *bayt* in the sense of an extended household' (ibid.); which term is, indeed, one of the specific cognates of é and *bîtum* (Gelb 1979; and see next chapter).

While there are several very strong indications of what seems to be a clear line of development from the Samarran to the Ubaid, Oates (1973: 172–3) cautions us against too easily assuming a direct linear succession, since the Transitional phase at Choga Mami might be contemporary with Ubaid I. She does, however, stress the process of 'local though not isolated development' (ibid.: 171). Employing this, we can envision a process whereby some Samarran groups who had *earlier* moved onto the southern alluvium, quite naturally underwent the same develop-mental processes as at Choga Mami, where the Transitional is very near, both artefactually and temporally, to Ubaid 1 and 2. In other words, the Choga Mami Transitional is a development of the Samarran, but so too is the Ubaid, and perhaps they are contemporaneous during Ubaid 0–1 (see putative 'Oueili chronology on p. 141). Certainly, Oates herself supports the possibility of parallel developments from a common Samarran origin by the observation that at Choga Mami

> the plant inventory, both of cultivars and weeds, is too rich . . . for the site to be considered as representing early experimentation with irrigation, a purely botanical observation that is confirmed by the complexity of the irrigation schemes observed in the area.
>
> (Oates 1982: 27)

Indeed, of Tell el 'Oueli, the site with the earliest Ubaidian levels so far known, and which reach right down into the present water table of the southern alluvium, J.D. Forest observes in the preliminary report on the fourth season (1983) that

> As may be seen by consulting the report which is dealing with the Obeid 0 ware, the latter is showing some similarities with the 'Choga Mami Transitional' culture which has been viewed as a kind of compromise between the Samarra and the Obeid 1 cultures. It is interesting to observe now that connections between the Obeid 1 and the Samarra cultures are to be found in the architec-tural field as well. We are dealing in both cases with complex multi-

room buildings. The three parallel rooms of our Obeid 1 level [building] belong to some unit, which may be compared only to some features from Tell es-Sawwan.

(J.D. Forest 1985–6: 65).

Indeed, in their summary of excavations in Iraq during 1989–90, Roger Matthews and Tony Wilkinson (1991: 179) observe of Oueili that

We now have the plan of three houses of the period Ubaid 0 [which has three main phases I to III, latest to earliest]. The general outline of the plan, as shown by these buildings, *is tripartite* (my emphasis). During phase II, a building measuring 12.4 m long covered an area of 233 $m^2$. Its northern wing includes a large hypostyle hall (6.3 × 5.2 m, 32.7$m^2$) flanked by a staircase. The central wing is also hypostyle [one where the roof is supported on posts or columns]. Two later buildings (phases IB and IA) have been excavated, also hypostyle constructions. This architecture is quite similar to that from Tell es-Sawwan, but there are original features at Oueili, the most spectacular being the systematic use of posts to support the roofs of the rooms which, in some cases, reached 5 m wide. These dwellings alter considerably the prevailing picture of the beginnings of architecture in lower Mesopotamia during the Ubaid period.

And to Mellaart writing a decade earlier (1975: 155), the fact that Choga Mami 'house plans show rectangular structures with external but-tresses, thin [internal] walls and two to three rows of rooms'; and overall 'vary in size from 9 × 7 m with twelve rooms and two doorways, to 7 × 6 m with nine rooms and three doorways, or 8 × 4.5 m with eight rooms and two doorways . . . suggests that more than one family lived in these houses'. By the Ubaid period this can no longer be regarded merely as a plausible suggestion – the architecture resists explanation otherwise.

Given the exigencies of discovery at the type site of Al 'Ubaid, near Ur on the southern reaches of the alluvium, Ubaid architecture is best seen in an area not far to the north of Choga Mami and at the same latitude as Samarra. Although it lies on the edge of the area of rain-fed agriculture, receiving annual rainfall not far short of 250 mm, the Hamrin Basin shares the semi-arid climate and poor ground cover of the alluvium. Here a large and therefore international programme of rescue archae-ology had to be mounted during the 1970s as a dam threatened to obliterate over seventy sites. As Jasim (1985: I; 2) describes it:

The Hamrin basin is an almond-shaped area measuring some 40 × 15 km. It lies in the Middle Diyala region in the east–central part of Iraq between Jebel Hamrin, the westernmost ripple of the Zagros mountains, and the ridges of Jebel Jubbah Dag, which run roughly parallel to the north of it.

With its western extension as the Jebel Makhul, the Jebel Hamrin marks the division between upper (or northern) and lower (central and southern) Iraq (ibid.). The Hamrin Basin, with an elevation between 80 m and 105 m above sea level, definitely falls into the dry-steppe category (Jasim 1985: 5). However, soils in the Hamrin basin are generally good, deep and scarcely salinized, so only require a secure water supply to be highly productive; and Choga Mami shows that irrigation had been mastered before the Ubaidian occupation of the Hamrin.

A particularly good site at which to see Ubaidian architecture is Tell Abada, excavated from December 1977 to July 1978 by S.A. Jasim of the Iraqi State Organization of Antiquities. This oval-shaped mound, about 190 m long and 150 m wide, rising only 3.5 m above the present surface of the surrounding plain,

> lies to the east of the Diyala river in the southeastern part of the Hamrin region, some 12 km southeast of the town of As-Saaddiyah, in a vast plain along the Zagros foothills. This fairly large site occupies a central position among the prehistoric sites found on this side of the region.
>
> (Jasim 1985: 16)

Tell Abada is doubly fortunate in that it is a substantial site which was especially well preserved in the two basic regards: in antiquity the site was not occupied after the Ubaid period; and subsequently it has not served as a burial ground (as tells were so used from the Halaf onward), nor has it been ploughed or used as a source of building material, due to local belief that the site is haunted.

Realizing both the importance and opportunities of the site, the excavators exposed no less than 80 per cent of it at the top building level (I), and over 50 per cent of the bottom level (III). During level III, founded on virgin soil, the western sector of the mound contained two large multi-room houses in very well-preserved condition (A and B), while the centre of the mound held a building (C) which was largely destroyed (Jasim 1985: 17). Levels I and II are dated to the early Ubaid 3 phase by the excavator (ibid.: 172); and he also observes that

> the earliest level [III] at Abada produced a number of vessels and a variety of sherds which are closely comparable to examples from Eridu XVI–XV [Ubaid I], together with some examples which resemble both Choga Mami transitional Samarra/Ubaid type and more classical Samarra pottery. They were also associated with more conventional Ubaid 2 pottery.
>
> (ibid.: 169)

The buildings of this level (III) were constructed in long slabs of sun-

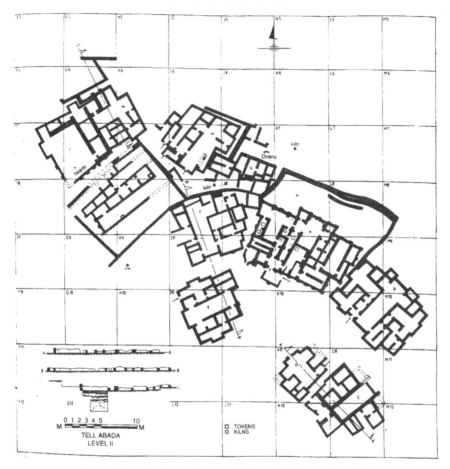

*Figure 7.4* Tell Abada (Jasim 1985: pt. 2.) Plan of level II.

dried mud, 50 × 25–27 × 7–8 cm, laid in alternate courses of headers and stretchers along the axis of the wall. The floors were of beaten clay, while the walls of buildings A and B were plastered inside and out with *jus* (gypsum). The walls of C were only plastered internally (ibid.: 18). However, as can be seen from Figure 7.4, building A manifests a regular tripartite plan, with a central hall of 8 m × 2.4 m, flanked on either side by small rooms. Characteristically, the outer walls (here on the north-eastern and northwestern sides only), are reinforced by buttressing. Right up against its northeastern wall is building B, of irregular plan and with no fewer than nineteen rooms of varying but small size, ranging from as little as 0.8 × 0.5 m to a still small 2.5 × 1.8 m; suggesting that this was not so much a habitation as a storage and workshop building. Indeed, although more rectilinear in plan, the building attending the

154

tripartite one at the early Ubaid site of Kheit Qasim III (Forest-Foucault 1980: 222) has been tentatively identified as a general purpose structure, housing workshops and possibly workers too (Maisels 1990: 167).

From the finds of large storage jars and large quantities of red ochre together with grindstones still bearing traces of ochre; a number of plano-convex discs which are possibly some sort of mould; a small basin in room 14 of building B coated with a very thick layer of gypsum; the proximity of two large pottery kilns and large quantities of sherds and debris; Jasim (1985: 18) infers that both buildings were associated with the manufacture of pottery. Since the plano-convex discs were concentrated in B, and the gypsum-coated basin was located there, this tends to support the suggestion that building B was the actual manufactury, while A was the 'residence', though a number of alternative possibilities cannot be ruled out.

Level II (opposite), which is separated from the level beneath by 50–70 cm of fill and gives a carbon-14 date of $5770 \pm 45$ BP, calibrated to $4670 \pm 70$ BC (Jasim 1985: 172) has, as so rarely, been excavated over the whole site, and it reveals a truly remarkable phenomenon: a nucleated settlement or township, consisting of ten well-preserved independent buildings (Jasim 1985: 19). With the exception of building I, the least well-preserved, the general plan of each building is tripartite, as observed in level III, and later in level I. However, some have this configuration reduplicated three times over in the same structure, with the T-form halls at either side of the central one, turned through a right angle in building B to produce perfect symmetry (see Figure 7.4 (from Jasim 1985: Fig. 13)). Other structures have permutations of this theme.

Central to the settlement is building A, at $20 \times 12.5$ m the largest, possessed of no less than twenty-nine buttresses on the exterior walls where they receive interior walls, and with large buttresses at each of the corners. Building A also displays a large terrace wall to its northeast, no doubt related to the nature of the site (Figure 7.5 (from Jasim 1985: Fig. 9)). Within the building were found groups of small clay objects, which may be calculi in a recording system, contained in pottery vessels. Building A, levels I and II, also contained fifty-seven urn burials, nearly half the total number (127) at the site; all were of infants (Jasim 1985: 34). Three were associated with elementary grave-goods in building A, level II: a few beads perhaps from a necklace; a clay figurine of human shape; and a small cup with burial no. 5 in building A, level I (ibid.: 36). Those items could be interpreted as status marking, but they could just as well be simple marks of affection.

As the asymmetric building I seems to have been a sheepfold and cattle barn, building B, to the east of A, can stand as ideal-type, given its symmetry and the fact that it is not the central one, with the special items just mentioned:

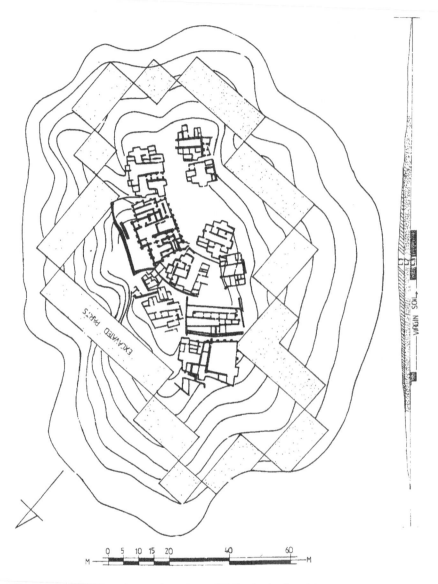

*Figure 7.5* Contour, plan and section of Tell Abada, level II (Jasim 1985: Fig. 9).

The plan is tripartite with a very symmetrical shape based on a central cruciform hall (194), measuring 10 m in length, and two lateral, smaller cruciform courts perpendicular to it (111 and 119), identical in shape and position. The entrance to the building is on the southwest side and leads to a small square room (118) which serves as the antechamber giving access in three different directions: to the main central court (104) to the right, to a large L-shaped room (114, 115) to the left, and to the cruciform lateral court (111) via rooms 117 and 116. The presence of a central access in the middle of the northwestern wall resulted in the creation of two small rooms (107 and 110) both projecting from the northeastern wall of the building; room (109) on the northwestern corner corresponds to room (108) on the northeastern corner. No doors have been found to the last four rooms which might have been used for storage purposes.

A glance at the method of communication between rooms in this building (B) shows a great similarity with building A . . .,

(ibid.: 24–5)

where, additionally, stone sockets still *in situ* (in rooms 33, 22, 16 and 28) indicate that doors of wood or wood-framed reed matting closed off access. This is important, for it demonstrates the possibility of separate suites of rooms within the same building.

In level I, the uppermost, seven coherent architectural units have been excavated, and all show considerable continuity from the previous level (Jasim 1985: 27). Innovations, however, are a water distribution network employing overlapping conical pottery pipes (50 × 30 cm in diameter) which linked to the Kurdurreh river several hundred metres away; and one formed from cylindrical pipes (50 × 20 cm in diameter) which fed from the north into a wide, 1 m deep, oval-shaped stone-lined basin measuring about 2.5 m in length and 1.5 m wide, the edges sealed with *juss* and reinforced with pebbles (ibid.: 32).

The new grain storage technique, which is clear in buildings E, F, H and J, is called *Baryat shilib*, still used in Iraq:

A small area of floor not exceeding 1.5 × 1 metre, usually in the main courtyard, is marked out and covered with straw or reeds and surrounded with standing mats tied together by means of strings or frond leaves. This mat container is filled with grain, covered with reeds or straw and sealed with a layer of clay, which was also used to seal the edges between the mats and the floor.

(ibid.: 29)

The parallels between Tell es-Sawwan and Tell Abada in terms of nucleation will by now be obvious, as also in the component houses. But the Hamrin has other Ubaid sites which must be taken into consideration.

A particularly well-preserved one is the house discovered at Tell Madhhur in the northeast part of the area to be flooded, a small mound of only 90 m in diameter, rising 2.5 m above the level of the surrounding plain, but 4 m below it (Roaf 1982: 41). Here was found, and fully

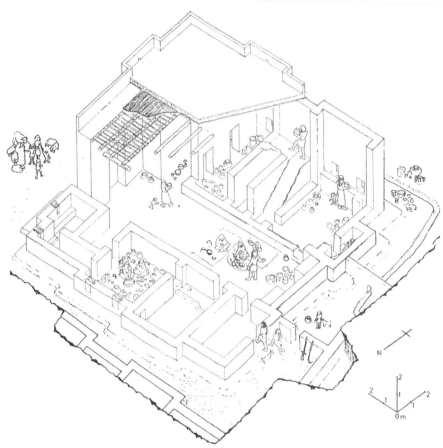

*Figure 7.6* Tell Madhhur (courtesy of Mike Roaf).

excavated with its windows and doors intact (!) 'one of the best preserved historic buildings ever to have been found in Mesopotamia' (see
Figure 7.6). At 14 m square

> It had a tripartite plan, consisting of a central cruciform hall run-
> ning the whole width of the house, with rows of rooms to the
> north and south. The walls were made out of rectangular mud-
> bricks [53 × 28–30 × 8–10 cm and 53 × 14.5–15 × 8–10 cm] and the
> outside wall stepped out wherever it was met by an internal wall.
> The building was reinforced by a heavily plastered low mud-brick
> revetment built at the base of the outer wall.
>
> (Roaf 1982: 42)

The entrance, as at Abada, was in the northwestern corner, leading
through an antechamber into the central hall. By counting the courses of

fallen bricks from the north wall of this hall, its original height could be calculated to be at least 3.5 m (ibid.). The excellent state of preservation not only of the building but of its contents – which included more than seventy pots, baked clay nail-shaped mullers, grindstones, stone hoes, blades of flint and obsidian, baked clay spindle whorls, a few animal figurines and over 3800 egg-shaped clay sling bullets – were due to destruction of the building by fire. Fortunately large quantities of carbonized grain, tentatively identified as six–row hulled barley, were recovered from one of the most heavily burnt rooms, and this yields a carbon-14 date of 5570 ± 55 BP, or 4470 ± 80 BC calibrated (ibid.), which puts this house fairly late in the Ubaid. The items recovered have been situated where found in this imaginative isometric partial reconstruction by Susan Roaf of the Ubaid house in level 2 (1982: 43 (Figure 7.6)).

The Hamrin Dam Salvage Project has been described by Michael Roaf (1982: 40), one of the British project leaders, as

> Perhaps the most exciting project undertaken in the last fifty years of Mesopotamian archaeology . . . other sites have produced more impressive finds, such as the beautiful ivories from Nimrud or the spectacular architecture of the temple at Tell al Rimah, but nowhere else in Mesopotamia has there been such successful international cooperation on such a wide variety of sites in such a small area producing such important and interesting results. When the results of the numerous excavations have been published the Hamrin Basin will be the area best known archaeologically in Mesopotamia and we will be able to discuss settlement patterns not only superficially, from surface collections of potsherds, but also in depth from the more complete and reliable evidence of excavations.
>
> (Roaf 1982: 40)

A few kilometres to the north of Tell Abada, members of the French Archaeological Mission, under Chantal Forest, in four months during 1978 and 1980 excavated the site of Kheit Qasim III, already referred to. They uncovered two buildings of early Ubaid date: one, of classical T-form, measuring 10.5 × 14 m and made of mud-bricks of 27 × 55 × 6 cm (standard for the period), the other, badly eroded, of roughly tripartite but not T-form, measuring 10 × 10 m (J.D. Forest 1984: 85). This site is important not only because a building of striking symmetry with three main halls is accompanied by another with barn-like rectangular spaces, but because the excavators have been able to work out a circulation pattern, which in its turn suggests the occupation pattern (Figure 7.7).

The central T-form hall, comprising rooms 1, 13 and 14, is clearly the

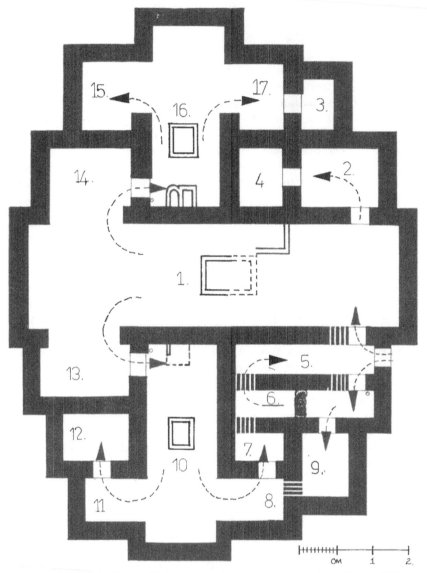

*Figure 7.7* Kheit Qasim III: Layout and access (redrawn from Forest 1984: 119 and 1980: 222).

dominant axis. Entry to the house is gained from the southeast through room 5, whence access could be had either directly to the main hall or by stair to an upper level. Rooms 2 and 4 open off the main hall facing the principal access. From the rooms 13 and 14 at the top of the T, access can be had to the two subsidiary halls: 10 (with 8 and 11) and 16 (with 15 and

160

17) respectively, the former giving entry to rooms 7 and 12, the latter to room 3 (from 17). Access to room 9 proceeds from the 'eastern' part of room 6, the low mud-brick wall in the middle of which would logically be the beginning of the staircase which continues above room 5 to the roof (C. Forest 1984: 86). Sherds, large stones, bone and flint refuse found in room 6 further suggest this was an 'understairs' dump.

As can be seen, each hall has a rectangular hearth in its centre, made of a row of mud-bricks set on edge. Each also has a storage bin against an interior wall. Taken with the fact that door-sockets exist in the doorways between the halls (and indeed at the staircase in room 6), this suggests that each hall is the centre of a separate unit of a common household.

J.D. Forest (1984: 85) observes, therefore, that 'the house cannot correspond to a nuclear family', and, since the halls are unequal in size and number of attached rooms,

> we can infer that there was some kind of hierarchy within the inhabitants. I think that there are only two ways of extending the household while respecting that notion of hierarchy: it is either by multiplying the number of wives living in the house with their husband, or by multiplying the number of generations. The first hypothesis is to be rejected for several reasons. For example, and I am thinking of Tell Abada, it would be impossible for every male in any village to get two wives. Therefore I retain the second hypothesis until another possibility would be suggested.
>
> (ibid.)

By developing the distinction between the domestic unit, the unit of human reproduction, and the household, the unit of economic reproduction, it is possible (Maisels 1987; 1990) to account for the structure not only of a multi-generational household, but one in which there are relations of power inequalities, and which include persons who are not, or are only tenuously related to the 'owners'. This *stratified* and *augmented* household, where a proprietorial patrilineage is resident with their dependants,[2] seems best to account for the large, independent T-form buildings found at Samarra–Ubaid settlements.

The eminent Sumerologists I.M. Diakonoff and I.J. Gelb had already suggested that evidence for such households, called é in Sumerian, and *bîtum* in Akkadian (and *oikos* in Greek) was present in textual materials from Sumer and Akkad (e.g. Diakonoff 1982; Gelb 1979). Using data from the last mentioned, I have tried in the following chapter to show just how a household might be constituted, and also what a society structured around such seminal nodes might look like. In this the work of that other pre-eminent Sumerologist, Thorkild Jacobsen, has been invaluable.

161

Prior to such an exposition, is there any archaeological evidence connecting the pre-historic Samarra–Ubaid periods to the historical materials, which begin with the third millennium? Intermediate between the Ubaid and the Jemdet Nasr period (which spans the last centuries of the fourth millennium) is the Uruk period. At Erbil (the town illustrated on the cover of Maisels 1990), the following houseplans (Figures 7.8 and 7.9) of the Uruk period were uncovered.

As can be seen, the excavated part (*c.* 34 × 60 m) of the site contains tripartite buildings, the best of which is in the centre, with rooms numbered 36, 37, 38 (central hall), 42, 43 (east side rooms) and 45, 49 (west side rooms). In the text Al-Soof states that 'The familiar tripartite form, the orientation of its four corners (directed to the four cardinal points), and the buttresses against its outer walls, together with its contents, all led the writer immediately to the conclusion that this was a temple' (Al-Soof 1969: 5–6).

Now in regard to what he calls the Eastern Temple (centred around room 11 in the southeast of the site), Al-Soof itemizes the objects which led the building to be so classified:

A clay female figurine with pointed head and conical body, and a small black stone cube (in room 11); another small cubic black stone, a clay female figurine, and a clay spiral object (in room 14); a stone cube, and a clay animal head (perhaps belonging to a bird) in room 17.

(ibid.: n. 8)

Perhaps this suggests some cultic (not necessarily exclusive) functions for this eastern building. However, not even this thin list supports the 'immediate conclusion' that the central structure is a ('western') temple. Apart from the mundane functions of a stairway leading up to the roof (from room 42), the other rooms contain nothing but the most workaday objects: overwhelmingly sherds from globular storage jars, cooking pots, bowls and plates.

Further: room no. 36 contained a flint core and 3 obsidian knives; room no. 37 contained a clay gaming-piece, 4 cm in length, 2 flint sickle-blades and 6 obsidian knives; room no. 38, the main hall of the putative 'temple ', contained: a clay ovoid sling-pellet, a small stone celt (usually for digging), 4 flint blades, 4 obsidian blades and 2 scrapers; and so on up to room 45 which contained: a small stone cube (*c.* 4 cm square), a stone pounder, a rubbing stone, one flint sickle-blade and two obsidian knives. Manifestly, one stone cube 4 cm square cannot alter the domestic/occupational character of all those artefacts which are found in equal measure in other structures, *including the so-called 'Eastern Temple'*! On the contrary, from their contexts

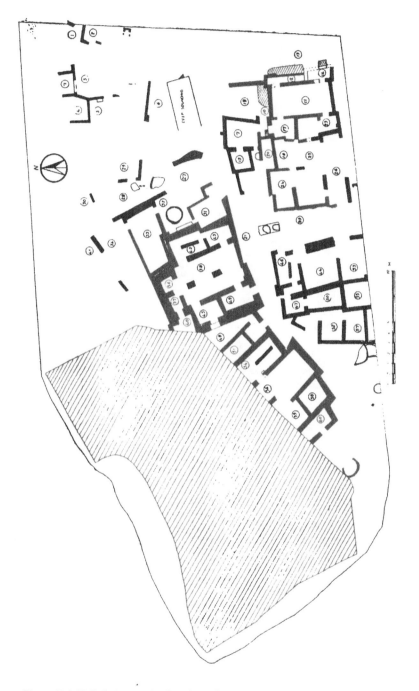

*Figure 7.8* Tell Qalinj Agha level III (from Al-Soof 1969: 39 – Plate IV).

163

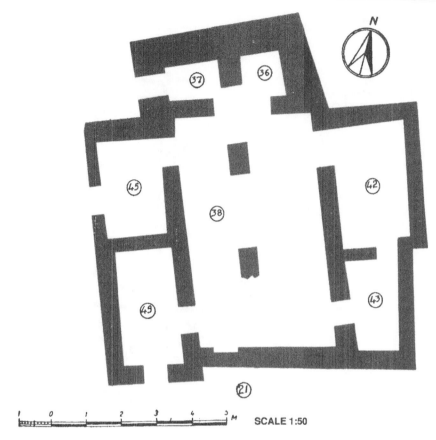

*Figure 7.9* Tell Qalinj Agha level III; so-called 'Western temple' (from Al-Soof 1969: 49).

they all look like 'working households' in which took place the whole range of activities necessary to support life for a number of people significantly larger than a nuclear or even an 'extended' family.

And in the Jemdet Nasr to Early Dynastic III periods there is evidence (thanks to the 'recovery archaeology' of Harriet P. Martin) from the city of Shuruppak, located in the Sumerian heartlands on the western branch of the Euphrates about halfway between Uruk and Nippur. In the Jemdet Nasr period, whence probably dates the key cosmological theme of the Flood whose crucial action is located at Shuruppak (with Ziusudra = Ut-napishtim = Noah), the city, covering around 70 ha, was one of the five largest settlements south of Nippur at the time (Martin 1988: 125). In the subsequent Early Dynastic II–III periods Shuruppak expanded to the west, reaching 100 ha, by which time

*Plate VI(A)* A cylinder-seal scene (Early Dynastic II, *c.* 2700) showing men fighting/controlling nature by violence and possibly shamanism.

*Plate VI(B)* An impression of a lapis lazuli seal of Early Dynastic III, *c.* 2600. Its complex imagery appears to show the perils (lion-headed eagles in the upper register, a vulture (?) in the lower) besetting husbandry, which only force can combat (a hero and a bull-man are attacking the eagles in the upper register).

Martin (ibid.: 127) estimates the population to be between 15,000 and 30,000.

Fara is the modern name of the site, which, excavated over a large area, has supplied the earliest readable corpus of texts; in such abundance indeed, that 'the terms "Fara period tablets" and "Fara style seals" came into common use to describe all similar Early Dynastic IIIa tablets and Early Dynastic II seals' (ibid.: 10) (Plate VI, A and B).[3]

Harriet Martin (1988: 127), who has carefully plotted the find-sites of the tablets, concludes that the excavators recovered tablets from a minimum of fifteen small to medium-sized households, one at least of which ('rent-a-donkey') could have been a shared facility. However, neither texts nor architecture clearly indicate the form of government obtaining, although kingship was already well established in Sumer. Nonetheless her analysis confirms the nodal presence of 'households', for she concludes that:

> Large temples and palaces undoubtedly existed at Shuruppak. The building in IIIb–c was probably a temple; it is almost as large as the Shara temple at Tell Agrab. The palace of the city-ruler cannot be traced, but there are a number of texts hinting at the city's administration. On the ED IIIa texts there are references to the é-lugal, the é-ensi, the GAR-ensi, the GAR-ensi-gal, and the ensi-gal while legal documents are dated after the balas ['turns' in office] of yet another series of officials. None of these men appears to have been all-powerful; none is known to have held office for a long period of time and many did not even hold office alone. The appearance of some of these officials in ration lists from several 'households' even suggests that the various classes of ensís may have been 'household' rather than city officials at Shuruppak.

> (ibid.)

This last observation in particular, reinforces Jacobsen's (1957: 123) interpretation of the original role of the **ensí** being that of a manager of arable lands and coordinator of plough teams.

A further study of clay sealings from Fara (88 per cent of which sealed door-pegs, i.e. store rooms) by R.J. Matthews, concluded that

> The Fara evidence, architectural and other, supports the view of discrete or semi-discrete households as being the fundamental unit of society and administration at ED III Fara, while larger-scale communal activities are attested by inter-city cooperation and by structures such as the immense silos, probably for grain storage, found at several points on the mound.

> (Matthews 1991: 13)

And yet further evidence is available from the later Early Dynastic Period (EDII, EDIII and pre-Sargonic). Elizabeth Henrickson (1981; 1982) has undertaken a thorough restudy of the Chicago Oriental Institute's famous work in the Diyala during the 1930s (Delougaz 1940, Delougaz *et al*. 1967) concentrating on residential patterning and relating the find locations of artefacts to the groundplan of buildings in order to determine their functions. The residential areas are in the towns of Khafajah (around the Temple Oval) and Asmar, and they were compared to a residential area in Ur of the Isin–Larsa period (2017–1763).

Structures in all three sites fell into three groups: those less than 40 m², which are interpreted as shops or stalls; those ranging from 40 m² to 100 m², which 'would have been best suited to nuclear families' (1981: 76), while

> The third cluster consisted of houses larger than 130–140 m² and were interpreted in two ways, depending on their internal structure. Large single-suite houses possibly belonged to large wealthy nuclear families, while large multi-suite dwellings may have been designed or modified to suit the needs of extended families.
>
> (ibid.)

Further, 'almost all multi-suite houses were very large and located in temple or "palace" neighbourhoods, possibly indicating that most households living together as extended families possessed considerable wealth and status within their communities' (1981: 76–7).

Indeed in a subsequent examination of the so-called 'Palaces' at Tell Asmar and House D (within the outer wall of the Temple Oval) and the adjoining Walled Quarter at Khafajah, Henrickson (1982) came to the conclusion that the 'palaces' were certainly elite residences, but that there is no direct evidence for a conventional gubernatorial role. However, she did find evidence that the so-called Main Northern Palace (MNP, 1825 m² and built over the Early Northern Palace) was simultaneously an elite residence and manufacturing establishment:

> The MNP was, in any case, not a 'palace' as Lloyd assumed. Rather it was a combined industrial centre, as Delougaz suggested, and elite residence, probably for a wealthy commercial family without direct ties to the religious establishment, who had some responsibility for the operation of the production activities carried out in the rest of the building.
>
> (1982: 32)

By contrast the Early Northern Palace, with an area of roughly 800 m², and consisting of 'several ordinary house plans melded together to form a single unit' (1982: 20) does seem to be the residential establishment of someone with temple connections, while

> the southeastern suite, with its large hearth and cistern, may have been a service or small industrial area where a family of servants or clients lived and worked, providing for the daily needs of the priest's family and possibly for the temple as well.
>
> (1982: 23)

Thus both 'palaces' are the residences and economic loci of expanded and stratified households, and the proprietor of the ENP looks very much like an **en** or **sanga**.

Another city of this period, though smaller than Shuruppak (Fara), has yielded a very important collection of tablets and, under Nicholas Postgate, has been in continuous excavation since 1975. This site at Abu Salabikh, which has its origins in the Uruk period, is possibly the ancient Eresh, and lies on the eastern fringes of cultivation, by the Daghghara branch of the Euphrates, only 20 km to the southeast of Nippur (Postgate 1982: 50). Although the tablets, recovered from a huge building that might have been the temple of Nisaba (the goddess of reeds and writing), are contemporary with those from Shuruppak which are in the mainstream of Sumerian tradition, those from Abu Salabikh show Semitic elements in, for example, numerals, connecting this (proto-Akkadian?) tradition with cities to the north and west, notably up the Euphrates to Mari and Ebla (ibid.).

The ancient city extends over at least 50 ha, yet the aim was to expose a representative, that is an extensive, city plan, as none such exists in Sumer. Conventional vertical digging of squares would not have achieved this in the lifetimes of any of the participants, so a new technique of 'scrape and plan' was adopted (ibid.: 59). Since later occupations have been eroded away, the Early Dynastic levels lie immediately beneath the exposed surface. Thus 'by scraping away quite a shallow layer of loose soil, one can generally expose clear layers and wall-lines, which can be planned quite as accurately as after actual excavation, and very much faster' (ibid.); especially when the surface has been damped by rain, bringing up the distinguishing colours.[4]

When this technique was applied to the West Mound (see plan in Postgate 1982: 58), walls up to 4 m thick and composed of characteristic plano-convex Early Dynastic bricks were found. They formed

> three or four enclosures or compounds within which stood independent ordinary rectangular houses and courtyards, storerooms, and drainage and fire installations. This suggests that at the beginning of the Early Dynastic I period we should envisage a city composed of large, self-contained compounds, and socially of corresponding groups of persons. Inevitably we are reminded that the Sumerologists, especially Diakonoff and Gelb, have recently laid great stress on the importance of the extended family in Sumerian city life, and agree that the word 'house' (é) embraces not merely the building and its owners, but their servants, animals, sheep-pens, etc.
>
> (Postgate 1982: 59)

Since, however, servants and dependants are included, the term 'extended household', which has particular meanings in anthropology, is inappropriate, and so I have referred to those *oikiai* as 'augmented and stratified households'. Their internal composition and their role in constituting the polity is the subject of the following chapter. (See Plate VII, A and B.)

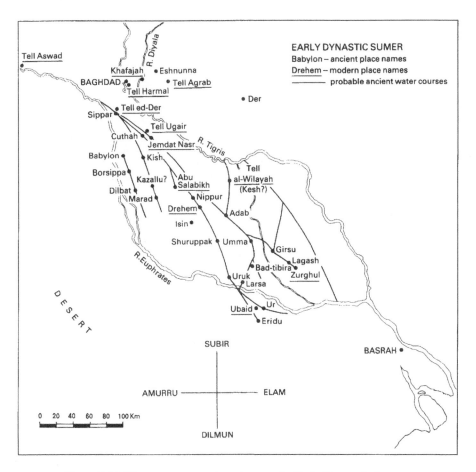

*Figure 7.10* Watercourses and settlement in Early Dynastic Sumer
(Maisels 1990: 152).

169

*Plate VII(A)* One side of the 'Standard' from the Royal Graves of Ur, *c.* 2600, showing feasting in the upper register, and the supply of sheep, cattle and grain in the lower two.

*Plate VII(B)* The obverse of the 'Standard' in the fullest sense, this side showing warfare.

# 8

# THE HOUSEHOLD AS ENTERPRISE

In 1979, the contribution of that most eminent Sumerologist, the late Ignace J. Gelb, to a symposium held the previous year in the University of Louvain, Belgium, was published along with the other papers, under the heading of *State and Temple Economy in the Ancient Near East* (Lipinsky, ed., 1979). For many decades Gelb himself, in parallel with other eminent Assyriologists – notably the Russian scholar I.M. Diakonoff and the Dane Thorkild Jacobsen – had been working to elucidate the social structure of ancient Sumer and Akkad. Some progress had been made: by Jacobsen principally on political and religious structures; by Diakonoff mostly on economic organization; and by Gelb on a variety of subjects, famously, for instance on the 'Ancient Mesopotamian ration system' (1965), and on the 'Alleged temple and state economies' (1969). Indispensable as all those contributions were, however, in my opinion it is Gelb's lengthy (1979) contribution (to the aforementioned symposium) entitled *Household and Family in Early Mesopotamia* that enables us to clearly identify, and to 'see inside' as it were, the social molecule of early Sumero-Akkadian society.

In the previous year, 1978, there appeared the significantly titled volume *Social Archaeology: Beyond Subsistence and Dating*. In it, as mentioned earlier, Patty Jo Watson conducted a review of the domestic architecture from a number of Near Eastern communities, prehistoric and contemporary. Using quantitative data (such as Table 7.1) she concluded that

> There are striking contrasts in the overall nature of the dwelling complexes in these communities. At Hassuna, Matarrah, Hacilar, and [contemporary] Hasanabad the rooms making up a household are agglomerated around courts; at Sawwan and Choga Mami the houses are separate or detached,
>
> (Watson 1978: 156)

as well as containing two to three times as many rooms as the others.
Sawwan and Choga Mami are of course Samarran settlements, and

the social implications of detached, multi-chamber households have been outlined in Chapter 7. However, beyond the suggestions of Diakonoff, Gelb and Jacobsen (cf. Maisels 1990: 146–56) which initially enable us to connect social organization with architectural form, it is Gelb in the article cited above who provides us with the key to unlock the door to the Mesopotamian household; called in Sumerian é and in Akkadian *bîtum*, and which for convenience we can call, as Gelb did, the *oikos*.

The key document translated and discussed by Gelb is a *kudurru*, a boundary marker. This one, involving purchases by King Maništušu of the dynasty of Agade (founded by Sargon), is conventionally called the *Maništušu Obelisk*. Earlier and much later *kudurrus* are known, but this one is particularly revealing (so much so that Gelb calls it 'a unique document in the whole history of Mesopotamia') being a four-sided stone record of the sale of fields to the eponymous king. It registers the sale of fields by ninety-eight 'sellers' to Maništušu, but Gelb makes it plain that ninety-eight fields did not change hands. Rather that number are present as participants or witnesses in the alienation of property in which they have some interest as members of what can be called a 'clan' (in terms of descent; all are identified by at least three levels of kinship relations), but which in economic actuality is divided into a number of over-ranking households, the dominant amongst which are themselves internally stratified around a proprietorial axis. In other words, the property which is being sold is not the 'common' property ethnographically associated with clanship, wherein every member has a share, but property which is controlled and thus effectively owned by the heads of the dominant households. Although the kin have a claim on 'their' patrimony, by this time in the middle of the twenty-third century, it is but a residual claim.

Gelb (1979: 44–5) was able to unlock the relationships of the parties to the sale by pinning down the meaning of such crucial (Sumerian) terms as **dumu** to mean 'son' or 'daughter' of (really 'child'), **dumu-dumu**, 'descendant', and *šu*, 'Of', that is belonging to or affiliated with (a household). **Dumu-dumu** can also have the associated meaning of 'member' in a clan, and the extended meaning of 'citizen'. Thus: x DUMU.DUMU *A-ga-de* [ki], 'x citizens of Akkade'; and 539 **dumu-dumu** 7 **im-ru**, '539 members (in) 7 clans' (Gelb op. cit.: 39).

Figure 8.1 is the scheme worked out by Gelb from side A, group 1 of the Obelisk, which records seventeen sellers in twelve families in two groupings (plus four attached families), where each grouping is called DUMU.DUMU P(ersonal) N(ame); i.e. 'descendants of PN' and all of them are called DUMU.DUMU Me-zi-zi, that is, 'descendants of Mezizi', who features as the originating ancestor. The descent lines of which the 'clan' is composed are clearly patrilineages, meaning that only

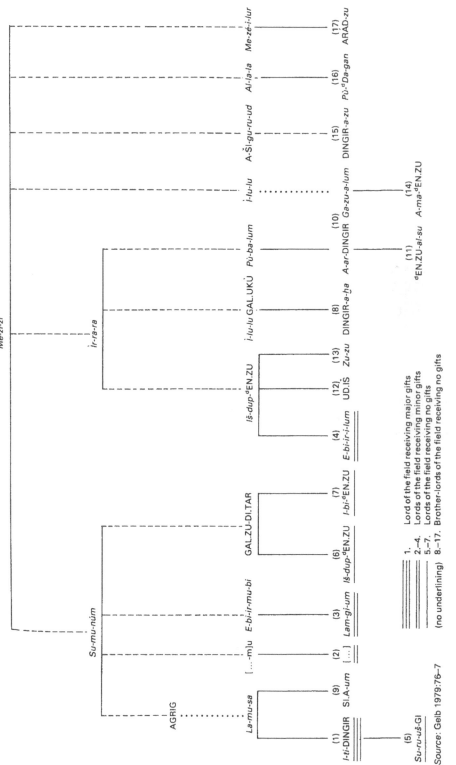

*Figure 8.1* Gelb's lineage scheme from the Manishtushu Kudurru (previously in Maisels 1990: 157).

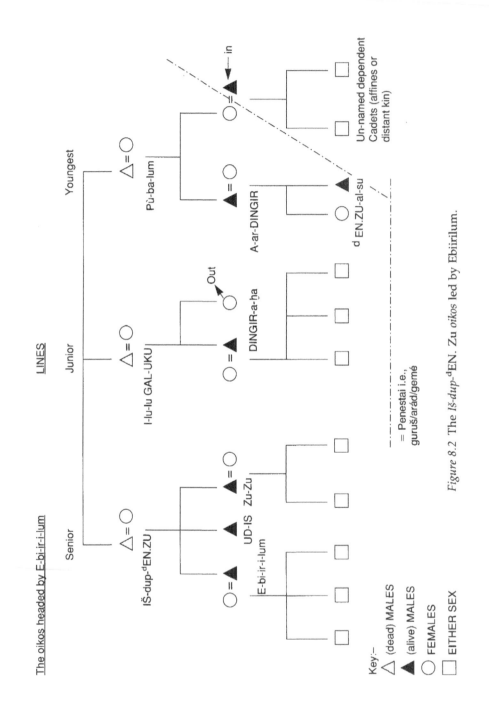

*Figure 8.2* The *Iš-dup-*<sup>d</sup>EN. Zu *oikos* led by Ebiirilum.

males are listed, and so the bulk of the population concerned – women, children, the very old – are effectively invisible. Of the adult males some are clearly senior and pre-eminent, some senior and significant, while others are merely present as witnesses. This inequality is recognized in the diagram by underlining, for the Obelisk states that, in addition to the price, those marked by three lines receive major extra gifts, two lines receive minor gifts, while single underlinings receive no extra gifts. This occurs despite all those whose names are underlined being termed: **lugal gán me**/*bêlū eqlim*, that is, 'Lords of the Field', so called as the 'chief owners' or main representatives of the patrilineages concerned. Accordingly, mere members of the patrilineages are called 'Brother-lords of the Field': **dumu gán-me**/*aḫū-bêlū eqlim*.

Those lineages are of course descent groups and not *per se* co-residential groups, except at the level of the minimal lineages which (by definition) have only a few generations' depth. Descent groups after all exist to transmit position and property, and this need not affect residential pattern or even household composition. Now, *kudurrus* record only the sale of land, and Gelb himself recognizes that coparcenary rights in land tell us nothing about co-residence. He does, however, address this question directly from clay records of the sale of orchards, animals, slaves and houses (ibid.: 68), concluding that 'The evidence to be derived from the study of clay tablets of sale of lands and houses favours the existence of extended-family type [households] in earliest Mesopotamian times up to and including the Sargonic period' (ibid.: 79).

The Sumerian term **dagal**, and the Akkadian equivalent *rapaštum*, both meaning 'wide' or 'broad' and thus 'extended', may be the terms that refer to such households. Certainly Diakonoff (1969: 179) had previously argued for the existence of 'extended patriarchal families or family communes'; and Jacobsen (1957: 119) contended that **lu-gal**, the term for king, originally denoted the great householder, great because he commanded the 'great house', **é gal**, *ekallum* (which became the palace), and which was a real political resource because it 'contained his personal servants and retainers bound to him by exceptionally strong ties of dominance and obedience'. Further, Gelb (1979: 49) sees in the genealogical structures of the Maništušu Obelisk, 'an intermediate size grouping for the individuals comprised under a given *šu* PN (i.e. of PN) designation, not a large overall grouping of the size of a clan'. So in total we are looking for the constitution of an augmented and stratified household, and one, indeed, where completed family size is only around 2.2 (ibid.: 75).

In *The Emergence of Civilization* (Maisels 1990: 159) one such putative household with *l-ti*-DINGIR as paterfamilias was sketched. He was chosen because he was the only one to receive major gifts in recognition of his station. But in the other main branch of the clan, grouped under

*Ir-ra-ra*, we find that only one man receives any gifts at all, and that none of the other names even rates as 'Brother lords of the field', so clearly they are in a subordinate position. Thus if there exists another major household within the 'clan', then it looks as if this is the one founded by *Iš-dup*[d]EN.ZU, and presently headed by *E-bi-ir-i-lum*. As this *oikos* is structured around three named individuals, as was the *La-mu-sa oikos* (and in this case the three individuals are of the same generation), it seems worthwhile to attempt an internal reconstitution of the household from the 'bare bones' of the named individuals, to see who might inhabit those major pieces of domestic architecture within enclosures, such as were encountered by Postgate and Moon at Abu Salabikh. In Figure 8.2, we see that the 'proprietors' consist of three lineages – Senior, presently headed by Ebiirilum who received gifts; a Junior lineage represented by Dingir-aha (who did not) and a Youngest lineage with Aar-Dingir as its contemporary representative. The four 'attached' descent lines (left-hand side of the previous diagram) could have been subordinate either to the La-mu-sa *oikos* (Maisels 1990: 159) or of the *Iš-dup*[d]EN.ZU *oikos* headed by Ebiirilum (Figure 8.2), or to both.

Speaking of Abu Salabikh (possibly ancient Eresh) during the Early Dynastic I Period, Postgate and Moon say that

> one is forced to the conclusion that each compound housed a single 'private' establishment and if we seek to interpret our plan in human terms, we must visualize a city composed architecturally of large enclosures and socially of corresponding groups of persons, presumably extended families.
>
> (1984: 731)

As Postgate and Moon (1984) go on to suggest, however, such large formative establishments at the centre of cities would tend to break up in subsequent periods, and the sale which the Maništušu Obelisk records may be part of this process (or merely contingent on that ruler's desire for land).

A king may have been acquiring land on his own account – to add to his personal, originally familial holdings – or to add to public or state ('palace') holdings; all of which he would have administered. The 'public' land holdings are those centred on temples, and for this reason are often called '*ensíal*', from the term **ensi**, originally the leading official of temple (and thus city) property, a name which was later used to refer to a 'governor' of a city, subordinate to a king (**lugal**).

By such alienations of land as that above (and probably also donations of land to the temples, as to the Church in medieval Europe) a 'private-individual' sector of land-ownership formed alongside the two pre-existing sectors: namely the diminishing private–communal ('clanship') sector and the augmented 'public', later state, sector of temple holdings.

| PERIOD | | YEARS BC |
| --- | --- | --- |
| Ubaid I | (beginning) | 5,500 |
| Ubaid IV | (end) | 4,000 |
| Uruk | | 4,000–3,350 |
| Jemdet Nasr | | 3,350–2,960 |
| Time of city-states | Early Dynastic I (EDI) | 2,960–2,760 |
| | Early Dynastic II | 2,760–2,650 |
| | Early Dynastic IIIA | 2,650–2,480 |
| | Early Dynastic IIIB | 2,480–2,365 |
| | Lugalzagesi | 2,335–2,310 (25-yr reign) |
| Sargonic 'Empire' | Sargon of Akkad | 2,310–2,273 (37-yr reign) |
| | Rimush, younger son of Sargon | 2,272–2,263 (9-yr reign) |
| | Manishtushu, elder son of Sargon | 2,262–2,247 (15-yr reign) |
| | Naram-Sin, son of Manishtushu | 2,246–2,190 (56-yr reign) |
| | Sharkalisharri, son of Naram-Sin | 2,189–2,164 (25-yr reign) |
| Gutians | Uruk-Lagash Period (Gudea, Ur-Ningirsu, Pirigme, Nammahani) terminated by: | c. 2,160–2,120 |
| | Gudea ensi of Lagash | 2,141–2,122 |
| Ur III or 'Neo-Sumerian' Period | Utuhegal, king of Uruk | 2,122–2,114 (7/8 yr reign) |
| | Ur-Nammu, king of Ur | 2,114–2,096 (18-yr reign) |
| | Shulgi, son of Ur-Nammu | 2,095–2,047 (48-yr reign) |
| | Amarsuen, son of Shulgi | 2,046–2,037 (9-yr reign) |
| | Shu-Shin, brother of Amarsuen | 2,036–2,027 (9-yr reign) |
| | Ibbi-Sin, son of Shu-Sin | 2,026-2,001 (25-yr reign) |
| Isin & Larsa Period* | Isbi-Irra of Isin | 2,017–1,985 |
| | Naplanum of Larsa | 2,025–2,005 |
| | Damiq-ilisu of Isin | 1,816–1,794 |
| | Rim-Sin of Larsa | 1,822–1,763 |
| First Dynasty** of Babylon (old Babylonian) 'Hammurabi Dynasty' | (1) Sumuabum | 1,894–1,881 |
| | (2) Hammurabi | 1,792–1,750 |
| | (3) Samsuditana | 1,625–1,595 |

Four centuries of Kassite rule in Babylonia were ushered in by the Hittite raid on Babylon in 1595, when Samsuditana was defeated by Murshili I (1620–1595). The Hittites, Indo-European speakers from Anatolia, withdrew after their victory, leaving the way open to the Kassites. In the extreme south, the indigenous Sealand Dynasty lasted from 1793 until 1415, when integrated into Kassite Babylonia which they called Karduniash. Kassite hegemony lasted until 1155, when attacks by Assyria and Elam terminated it.

Key: Z denotes disturbed period of fragmentary and shifting power(s).
* beginning and ends only.
** beginning, middle and end rulers only.

Source: Brinkman 1977:335–7, and Hassan and Robinson 1987:127–8, as discussed in ch.4, sect. 4
Note: See Whitehouse 1983:320–1 for an exposition of 'high' (early) compared with 'middle' chronology

*Figure 8.3* Periodization of Mesopotamian history (Maisels 1990: 133).

All used dependent labour: clients and slaves, with the temple house-holds incorporating into their finely structured divisions of labour the outcasts: old and unmarried women, cripples etc. But in their hierarchy and controls, the temple estates can be seen as larger-scale enterprises than 'ordinary,' household ones, whose economic basis has been so well indicated by Foster's analysis of their accounts, drawn from Gasur in the Sargonic period. Foster (1982: 17) distinguishes three main types of archive: the family or private, the household and the great household, and states that the differences between them relate not to behaviour, but to the amount of property handled. In other words, the differences are not of kind but of degree and scope. That scope is illustrated by a profile of an archive from an 'ordinary household', indicating the household's economic activity (see Table 8.1).

*Table 8.1*  Profile of a household archive, Gasur

| Subject category | Including | Percentage of subjects counted |
|---|---|---|
| Grain | | 43 |
| Food | Beer, oils and fats, legumes, flour, brewing ingredients | 12 |
| Land | | 10 |
| Personnel management | | 9 |
| Livestock | Sheep, cattle, goats, pigs, hides sinews | 9 |
| Industrial products/materials | Pottery, textiles, wood, metals | 4.5 |
| Legal, commercial | | 4.5 |
| Learner's exercises | | 4 |
| Letters, bullae | | 4 |

*Source*: Foster 1982a: 9

A 'great household' archive, by comparison (Foster 1982: 11) shows grain references down from a dominant 43 per cent to a mere 6 per cent, food rising from 12 to 29 per cent, industrial materials and products tripling from 4.5 to 13 per cent, while personnel management references jump from 9 to 22 per cent. What this shows is not only an obviously larger workforce, but the reorientation of the large households away from primary towards much more 'value-added' and specialist production.

One specialism that must be noted is literacy and numeracy itself without which there could be no such archives. The presence of 'learners' exercises', in addition to the records and correspondence, indicates that every household of any size required at least one person so qualified. While places in the bureaucracy may have been confined to those with formal schooling in the **édubba** (lit.: 'tablet house', by exten-

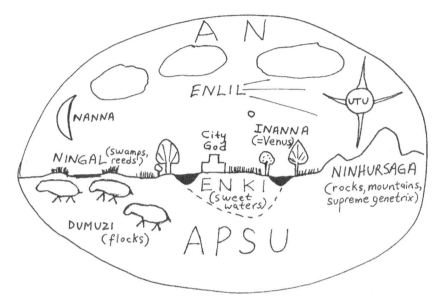

*Figure 8.4* An encapsulation of the Sumerian cosmos.

sion scribal academy), household recordkeeping could have been taught *in situ*.

The temple, of course, required both priests and administrators in addition to the dependants it needed for production activities; it was after all the household of (at least one) god, and as such contained sanctuaries. In addition to the god representing the city in which the temple was located (often one of several temples), they might also contain sanctuaries of one or more of the chief gods from the pantheon. In the historical period the leading gods were Enlil ('Lord Wind', the chief executive), Inanna ('Queen of Heaven' and the principal goddess of fecundity), and Enki, whose name means Lord Earth, but whose principal role was that of 'Lord of the Sweet Waters', basically the fresh (non-saline) water table *in* the earth (and hopefully at the root-zone of crops). As a fairly comprehensive account of the Sumero-Akkadian pantheon is given in *The Emergence* (Maisels 1990: Appendix A), a summary of the key forces in Mesopotamian life is provided in pictorial form (see Figure 8.4).

As Gelb (1979: 16) states: 'At the top of the temple-household hierarchy stands the **sanga**, "priest", or the **sabra**, "temple steward". In his capacity as the head of a household, the word **sanga** may be interpreted as the chief administrator of a temple-household'. The high officials, seven in number in each household (listed below), are called **ab-ba-ab-ba-me**, 'elders', just as the heads of private households would be. The

179

whole hierarchy can be seen in developed form from temple-households
of Lagash in the Ur III period (end of the third millennium). Gelb's (1979:
14) synopsis of ten texts supplies the following:

(1) **ab-ba-ab-ba-me,** 'elders', in the sense of top officials:
  (a) Managers:
  1 **sanga** 'priest', or 1 **sabra**, 'temple-steward'
  (b) Officials, Class 1:
    1 **GÁ-dub-ba,**          'archivist'
    1 **sag-du5,**            'field-surveyor'
    1 **ka-gur7,**            'grain-store supervisor'
    1 **nu-banda erín-na,** 'overseer of workers/soldiers'.
  (c) Officials, Class 2:
    1 **dub-sar gud-apin,** 'scribe of the plough animals'
    1 **sár-ra-ab-du,**      'treasurer'(?)
(2) **engar nu-banda gud-me,** 'chiefs of plough teams and overseers of
  plough animals'
  2–28 **nu-banda gud,** 'overseers of plough animals'
  4–100 **engar,** 'chiefs of plough teams'.
(3) **8–450 erín-me,** [general purpose] 'workers/soldiers'
(4) Miscellaneous personnel.

(see Plate VIII)

Income derived from belonging to the temple was characterized by
marked differentials. Higher officials received one-half of the grain
allotted to the 'priest' or temple steward, with the temple officials
allotted only one-fifth of this amount (ibid.: 16–17). But even low grades
in the hierarchy did well compared to the ordinary workers, whose
rations – pretty standardized throughout Sargonic and Ur III periods
(that is, during the latter part of the third millennium) – were as follows:

| Kind | Time | Men | Women | Children | Measure |
|---|---|---|---|---|---|
| barley | once a month | 60 | 30 | 25, 20, 15, 10 | quarts (sila)* |
| oil | once a year | 4 | 4 | 2, 1.5, 1 | quarts |
| wool | once a year | 4 | 3 | 2, 2.5, 1 | pounds |

[* A current working equivalence is 1 sila = 1 litre, approximately.]
(Gelb 1965: 233)

Those, of course, are only basic rations, which were supplemented
both regularly and periodically, for example during festivals, and they
relate to the temple's own dependants. However, Halstead (1990: 190–1)
has argued that very high yield/seed ratios found in Mesopotamian
cereal agriculture, which could have been as high as 76:1 in the first part

*Plate VIII* A wall plaque of the EDIII period from Ur, showing, in the upper register, a naked priest, followed by three worshippers, pouring a libation in front of a naked god; while the lower register again shows three worshippers, two of whom carry animal offerings, behind a naked priest pouring a libation onto a sacred plant before a temple.

of the third millennium, perhaps falling to 'only' 30:1 in the latter part, are due in large measure to a sparing application of seed, exactly applied with a seeder plough. This 'seed-saving' technique he sees as an efficiency measure in the provision of reserves of staples (mostly barley) to the community at large by the temples, in the event of a bad harvest; even as late as the Ur III period. This was done every year, and in years of generally good harvests, when the grain was not required, it was fed to animals; a further efficiency being that enormous, pest-prone silos were not required for buffer stocks. Thus

> the combination of sparse sowing and a variable labour supply [those working for food in bad years] would make public-sector cereal agriculture partly self-regulating, with crops being neglected

at times of low demand and receiving careful husbandry in bad years.

(ibid.)

Though the temple was the household of its god or gods – **é dingir**, 'household of a divinity', **èš dingir-ri-ne** 'sanctuaries of divinities', the institution encompassed, of course, the households of the human functionaries also, from **sanga** or **sabra** down. Indeed chief administrators were likely to have their households within the temple complex itself, as Zettler (1987: 121) has indicated for the Ur III temple of Inanna at Nippur (the cultic heart of Sumer), a pattern Zettler sees as going back at least to the Early Dynastic period (Plate IX, A and B). And in what may well be

*Plate IX(A)* A cone inscription of Ur-Bau, ruler of Lagash from 2155–2142. Such clay cones were driven into temples upon building or restoration to continuously notarize the gods as to who had done such a pious deed.

*Plate IX(B)* Terracotta foundation peg (from the city of Bad-tibira) of Entemena (2404–2375), mentioning a treaty with the king of Uruk.

typical of the interlocking functions of elite families, the chief administrator of the Temple of Inanna in the Ur III period attained this position
by inheritance from an earlier chief administrator in his lineage, one
**Ur-Me-me**, while another branch headed by one **Lugal-engar-du$_{10}$** (in
the second generation of this five-generational succession) 'monopo-
lized the post of **ensi** or governor of Nippur under the kings of the Third
Dynasty of Ur' (op. cit.: 126). Further, not only those family members
actually 'employed' by the temple acted on its behalf and benefited from
its resources, but family members with no formal role in the temple did
likewise, leading Zettler (ibid.: 130–1) to conclude that

> the Ur-Me-me family evidently manipulated the resources of the
> temple of Inanna at Nippur in a sense to guarantee its continued
> prosperity and prominence. That being the case, I think that bur-
> eaucratic is hardly an apt description for the administrative organ-
> ization of that institution. It is rather what Weber called
> patrimonial administration.

By the Ur III period, the days of the city-state were indeed numbered.

## WHY HOUSEHOLDS?

We have seen that when the Sumerians and Akkadians used the terms é
and *bîtum* – 'household'- to refer to the temples, this was not just a figure
of speech, but meant that those households containing public shrines
were also, and necessarily, engaged in the same sorts of economic
activity as 'ordinary' households, albeit on a larger scale and with a
greater range of specializations. Indeed, in the Ubaid and Uruk periods,
when the temple buildings were still quite modest, the very tripartite
layout of private household structures was reflected in temple architecture. Palaces too, which are known from early in the ED III period, have
similar forms. The isomorphisms are clear from a comparison of two
Ubaidian structures: the house at Tell Madhhur (Susan Roaf) and a
temple (VII) at Eridu (Seton Lloyd 1978: 42), from a long sequence of
temples there (see Figure 8.5).

Michael Roaf (1990: 56), who excavated the Ubaidian house at Tell
Madhhur, (Chapter 7), states that, in general, 'Ubaid houses were quite
large, occupying about 200 square metres, and probably accommodated
an extended family of around twenty people. *The tripartite plan (or the
triple tripartite plan of Abadeh and Kheit Khasim) must have, in some way,
reflected the social structure of the time'* (my emphasis); and if there are
manifest continuities subsequently also.

The domestic unit (female–children–male) is the unit of human reproduction in both the obvious biological sense and in the less obvious
sense of being the locus of primary preparation for membership in

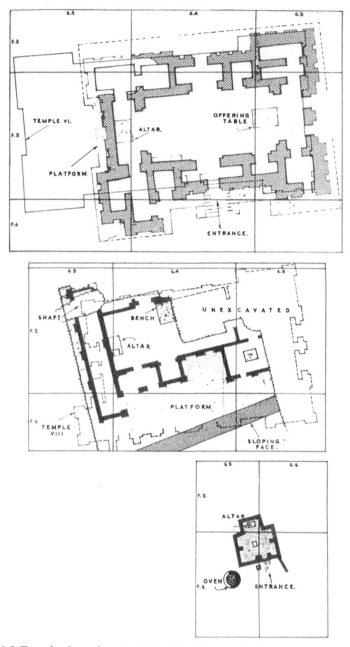

*Figure 8.5* Temple plans characteristic of the three main phases recognized in the sounding at Eridu: top, 'Ubaid 4' (temple VII), middle, 'Ubaid 3' (temple IX) and, above, 'Ubaid 1' (temple XVI), dated respectively to *c.* 3800, 4100 and 4900 BC. Temple XVI (not shown) is no more than a chapel, but already has a niche for the altar and offering-table. (Lloyd 1978: 42.)

society (a process called socialization). It has as its physical basis the household (dwelling structure, stores, animals etc.) but on its own such a household is unviable. Agriculture is a very risky business and on their own individual households based only on the domestic unit will not survive and prosper. That is why in all agricultural societies known to anthropology and history a dense kinship network has grown up, tying domestic units into chains of obligatory assistance; useful on an everyday basis, vital in times of hardship.

Kinship networks therefore are a form of comprehensive insurance policy, and like insurance policies involve costs: investments of (at least) time and effort have to be made in the system of social relationships binding kin together. For what is the alternative: simply that each household must continuously labour to lay down enormous reserves in order to guarantee its own security in the worst conditions. However, if the risks are spread over a number of producing households, cooperating with their neighbours, clustered over fair distances, then a disastrous flood or pestilence in one locality would still leave sources of succour in others. In normal times the process of investment in social relations (assistance in rites of passage, festivals, etc.) would simply be regarded as pleasure, not pain.

However, in certain circumstances it may not be possible to 'externalize' the risks by spreading them across a large number of linked households. Conditions may be such that households exploit resources nucleated in certain localities which can be a considerable distance from the next similar. In such circumstances the household would need to incorporate within itself all needful to surmount the 'worst of times'. In other words it would be composed of a number of domestic units which were united in exploiting a range of resources employing a division of labour in which effort could be switched from one set of tasks to others as needful.

Netting (1990: 59–60) has argued on the basis of cross-cultural ethnographic comparison, that where sustained rural population density exceeds the range of around 150–250 persons per square mile, agricultural intensification takes place, characterized by the investment of considerable amounts of labour in the likes of ditches, dykes, terraces and canals. Under those circumstances, while corporate unilineal descent groups (i.e., lineages and clans)

> may function to secure and defend resources. . . . The major social
> unit of production and consumption in intensive agriculture is the
> family household, including children, women, and men, in which
> work effort, disciplined cooperation, and effective management
> receive the direct incentive of higher and more sustained material
> production.
>
> (ibid.)

*Plate* X A votive monument of the Old Babylonian Period (1894–1595), showing Hammurabi (1792–1750) with his right arm raised in worship. Despite ethnic shifts from the middle of the third millennium onwards, the continuity of religious traditions is remarkable.

Although in the Samarran/Ubaidian periods such levels were only encountered in restricted areas (and in settlements such densities could be encountered in each *hectare*), the very non-uniformity of the resource-terrain did concentrate populations in excess of 150–250 per square mile in favoured localities and did demand household autonomy and thus scale, for the reasons already given. And the demands of scale meant that non-lineal or even affinal outsiders had to be incorporated as dependants.

Further, in a computer simulation study of the similarly nucleated Hopi in the arid southwestern United States, Hegmon (1985; cited Plog 1990: 189–90) found that in the absence of sharing between households

186

dependent on agriculture, only 44 per cent would survive after twenty years, largely because 'independent households often could not recover from a bad year in which their storage buffer was depleted'. This much is intuitive, but it is counter-intuitive to discover that with complete sharing the survival rate after twenty years only rises 6 per cent to 50 per cent because, although 'a household is protected against the chance of having an unusually low yield . . . it also loses the benefits of having an unusually high yield. The result is a survival rate for groups that is scarcely higher than for individual households'. Accordingly, 'it appears that the advantage a household gains by having a low yield supplemented by the group is outweighed by the disadvantage of the household being pulled down with the group'.

However, when Hegmon 'modelled a form of restricted sharing in which households only share surplus production . . . the survival rate of households increased considerably to an average of 60%' (Plog 1990: 190). The optimal number of sharing households appears to lie between six and eight, with minimal change occurring above this number, though there may well be hidden 'cooperation overheads'. As it happens there are 'ten well-preserved independent building units' (Jasim 1985: 19) in the completely excavated level II at Tell Abada, the mid-Ubaidian (i.e. early Ubaid 3) site in the Hamrin region. Level I (the uppermost) has seven such architectural units, all showing considerable continuity from the previous level (Jasim 1985: 27), and all being tripartite in some form; that is, structured around a central T-form of long hall ended by transverse rooms (and with side rooms off the long axis). Whether this number is typical for Ubaid settlements or not, such a group of cooperating households might then, on the southern alluvium, function as the core or 'home unit' around which cities formed, with temples assuming more of the production-smoothing burden as populations grew (Plate XI, A and B). But the key thing is *surplus production* (supra), which not only smooths the troughs without dragging down each household with the others, but which has the added (if originally unintended) bonus of providing generally disposable surpluses. This means that in good years or in normal times they are available for external trade (out of the alluvium) or to feed to herds of sheep and cattle, with their secondary products (wool, hides, etc.) available later for craft and again for trade. Indeed Kathryn Bard (1990: 481–5) sees an analogous mechanism operating 'between formerly autonomous villages' generating stratification and the state in Egypt. There

agricultural surplus would not only feed a community in times of crop failure, resulting from high or low Nile floods . . . or the various other calamities that face agricultural specialists (blight,

187

*Plate XI(A)* Impression of a limestone cylinder-seal of the Uruk Period (*c.* 4000–3350), probably from Uruk, showing a robed figure (left), who is probably a priestess, grasping a reed bundle, which is the symbol of the fecundity goddess Inanna. Between her and the other figure, who is probably an *en* (priest-king), holding an ear of wheat, stand two large containers (baskets ?) probably holding grain.

*Plate XI(B)* A seal in the style of the succeeding Jemdet Nasr period (3350–2950), showing a temple façade. On either side of the gate-post, symbols of the goddess Inanna are again present. Two goats and a sheep approach, while around them stand four spouted vessels used for pouring temple libations. Beneath them are a snake and two scorpions, symbols of fertility.

insect pests, increasing aridity etc.), but such surplus could be used in exchange for craft goods.

The demands of the natural and agricultural cycles on the alluvial plains of Mesopotamia are clearly seen in Table 8.2 (from Hunt 1988: 191).

The division and aggregation of labour required for ploughing, sowing, irrigating, flood-control, harvesting, storing etc., could be arranged

*Table 8.2* Mesopotamian natural and agricultural cycles (Hunt 1988: 191)

| Euro months | Jan. | Feb. | Mar. | Apr. | May | June | July | Aug. | Sept. | Oct. | Nov. | Dec. |
|---|---|---|---|---|---|---|---|---|---|---|---|---|
| Temp[1] | | | | | | | | | | | | |
| Max | 16 | 19 | 20 | 29 | 34 | 40 | 42 | 44 | 40 | 36 | 27 | 19 |
| Mean | 10 | 11 | 15 | 20 | 27 | 31 | 35 | 36 | 31 | 27 | 19 | 11 |
| Min | 5 | 6 | 8 | 12 | 19 | 21 | 24 | 24 | 21 | 18 | 11 | 6 |
| Rain[2] | 24 | 25 | 29 | 10 | 2 | 0 | 0 | 0 | 0 | 2 | 21 | 27 |
| Tigris[3] | 1000 | 1800 | 2200 | 3100 | 2900 | 1400 | 600 | 400 | 300 | 400 | 500 | 800 |
| Euphra-tes[4] | 500 | 600 | 1000 | 2000 | 2200 | 1100 | 500 | 200 | 200 | 200 | 400 | 500 |
| Agri. cycle | Irrig wint crop | Irrig wint crop | Last irrig  Harv earl barl | Harv barl  Begn wht harv | Harv wht  & lin  Cart cere | Thrsh barl  &  wht | Thrsh &  win barl  &  wht | Thrsh &  win barl  &  wht | Prep land, Irrig Plough Sow barl | Prep land, Sow barl wht | Sow barl wht lin |

[1] Temperature (C) at Baghdad Airport. Dieleman, 1977: 15

[2] MM of rain at Baghdad Airport. Dieleman, 1977: 15

[3] Flow rates in cubic meters/second, measured at Samarra. Dieleman, 1977: 16 (interpolated)

[4] Flow rate in cubic meters/second, measured at Hit. Dieleman, 1977: 16 (interpolated)

[5] Phases of the agricultural cycle as of the 1950s. Adams 1965: 16

on a democratic-collaborative basis, as was probably the case during much of the Ubaid period. However, given that the processes of state formation were well under way in the Uruk period, it seems logical to assume that by now the augmented households had become internally stratified under an 'owner', the most senior member of the dominant or axial lineage, whose patrimony the house and lands were. In turn this, by disenfranchising many, would enable households to grow in size by incorporating outsiders under disadvantageous terms. But the coordination of palm and fruit tree, legume and vegetable polyculture on the optimum levee soils, integrated with the farming of the immediate backslopes that made the best cereal fields, would be most effectively accomplished under unitary control. Under unified management there could be no disputes over irrigation water.

And while the temples saw to the reproduction of society in the cosmos (central to which may well originally have been the promotion of inter-household cooperation) the resources of the temple-household, later the underpinning of the state, could have provided back-up reserves. Indeed, the earliest position of public leadership in Sumer is that of the **ensi**, which later referred to a city governor, but earlier, Jacobsen (1957: 123) has argued, referred to the chief steward of the temple, where he was 'manager of the arable lands', and, significantly, 'leader of the seasonal organization of the townspeople for work on the fields'. He was thus always a manager (cf. **sabra**), not principally a priest (cf. **sanga**), the most potent of whom were designated **en**, a priestly title potent enough to be applicable to gods (notably Enlil). Though particularly pious kings such as Gudea of Lagash, might readily refer to themselves on inscriptions as 'the great **en** of Ningirsu' (the city-god of Girsu and god of the hoe), **en** is not a synonym for **lugal** – king – as **ensi** could be in some cities.

So what might those ecological circumstances have been that favoured the formation and longevity of the augmented and stratified household? Though it is conventional to state that the alluvium begins roughly in a line from present Hit on the Euphrates to Samarra on the Tigris, in fact alluvial soils extend up the east bank of the Tigris across the Diyala, Little and Great Zab Rivers to Nineveh (as can clearly be seen in Roaf 1990: 83). It happens that the reliable 200-mm isohyet needed for rainfall farming crosses the Tigris just north of its confluence with the Lesser Zab (and not far south of Hassuna); thereafter this crucial isohyet skirts the plains. It is this alluvial band south of the isohyet which is of course the Samarran heartland (and the Tigris itself was originally braided and meandering immediately below Samarra; Wilkinson 1990: 126); though where similar conditions exist, as at Baghouz on the Euphrates, then the same strategies for exploiting hydromorphic conditions on river and swamp margins could flourish. If then an expanding Samarran population, working south along the alluvial soils and the tributaries of the Tigris, found its favoured sites highly localized – and the incision, rate and rise of flow of the Tigris make early irrigation practicable only around the Diyala – then we can readily see the logic for the sort of households occurring at Tell es-Sawwan on the Tigris below Samarra. There we see the tripartite households clustered into a nucleated settlement implying that the benefits of cooperation even between substantial establishments (perhaps assisted by the presence of the original 'clanship' relations) outweigh the costs in loss of autonomy and heightened political complexity. Indeed, it is probably the heightened cultural and political (as well as technical) complexity with which the Ubaidians surmounted the challenges of the southern alluvium, that made their culture so fascinating to their contemporaries, and the very matrix of cities.

Those cities were, at least initially, clustered on the southern alluvium, and Eridu the furthest south was, by traditional account at least, the very oldest. Like all the early cities, Eridu lay on one of the channels of the Euphrates which, being depositional, ran between its levees above the level of the surrounding plain. Thus it frequently changed course in finding a lower level, making half a dozen channels active at any one time, in addition to forming relict channels, oxbows (mortlakes) and the other water-bodies or hydromorphic features left behind when rivers meander; for the slope of the lower valley as a whole is only about 10 cm per kilometre; i.e. 1:10,000 (Hunt 1988: 190).

Hence, an admittedly speculative scenario for the early Chalcolithic colonization of the southern alluvium would be that populations initially spread where (and only where) such relict features were available to supply hydromorphic soil conditions; and the moistest soils of all (and likely the most fish, waterbirds and wild pig) would be found not far north of the then shoreline, at Eridu, Ur and Ubaid itself. The situation of Tell el-Oueili (north of Tell al-Ubaid and east of Uruk) on its levee or sandbank, relying for two-thirds of its animal domesticates on cattle, one quarter on pigs (Desse 1985–6: 125) thus indicating a marshy ennvironment, supports this construction.

Ubaid culture would accordingly be a reflex from the deep south to the north and northeast of the alluvium. Only when such successes had led to population growth and heightened nucleation, outgrowing or exhausting the local hydromorphic soils which would have been progressively fed with sustaining water, would significant canal construction be necessary. Breeching a levee which could be a kilometre or more wide and then leading water along the backslope to where it is required, is not something that can be undertaken without a lot of experience, labour and necessity.[1]

# 9

# WHAT WE'RE GETTING TO KNOW AND WHAT WE NEED TO DO

France has a High Council for Archaeological Research chaired by the Ministry of Culture. Its Centre National de la Recherche Scientifique has a special section promoting archaeological research and publication. In Britain there has never been a public agency devoted to archaeology, not even to the archaeology of Britain. Presently certain archaeological responsibilities are scattered between the Department of Education and Science (for funding university teaching), the Property Services Agency (maintaining monuments) and the Department of the Environment (ensuring that archaeology does not hinder development, though it has an Ancient Monuments branch which is supposed to protect sites). Some research funding is available from the British Academy, though in general university departments and museums have to manage as best they can, and all initiatives rely on the energies of the individual archaeologist.

In India the record was better. As early as 1862 General (Sir) Alexander Cunningham was temporarily appointed Director of Archaeology in order 'to make an accurate description of such remains as most deserve notice' (Wheeler 1955: 179). In 1871 he was made Director-General of the Archaeological Survey of India with the duty of conducting 'a complete search over the whole country and a systematic record and description of all architectural and other remains that are remarkable alike for their antiquity or their beauty, or their historic interest' (ibid.: 180). For a quarter of a century between 1862 and 1885, he conducted field-survey personally and with great vigour, confining his activities to North India, as in 1874 the survey of South India was delegated to Dr James Burgess. When Cunningham retired in 1885 he was succeeded by Burgess, but when the latter retired in 1889 the Department became moribund (ibid.). It was, however, revived on the initiative of the Viceroy, Lord Curzon, who appointed a very young John Marshall to bring the Department back to life. He it was who brought the Indus Civilization to light, drafted the (Indian) Ancient Monuments Act, built up an epigraphic section of very high quality, and thoroughly excavated the famous site of Taxila (ibid.: 181). However, when he retired in 1929 the Department once again fell into decrepitude, for reasons to which I shall return. Further, with field-experience prior to India only in Greece in the first years of this century, Wheeler (ibid.) remarks that Marshall's 'immense task in India inevitably barred close or continuous contact with international development, and in excavation his technical standards remained to the end substantially those of Greece and the Near East in 1900'. This is one of the reasons why the major Harappan sites are less informative than they could be for modern archaeological enquiry.

But help was on hand from the Near East. After Indian government financial cuts in 1932 (the standard response to the Depression), the Department disintegrated. To propose a remedy Leonard Woolley, who was by then famous for his work in Mesopotamia, was summoned to advise. He spent three months in India during 1938 and his Report was issued in February 1939, then withdrawn because of the criticisms it contained. For instance he declared that:

> The departmental policy in regard to museums had been 'radically wrong and detrimental to the real interests of archaeology'. Excavation had been 'haphazard, initiated for no good scientific reason on new sites or carrying on the clearing of old sites which had already yielded their essential information'. The vital study of pottery had been neglected; in particular 'for the historic periods no information was available and a pottery type could not be dated within a thousand years. . . . On almost every [excavation] site which I visited there was evidence of the work having been done in an amateur fashion by men anxious indeed to do well but not sufficiently trained and experienced to know what good work is.'
>
> (Wheeler 1955: 183)

To make matters worse he cited many examples of each of those failings, and others too.

A key part of a comprehensive package of reforms affecting everything from museums to techniques of excavation, was that 'a European Adviser in Archaeology be appointed for a strictly limited term of years'; and this Adviser he suggested be Mortimer Wheeler. However, by the time this was acted upon Wheeler was on active army service in the Mediterranean, and did not take up his post until 1944. With characteristic energy he tried to make up for lost time by restructuring to bring new life to the Department, through digging at major sites, notably Harappa, and by establishing a permanent training base and programme. And while the Indian Department survived Partition, the Pakistan Archaeological Department on which he spent his last years in the subcontinent (until 1951) did not thrive. Yet even in India the controversies started by Woolley's report and continued by Wheeler's energies were such that when, in 1973, S.P. Gupta and B.B. Lal planned to bring out a comprehensive volume on the Indus culture, to be entitled 'Fifty years of Harappan civilization', and with the intention of dedicating it as a Wheeler felicitation volume, in the words of Lal, Gupta and Asthana (1984: vii), 'members of the very organization which Sir Mortimer nourished for a full four years between 1944 and 1948, declined to cooperate. Even personal entreaties to individuals were of no avail, and it became clear that the book was doomed'.

Eventually what the editors (op. cit.) termed an 'attenuated' volume appeared in 1984 thanks to the Indian Archaeological Society and the Indian History and Culture Society.

Here, as so common elsewhere, what should have been done in the public domain for the advancement of knowledge, fell to private parties to accomplish. Even someone as influential as Sir Max Mallowan (also the husband of Agatha Christie), who was instrumental in getting British Schools (local excavating institutes) of Archaeology established in Tehran and Kabul, had to conclude his Memoirs (1977: 297) with the complaint that he could not 'but lament that we have as yet not [even] attempted to establish a British Institute of Archaeology and Linguistics in India'.[1] But this is scarcely surprising since the British School of Archaeology in Iraq (founded in 1932 as a memorial to Gertrude Bell and funded by her own bequest of £6000 to the British Museum), and which mounted its first campaign in 1933 (Mallowan's at Arpachiyah), had no premises of its own in Iraq until 1948 and no grant from the British government, incredibly, until 1965 (Oates and Oates 1981: 30).[2]

The usual excuse is 'lack of funds' or 'budgetary responsibility' – clearly seen in the refusal of public funds to save Shakespeare's Rose Theatre in central London – but what this really means is at best an indifference to, and at worst an ideological hostility towards, archaeology (seen, for example, in the resistance of the Irish Government to the preservation of Dublin's Norse origins); for, based as it is on palpable remains, it tends to be politically intractable, while 'text-based history' is more pliable, at least as it is written up for the general public.

Bruce Trigger (1990: 785), surveying the prospects for North American archaeology in the 1990s, concluded with an overview relevant to all archaeological theory and practice:

> Some totalitarian regimes have regarded the interpretation of archaeological data as so sensitive politically that it has been controlled by those in power. Some archaeologists have been more influenced by social prejudices than by archaeological evidence in their interpretations. Yet as archaeological data accumulate and methods for interpreting these data are elaborated, archaeological

findings increasingly resist subjective manipulation. A growing core of objective knowledge makes archaeology essential to understanding better the nature of human beings and their place in the world. Archaeological interpretations reflect the ideals of their societies, they also contradict those ideals and play a significant role in the formulation of new ones. Yet archaeologists can only do this effectively by grounding their interpretations in facts, by a willingness to abandon theories that their data do not sustain and by cultivating an awareness of the subjective elements that influence their thinking.

## WHOLE WORLD ARCHAEOLOGY AND PIECEMEAL EXCAVATION

One such is whether all complex societies must necessarily be class stratified and state dominated. I have argued (1991, 1998: ch. 4) that this is a matter of evidence, which speaks to the contrary in regard to Indus civilization, the most extensive of third millenium civilizations and, after Mesopotamia, the most urbanized.

A state consists of control over people and territory exercised from a centre through specialized apparatuses of power: (1) military; (2) administrative (mostly tax-raising); (3) legal and (4) ideological. A fifth element is the centre itself, possessing a double aspect: the ruling engine (palace, elite establishments etc.) situated within a settlement and hinterland that provide core resources. Indus civilization manifests none of this. Neither Harappa nor Mohenjo-daro, the principal cities, possess anything so far identified as ruling engines (palaces) or symbolic/cultic centres (temples), and there is no evidence of armed forces or a bureaucracy. Instead the society has the characteristics of a commonwealth: a non-hierarchical society produced by an organic division of labour resulting in an economic, political and cultural community of interests.

The sort of state which obtained in Mesopotamia was the city-state. As in ancient Greece, it remained a 'community state' to the extent that citizens' representative bodies had key decision-making functions. Thus the contrast between city-states and the commonwealth is less stark than between it and territorial states like Egypt and China. None the less, city-states are still states with the apparatuses of power that define them. Indus civilization then looks utterly anomalous. Although it has a symbol system inscribed on seals, Indus society has left us no readable texts illuminating its politico-economic structure. So everything is down to field archaeology to elucidate or dissolve its unique status. And this crucial research gets nothing like the effort it deserves.

The foundation levels of even Harappa and Mohenjo-daro remain undug. Either the lowest levels are waterlogged, and thus require special engineering resources (i.e. finances), or stretches of the higher level still remain unexcavated. Now this is a particular problem on the Mesopotamian alluvium also (and on the Nile): silt, either water-deposited or wind-blown or both, buries sites quite quickly under metres of deposits to the extent that they are not known to exist unless and until they are accidentally hit when irrigation ditches, roads or houses are being built. Then of course it may be too late. Even if archaeologists are promptly called in, much of the site may have already been destroyed, and if it hasn't the archaeologist's breathing (i.e. working) space may be all too brief before construction work proceeds and the site is obliterated.

The type-site of Al'Ubaid

> is situated about four miles west of Ur, and a mile and a half southwest of the railway from Ur to Samawah. The whole desert margins hereabouts, on the borders 'of the town', is dotted with tells, or mounds marking ancient sites of various sizes and dates, from the Sumerian period to early Arab days.

This is from the account of its discoverer, Captain H.R. Hall (1930: 229) who was already working for the British Museum on the nearby sites of Abu Shahrain (Eridu) and Ur (Plate XII, A and B). The mound of Al'Ubaid was thus very conspicuous as also was its likely significance. Thus, Hall relates (ibid.: 230),

*Plate XII (A)* A spouted jar from Ur, Ubaid period (*c.* 5500–4000).

*Plate XII(B)* A jug and a miniature jar from Tell al-Ubaid.

The mound roused my interest by the close resemblance of the ancient objects lying on the surface of the desert round it to those found at Abu Shahrain [Plate XII, A and B].

No previous visitor had noted the spot or had picked up any of the thousands of fragments of painted pottery, flint, chert, obsidian, carnelian and crystal flakes, disk-heads, nails and pegs, fragments of aragonite vases, inlay plaques of aragonite and redstone, copper nails and so forth which strewed the desert as at Shahrain.

Indeed, after Woolley had taken over the work in his 1923–4 season centred on Ur, he uncovered a massive temple platform, enclosing a prehistoric shrine. Such incorporation was standard Sumero–Akkadian practice, since once consecrated it was sacrilege to abandon a site and build elsewhere. Accordingly the platform, which would have supported a number of temples, was several times rebuilt, and yielded building inscriptions from foundation texts of Anepada King of Ur, son of Mesanepada King of Ur (the First Dynasty of Ur), and of Shulgi (2094–2047) in the Third Dynasty. This massive platform, as subsequently became apparent from the work of Delougaz (1931–2) was included within a temenos enclosure of 80 × 65 m (Woolley 1982: 111), to form a temple precinct, such as clearly delineated at provincial Khafajah (Delougaz 1940).

Ziggurats and temple-platforms leave highly visible tells, but for most of the alluvium discovery is a matter of chance since most sites, especially those that were only of village size or were occupied for a relatively brief period and so did not generate a sizable tell, are buried beneath the present surface and await merely chance discovery. Thus today, despite the energies of the Iraqi Department of Antiquities, for a view of an

*Plate XIII(A)* An Ubaid dish from Ur.

Ubaidian village on the alluvium, we still must rely upon Ras al'Amiya, discovered only because

> In the late 1950s two drainage canals, cutting across a once occupied area, happened to bring to the surface a quantity of Hajji Muhammad sherds. This circumstance at once extended the known distribution of Ubaid 2 pottery and at the same time narrowed the physical gap between the northern and southern ceramic sequences of Mesopotamia.
>
> (Stronach 1982: 37)

Nonetheless, the excavator (op. cit.: 39) concludes that

> it would seem bizarre indeed for Ras al-Amiya – a modest link in a long chain of discovery – to remain for much longer the earliest known site in the long stretch of low lying alluvium between Nippur, 80 km to the south, and Tell es-Sawwan, 180 km to the north.

Yet this 'bizarre reality' obtains in a location where people are alive to the needs of archaeology and there was until recently major national and international effort.

When buried sites are thus come upon, an exercise in rescue archaeology must take place; assuming of course that there is the political will plus the economic and manpower resources available. If, however, there is already a large programme of planned rescue archaeology under way, such as the

198

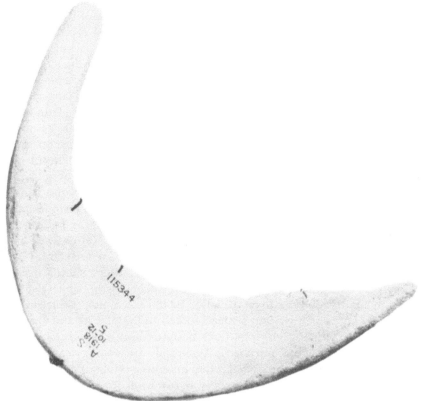

*Plate XIII(B)* A clay sickle from Ur, probably of the Ubaid period. Such tools indicate the ingenuity required to overcome the dearth of raw materials on the alluvium. Axe and hammerheads, fasteners and spindle-whorls were also made from clay.

admirable Hamrin Dam Salvage Project which began in the late 1970s (and which supplied so much of our information on the Ubaid), or at the Haditha Dam Salvage Project on the middle Euphrates, or again at the Eski–Mosul Dam Project – all relying on the cooperation of international teams of specialists – then there may well just not be sufficient expertise available for unplanned rescue archaeology on any scale.

In Iraq, which has a good record in such matters, only a couple of universities now teach archaeology, while in Britain the position is proportionately worse. Every British college, polytechnic and university teaches history (and now *all* can call themselves 'universities'!) but that history is merely text-based and relatively recent in period, under the assumption that this is somehow 'more relevant'. Relatively few seem to consider either that prehistory, that is history before the advent of texts, is relevant to the historical process, or that in periods and places where textual sources exist a whole new dimension of evidence is supplied by the recovery of the material record. But the shallowness of the textual record is quite remarkable, if too seldom remarked. As recently and 'relevantly' as in Medieval Europe for instance, literacy is but a thin veneer on society provided by a tiny educated elite, making the study of pictorial representations so important. Even the study of societies such as Greece and Rome, which were literate in fully-known languages throughout their long existence, and which have for half a millennium now been the province of large numbers of scholars in classics and ancient history; even that field would be essentially static (since textual sources are very limited and partial) without the continuous input of archaeology. For instance we would know a great deal less about the *polis*, had not Aristotle's lost *Constitution of Athens* (and also parts of the *Phaedo* and *Laches* of Plato plus the lost *Antiope* of Euripides) been found in the course of excavations in Egypt in the 1880s. Papyrus, an Egyptian invention, survives best in the dry conditions of Egypt, and indeed has given rise to the discipline of 'papyrology' for their secure recovery. But again, only archaeology can recover ostrakons – pottery sherds used originally in fifth-century Athens as voting tokens – on which were written the names of those to be banished by the assembly ('ostracism'). The use of sherds as a writing surface spread to Egypt with the Greek conquest, where, being cheaper than papyrus and more durable, it served a variety of textual purposes. Again only archaeology can get to such sources behind the rhetoric of (often invented) public speeches and other literary compositions which serve as historical accounts.

But those uses are scarcely news. As Alexander Gordon wrote in the Preface to his widely read '*Itinerarium Septentrionale: or a Journey Thro' most of the Counties of Scotland and Those in the North of England* (Containing an Account of the MONUMENTS of ROMAN ANTIQUITY. Also, An Account of the Danish Invasions of Scotland, and the MONUMENTS erected there on the different Defeats of that people. With other curious REMAINS of ANTIQUITY; Never before communicated to the Publick)', published by subscription in 1726:

> Seeing Reason and Knowledge are the Characteristicks which distinguish Mankind from the more ignoble Part of the animal creation: it is certain, that the farther we advance in the improvement of the one and Pursuit of the other, the nearer we approach towards the great Fountain of Knowledge in which Wisdom itself dwells.
>
> Knowledge ought, therefore, to be one of the great and main Scopes of our lives, which by Nature are but short and uncertain, and, consequently, should be spent with all possible Assiduity to qualify ourselves in Things becoming the dignified Natures of rational beings. Amongst all the Varieties, which present themselves before us, in prosecuting of this grand and necessary Work,

those Studies which are most Improving, deserve our greatest Application: In the number of which Antiquity claims a great Share, particularly Archiology, which consists of Monuments, or rather Inscriptions, still subsisting; in order to prove demonstratively those Facts which are asserted in History; which being the Mirror that reflects to Posterity the objects of past Ages, by the Discoveries made from such Parts of Antiquity, we have often True History distinguish'd from Falsehood and Imposture, and its Narratives either confirmed or condemned.

Of course it was argued at the outset that archaeology is fascinating in its own right simply as a huge jigsaw-puzzle based on material culture. This is the equivalent of 'pure research'; and like pure research in other sciences fundamental research has its utility, nowhere better stated than in the opening lines of the first volume of *Archaeologia* (1770), the journal of the Society of Antiquaries:

The history and antiquities of nations and societies have been objects of inquiry to curious persons in all ages, either to separate falsehood from truth, and tradition from evidence, to establish what had probability for its basis, or to explode what rested only on the vanity of the inventors and propagators.

Indeed the whole Enlightenment rationalist approach is here lucidly condensed, and not just as it affects historiography.

## A PEACE AND KNOWLEDGE DIVIDEND?

As 'heritage' is now, with 'environment', near the top of the agenda of public interest in the developed world, it should not be too difficult given some determined campaigning, to have every university (at least) possess a Department of Archaeology and for each department to be a fully operational one, which comes from having funds dedicated to excavation. If every existing university in Britain received £100,000 annually just to dig, then the total cost to the Treasury would be less than £10 million. (Every government programme in Britain wastes more than this every year according to the Public Accounts Committee.)

But such expansion and 'seed-corn' funding would still not find the sites buried under the alluvium of the Nile, the Tigris–Euphrates and the Indus–Ghaggar, to name only those mentioned above. Nor would it suffice to get to the lowest, waterlogged levels of Mohenjo-daro beneath the water table investigated thoroughly, to say nothing of the large group of important sites in that area where Bolan, Nari and Mula rivers merge into the Indus system. This requires the sort of prioritized, problem-oriented *and sustained* archaeological work pioneered by the Braidwoods in the Zagros. But the few relatively well-funded and motivated institutions, like Chicago's Oriental Institute, cannot possibly tackle everything and develop the sorts of technology required for detecting sites buried in alluvium or under water, or below the water table on land. And, for political reasons, the Oriental Institute's inspired pioneering would not be possible over much of the Hilly Flanks of today. So too in the Levant, where, as generalized hunters and gatherers, there must be a significant Natufian presence in the Lebanon, and if none is found after detailed searches, this will tell us a great deal about the Epipalaeolithic environment of Lebanon and the state of Natufian culture.

There is, however, a method of getting around partial and parochial scholarly interests (such as the British obsession with the Romano–British period or the Israeli with the Biblical), and for balancing problems of world priorities for fresh survey and new investigation as against adequate and timely-rescue archaeology; while, and indeed as a condition of, surmounting political obstacles in the countries where the work must take place. Indeed there is even now in existence an organization charged with such tasks, which has done something of the sort in the past (notably at Abu Simbel on the Nile) but which many regard as having failed in the recent past to discharge its real (i.e. non-art-history) cultural responsibilities.

I am of course referring to UNESCO, which though established to promote the full range of development in matters educational, scientific and cultural, has too often confined itself to basic literacy at one extreme and matters of 'high art' on the other: the hundreds of millions of dollars that it cost to move the Abu Simbel sculptures were justified largely on the basis of their artistic merit. But the sort of money involved in that project would easily cover several years' work of the sort of World Archaeological Programme I am proposing. Namely, that under the auspices of UNESCO, archaeologists from all countries would draw up an action programme extending from now till the end of the millennium in the first instance. Areas to be investigated and dug would be prioritized according to a weighting of: (1) how threatened likely sites are by development or environmental degradation; (2) how *little* we presently know about a particular area; and (3) areas and sites where we know we can plug important gaps in our knowledge if only enough resources were devoted to them.

A 'world map' perspective would help apply resources where needs were actually greatest (such as in grappling with the enormous site of Uruk – the world's first city – with which generations of German excavators have been struggling for most of this century (Boehmer 1991)). Go into any decent bookshop and note the amount of shelf-space devoted to works on ancient Egypt: they will easily exceed those of

Southwest Asia, India and China put together. Likewise note how most provincial and university museums (such as Glasgow's Hunterian) have whole galleries of Egyptiana and little or nothing on Southwest Asia. Indeed, it was the acquisition of the Rosetta Stone and much else following Napoleon's defeat in Egypt, that forced Parliament to approve major additions to the British Museum (Wortham 1971: 51). Can all this be because Egypt's place in History is so much more important than Mesopotamia's, and as significant as developments in Mesopotamia, India and China put together? Of course not. Neither is it due to the key role of Egypt's dynastic lists in Eastern Mediterranean chronology prior to radiocarbon dating. Egyptian reign dates are derived via ancient authors from Manetho's 'Epitome' (3rd century BC). Also from the Kinglists in stone: Palermo, Karnak, Royal List of Abydos (with a near duplicate, the Abydos Kinglist) plus the Saqqara List of Tjunuroy, an official of Ramesses II (cf. Kitchen 1991), the reigns correlated with three heliacal risings of Sirius.[3] No, the overemphasis has two sources, neither relating to Egypt's undoubted historical and cultural importance.

The first is that Egypt has always been the most accessible part of the Near East to European travellers. In the days when sea and river journeys were the most easily accomplished, Egypt was ideal. This made Egypt the favourite tourist destination for Greeks and Romans too (Greener 1966). From the seventeenth century onward Egypt became an adjunct of the Grand Tour for the more adventurous or scholarly, and in 1831 Benjamin Disraeli spent four months in Egypt gathering material for a novel (*Contarini Fleming*).

Second was Egypt's exoticism. Precisely because she was an introverted, relatively isolated and non-urban society, the cultural practices developed there, from pyramid building to mummifying, the emphasis on death and the afterlife, divine kinship and sister marriage, all taken together with its unique geography, fascinated those from other traditions, as it has subsequently enthralled northern Europeans. On this popularizers (rather than archaeologists) are guilty of pandering to popular fascination with exotica (which debouches into 'ancient wisdom', 'secrets', 'curses', pyramidiocy, etc.) and they do not direct enough attention, for example, to China where a quarter of mankind inhabits the world's oldest continuous culture; nor for that matter to India, where the next biggest bloc of humanity inhabits a historically and geographically diverse subcontinent.

The scale of this challenge in terms of the number and diversity of sites can be imagined. Unfortunately, even were the material resources adequate, the conceptual resources needed by Chinese archaeologists have been denied them by ideology and insufficient institutional support, for example for research and training in anthropology, as well as in excavation and general site-handling techniques. Even using their traditional excavation techniques (which basically ceased to advance when communism gained power) and thus neglecting the full range of information now sought to be gained from any site, full excavation reports have usually not been forthcoming. This again reflects on the lack of a proper institutional structure for scientific archaeology in China.

Mere bilateral or multilateral 'contacts' are not going to be enough to effect the qualitative transformation required from an improved anti-quarianism to modern scientific archaeological practice. Only a coordi-nating and initiating centre able to deploy resources in its own name can achieve this; namely the UNESCO centre for archaeology, run not by officials but by working archaeologists.

Such a 'world map' drawn up and renewed by periodic archaeological conferences would be overseen by an executive composed of working archaeologists on a rotational basis (say on five-year contracts), answer-able to the standing conference, not to politicians. Paradoxically enough, a programme free from political direction should be best able to overcome political suspicion and opposition!

Now that political events have proceeded so far as to have dismantled the military blocs and so make a 'peace dividend' potentially available from the moneys not wasted on armaments, the developed countries which (in absolute terms) spend most on arms, could easily fund such a global UNESCO programme, where priorities would be agreed interna-tionally, but conducted locally with international support. Planning and funding through this agency would also provide coherence for archaeol-ogists working in the developed countries, who spend far too much of their time filling in applications and scratching around for funds (and getting visas) instead of scratching around in the earth.

Despite the achievements of archaeology against the odds, neither funds nor personnel exists, nor has ever really been allocated, to per-mit the *thorough* and *scientific* excavation of any major site (though Abu Salabikh might eventually be the exception to this rule), let alone a group of related sites. So fragmentary is the research effort, and so torn are archaeologists between digging, teaching, organizing, researching and trying to publish, that Wheeler's (1955: 199) strictures that 'unrecorded excavation is destruction, and [therefore] prompt and full publication must be regarded by the excavator as a point of honour', too often are not met; or where they are then something else has to be sacrificed[4] Thus the results of the important excavations at Fara (Shuruppak) by two major institutions, the Deutsche-Orient Gesellschaft (1902–3) and the University of Pennsylvania (1931), are only available to us because Harriet P. Martin made their recovery and analysis the subject of her doctoral thesis at Chicago (1972). And if this inadequacy is true of well-funded organizations from developed countries, secure funds for well-planned programmes would transform the prospects in developing countries presently shouldering the burden themselves (such as India), and also raise their standards to the best international practices (such as China). In China, where there is an embarrassment of sites needing speedy but rigorous work, even a translation and (full) publication service would be of enormous assistance. Presently the UN does a colossal amount of translation and even publishes some archaeology on an arbitrary basis. Adding a specialist unit for worldwide archaeological translation and for sustaining a bibliographical database, is the very least it should do.

Even in developed countries publication of a sufficient quality at a reasonable price is a permanent difficulty. Even Woolley's landmark work at Ur, despite the fame of both excavator and excavations (his *Ur of the Chaldees* [1929] became, according to Winstone [1990: 153] the most widely-read book on archaeology ever), suffers from this gross malnutrition, so what ought to be the authoritative and permanent source of information scarcely does the excavation justice, and the final volume has only recently appeared, although Woolley died in 1960. Despite the campaign being sponsored and funded by the University of Pennsylvania and the British Museum – pre-eminent institutions in their respective countries – Volume II of the Ur Excavation Reports appeared in 1934 only thanks to a grant from the Carnegie Foundation (Winstone 1990: 189).

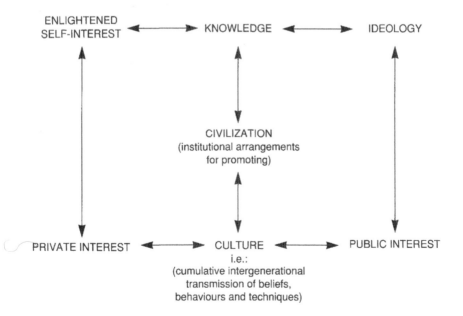

*Figure 9.1* 'Civilization' in popular understanding.

In *The Emergence of Civilization* (Maisels 1990), I used the term Civilization in the technical sense of any complex (and thus usually state-ordered) society. But the general public has an idiomatic and much more profound sense of the term. It takes the word to mean institutional arrangements that promote knowledge in the public interest as against ignorance and misanthropy seen to derive from the narrow self-interest of individuals and groups. And the public takes 'culture' to be the behaviours and beliefs that sustain and result from 'Civilization' in this full sense.

There is a straightforward way of representing this public wisdom which is self-explanatory (see Figure 9.1). At moments of decision people will always act in accordance with their perception of their own best interests. Objective knowledge, by informing self-interest (an instinctive imperative that cannot be wished away, for it is determined by the necessity of phenotypic success to propagate the genotype) can become enlightened self-interest. A current example is that of ecological information feeding 'green' consciousness, a self-interested movement from which everyone benefits, short- and long-term.

Finally, politicians in countries (which are many and rich) with a 'peace dividend' to hand, could not resist spending some of it to secure essential knowledge before much of it is irretrievably lost, *if* the professions of archaeology, anthropology and history were to wage a vigorous and sustained campaign for public awareness, paralleling and complementing that which is so successful in raising global environmental consciousness. Then the experience of archaeology worldwide would be transformed and the past secured for the future.

Why does this matter so much?

Consciousness has two aspects: awareness of environment, and self-consciousness: awareness of one's own thinking and feeling. Consciousness is particularly memory dependent, making its destruction by Alzheimer's Disease so tragic. Without memory – the imprint of experience – the person is lost. Personhood is lost with memory because one's biography is internalized as remembrances.

Societies, like computers, also need coherent memory to function properly. Culture in the anthropological sense: as the intergenerational cumulation of beliefs, institutions and techniques – what the Sumerians referred to as **me** – is obviously practical social memory.

Conceptual social memory, which provides overview, can only be constructed from the accumulation of hard data. For prehistory and for much of historical time, too, this can only be obtained through excavation. The findings, when analysed and interpreted, contribute to narrative explaining how things came to be the way they are. Thus informed, we can proceed in an enlightened manner.

# NOTES

## 2  AN ARTEFACTUAL BASIS FOR THE PAST

1 Yet Woolley's biographer, H.V.F. Winstone (1990: 145) could write of his subject's work at Ur in the inter-war period that there were even then 'still a lot of Bible readers in the world, and on the whole they were the ones who followed up Woolley's publicity efforts with expensive journeys to Ur-junction'. Woolley himself, the son of a reluctant clergyman, always retained a strong belief in the historical and religious truth of the Bible.

2 Based on Biblical genealogies, Archbishop Ussher of Armagh calculated 4004 BC at noon on 23 October, and rabbinical authorities at about 3700 BC; but all were heretofore agreed that the world was not of long existence and indeed had most of its time already behind it. Also most of the world's existence was 'historical', reaching from Creation itself to the Roman Empire in Biblical accounts, followed by the Dark Age interval, then medieval and modern times – all were documented in some fashion.

3 Indeed, in his *Descent of Man* (1871) Darwin made almost fifty references to the work of Lubbock, McLennan and Tylor (Stocking 1987: 179).

4 They had shared interests and accordingly were members of the same range of learned societies. For example, the title page of Lubbock's *The Origin of Civilization and the Primitive Condition of Man* (1870) describes him as a Fellow of the Royal Society, Vice-President of the Ethnological Society, Fellow of the Linnaean, Geological, Entomological, and other Societies. John Evans, one of those who vindicated de Perthes, and who was the manager of a paper-making firm in the home counties, in addition to trade organizations, was active in scholarly societies to the extent of becoming President of the Numismatic Society (1874), the Anthropological Society (1878) and, in 1885, the Society of Antiquaries (Levine 1986: 32).

5 Indeed it can be argued, as does Trigger (1989: 146–7), that the mid-century problem was the too-close linkage of archaeology to anthropology, such that once anthropology had made its unilineal evolutionary seriation of extant societies by 'degrees of primitiveness' back to a putative Palaeolithic, little then remained to archaeology except the finding of artefacts in confirmation. And current fashions in archaeology for *a prioristic* formulations again serve to reduce the novelty of what excavation or survey might reveal.

6 In 1766 Olympia, the site of the Olympic Games, was discovered by Richard Chandler, during a mission to Greece on behalf of the Society of Delettanti (of London). This society for the cultivation of taste was very much associated with the aristocratic Grand Tour, a kind of eighteenth century finishing

school for wealthy young gentlemen, who spent a few years touring the Continent – especially those parts with classical associations – in order to broaden their outlook and deepen their historical appreciation. This helped foster a climate sympathetic to the spirit, if not the practices, of antiquarianism.

7 The Ashmolean was founded in 1675, while the museum founded by Ole Worm in Denmark, which formed the basis of the Kunstkammer Royal Collection, was opened to the public in the 1680s. The third public museum would then probably be the British Museum established after the Sloane bequest of 1753; and fourth that established by William Hunter of Glasgow, and dating from 1768 (subsequently the much neglected Hunterian Museum of Glasgow University).

8 Thomsen was not, however, the first Scandinavian clearly to articulate those concepts. According to Daniel (1967: 79–80), the clearest statement was that of L.S. Vedel Simonsen in his *Udsigt over Nationalhistoriens aeldste og maerkeligste Perioder*, published in 1813–16:

> At first the tools and weapons of the earliest inhabitants of Scandinavia were made of stone and wood. Then the Scandinavians learned to work copper and then to smelt it and harden it . . . and then latterly to work iron. From this point of view the development of their culture can be divided into a Stone Age, a Copper Age and an Iron Age. These three ages cannot be separated from each other by exact limits, for they encroach on each other. Without any doubt the use of stone implements continued among the more impoverished groups after the introduction of copper, and similarly objects of copper were used after the intoduction of iron. . . . Artefacts of wood have naturally decomposed, those of iron are rusted in the ground; it is those of stone and copper which are the best preserved.

9 It can be argued that it was the traditional Chinese reverence for antiquity, in addition to the lack of the institutional supports mentioned, which meant that even a polymath of Shen Kua's (AD 1031–1095) brilliance, who anticipated Huttonianism and whom Needham (1969: 27) has described as ' one of the greatest scientific minds in Chinese history', could not get an empirical, non-art-focused discipline started, despite his great work on antiquities and other phenomena: the Meng Chhi Pi Than (Dream Pool Essays). Only societies with simultaneously expanding economic, technological and geographical horizons could launch such a revolutionary discipline.

10 This last 'objection' in particular alerts us to a favourite device of ideological 'argumentation', namely responding to an (*a priori*) 'inadmissible' proposition with a heap of calumnies asserting that its very consideration threatens 'the whole of civilization as we know it'.

11 Based on measurements of the Great Temple at Giza, 'by the use of correct mathematical formulas, Smyth intended to unlock the secrets of the pyramid, secrets that included information about the past history of man, his future, and the Christian dispensation' (Wortham 1971: 79). In 1874 the Royal Society of Edinburgh refused Smyth permission to read a paper on the Great Pyramid and he resigned in protest. But significantly Smyth received support from other streams of obscurantism, principally two: anti-evolutionists (since he claimed that the Great Pyramid was the oldest building in the world and thus manifested a primal high intellectualism – with God's aid – in Man); and from those resisting the introduction of the metric system to Britain (Smyth

having claimed that 'the English inch was a close copy of the "pyramid inch",
a perfect unit of measurement inspired by God' (Wortham 1971: 80)). Petrie
also disproved the Lepsius/Wild 'accretion theory' of pyramid construction,
in which, during the lifetime of a Pharaoh a small steep pyramid initially
constructed had outer layers of stone added until the Pharaoh died, at which
time a small pyramid was added to complete the top previously left exposed.
The pyramid was then finished by adding an outer casing of stone from the
top down to the ground (Wortham 1971: 67–8).

12 Archibald Henry; Professor of Assyriology at Oxford.
13 The Comparative Method, according to Evans-Pritchard (1981: 35) is 'a
method which gives us a schematic typology (stages), each stage having its
special features by which it is defined'. It is comparative in that any particular
society can be compared to this scheme of ideal-types; but also because the
stages themselves are constructed from the combination of the characteristics
of different societies to get at their common features. Daniel Wilson
employed the comparative method so successfully that in his pathbreaking
books of 1851 and 1862 he

> made two radical breaks with conventional studies: where 18th century
> philosophers had privileged logical deduction to reconstruct man-
> kind's history, he insisted upon induction from archaeological data,
> and where antiquarians had sought only particular identifications of
> objects, he placed antiquities in a sociological narrative.
>
> (Kehoe 1991: 473)

## 3 DIGGING BEFORE EXCAVATION

1 The lack of creative contact may be why the pioneering ethnological work of
Gustav Klemm (1802–67) and Theodor Waitz (1821–64) was not properly
followed up in Germany; with the partial exception of the Swiss lawyer, J.J.
Bachofen (1815–87), whose *Das Mutterrecht* (1861), was very influential.
However, in addition to the problem of nationalism already alluded to, the
underlying problem might just be the anti-rational, anti-evolutionary, anti-
pragmatic 'myth- and system-making' nature of the so-called Romanticism
and Idealism that so predominated in Deutsche Kultur (cf. Heltzman 1975).

Thus the undisputed leader of German anthropology in the latter half of
the nineteenth century, Rudolph Virchow (1821–1902) – pioneering cellular
pathologist and public health campaigner – violently attacked all evolutionary thought, and Darwinism in particular, on explicitly political grounds. It
led, he claimed, to atheism and that in turn resulted in socialism and civil
war, as seen in the Paris Commune of 1871! A particular target of his venom
was Ernst Haeckel (1834–1919), Professor of Zoology at Jena, materialist,
evolutionist, nature-worshipper and campaigning secularist, whose phylo-
genetic (his coinage) 'evolutionary trees' became central to Darwinian
thinking.

Though a Liberal, anti-Bismarck member of the Reichstag (1880–93), for his
anti-evolutionary rhetoric Virchow

> was widely extolled as a public spirited hero who had turned the
> dangerous tide of Darwinism; and Bastian [whose Elemetargedanken
> prefigure the 'elementary structures of the mind' of Lévi-Strauss] jubi-
> lantly recorded in the *Zeitschrift für Ethnologie* [which he co-edited] that
> Virchow had freed science from a nightmare by banishing 'the incubus

called Descent'. From the late 1870s onwards, then, a principal sector of German anthropology was inveterately opposed to Darwinian theory, and in Berlin in particular there was, as Haeckel noted, a 'sovereign disdain' for evolutionary thinking.

(Freeman 1984: 25–6)

This was the climate in which Franz Boas (1858–1942), who became the founding-father of American anthropology (not L.H. Morgan), was an undergraduate. In 1885 Boas became assistant to none other than Adolph Bastian (1826–1905) at the Royal Ethnographical Museum in Berlin, and an associate of Virchow. Not surprisingly then, Boas was a lifelong anti-evolutionist (cf. Maisels 1990: 6–13).

2 Similarly, Schliemann's destruction of Troy by digging out the mound of Hissarlik in the 1870s was done to establish the full 'historicity' of Homer's Iliad. He went on to establish the reality of Mycenae by similar methods, which meant that Mycenae was no more, and was only stopped from tackling Olympia – the green site in Elis sacred to Zeus where the Games were celebrated for a thousand years – by the German Archaeological Institute, who forestalled him. They introduced rigorous modern methods to Greece, which Cleator (1976: 121), describing Petrie's innovations, summarized as:

an entirely new scale of values, in which the emphasis was placed, not on the acquisition of imposing exhibits for display in museums (those 'charnel-houses of murdered evidence') but on the retrieval of all artefacts, no matter how trivial or seemingly insignificant, with particular reference to pottery fragments, which he acclaimed as the universal alphabet of the archaeologist. The great importance of this last item, he maintained, derived from its fragility and its low replacement cost (i.e. from its apparent worthlessness), in conjunction with the fact that it had been in everyday use from the earliest times. Constant breakages could thus be relied upon to label an ancient site throughout the period of its occupation, thanks to a steady discardment of broken bits and pieces, recognizable one from another bv such criteria as mode of manufacture, decorative design, shape and colour. These distinguishing features, taken in conjunction with stratigraphical and contextual considerations, enabled a reliable history of a site to be constructed, including the all-important question of its chronology.

3 Reported in the monumental and still valuable *Denkmaeler aus Aegypten und Aethiopien*, published at Leipzig in twelve volumes between 1849 and 1859.

4 One wonders what the results could have been if Joseph Bonomi the artist had been chosen. Even now, choosing the right person for a particular archaeological task plays a larger part than the public realizes in getting worthwhile results. By contrast, Botta's excavations were excellently served by his illustrator Eugene Flandin, made possible by generous government funding. Speedy, comprehensive and artistic publication in 1849–50 of Botta and Flandin's five-volume *Monument de Ninevé* was effected by support from the Minister of the Interior and the Institut de France.

## 4  PRACTICAL PIONEERS AND THEORETICAL PROBLEMS

1 For the background see Braidwood (1989: 89–99).

2 This is reflected in the remarkable diversity of plant species present in the Levant, where the phytogeographical zones – Mediterranean, Irano-Turanian

and Saharo-Sindian – represent southern European, west Asian and African plant communities (Henry 1989: 63). The Mediterranean zone of the Levant receives annual rainfall between 1200 mm and 350 mm, the Irano-Turanian zone from around 350 mm to 200 mm, and the Saharo-Sindian zone less than 200 mm, which makes desert of this most extensive zone of the Levantine area and the Near Eastern region as a whole. Not surprisingly plant species' environmental preferences are 57 per cent for the Mediterranean zone, and around 20 per cent for the other two (ibid.).

Accordingly, while the British Isles contains about 1750 species of plant, Denmark 1600, Germany 2680 and Poland 2000, Zohary (1962: 39) records 718 genera and around 2250 species of vascular plants in Palestine, and no fewer than 2865 species in Syria and Lebanon (Henry 1989: 63).

3 Those ideas did not originate with him, however, but, as Trigger points out (1989: 8), had their source in the well-known works on Turkestan edited by Raphael Pumpelly (1908); thence to Harold Peake and H.J. Fleure's *Corridors of Time* (1927: Vol. 3) and Childe's 1928 work: *The Most Ancient East: The Oriental Prelude to European Prehistory*. Further background is given in Childe (1989: 12–18).

4 Palestinian oak, *Quercus calliprinos* (a form of Kermes oak, *Q. coccifera*, Hepper 1981: 13), is an evergreen oak of elevations exceeding 300 m.

5 The patterns of mobility and landuse modelled above relate specifically to the Levant. The one in *The Emergence of Civilization* (Maisels 1990: 119) relates specifically to the Zagros, as can be seen from the high ground/low ground contrast which is less important in the Levant, and from the indicative dates, which lag several millennia behind the equivalent phase in the Levant. Further, full development of the Mesopotamian Neolithic took place not in the Zagros mountains, but down on the piedmonts and northern margins of the Jezirah plains, as at Nemrik 9 (Koslowski 1989: 25–42) and at Qermez Dere (Watkins, Baird and Betts 1989: 19–24).

## 5  HARBINGERS IN THE LEVANT

1 This may, none the less, be a consequence of depositional and erosional circumstances, coupled with relatively little research in the area (cf. Watkins, Baird and Betts 1989: 24).

2 The important mid-Euphrates site of Tell Mureybet with its long time-depth, as also those of Deh Luran (in Khuzistan, Iran) and the Zagros, have been extensively discussed in Maisels (1990), and so will not be further treated here.

3 A classification of PPNA arrowheads into three types which between them span the entire range of climatic and topographic zones in the Levant, has been proposed by Nadel, Bar-Yosef and Gopher (1991).

They are the El Khiam point, which is notched (see Figure 5.2); the Jordan Valley point, which is tanged and is the largest of the three; and the Salibiya point, which is the smallest in size (though dimensionally all overlap since their variability is considerable) and is straight-sided or shouldered, without notches or tang.

4 *Descent* is the principle (matriliny, patriliny, or cognatic) for the construction of ties between people thus reckoned to be members of a descent group (i.e. a clan or a lineage), through the recognition of a chain of filiation (i.e. accreditation) between children and their parents who are representatives of the 'line'.

5 Residence with the wife's group after marriage.

6 Finding a wife within one's own group.

7   There are at both Sha'ar Hagolan and Jebel Abu Thawwab figurines with 'coffee-bean eyes'. Somewhat different figurines with such eyes are discussed in Maisels (1990: 313-14) as perhaps, in their Samarran and Ubaidian incarnations, representing an early form of Inanna, Sumerian goddess of fecundity, who is particularly associated with dates (here 'date-stone' eyes?). However, in the two Jordan Valley sites, the references seem to be directly to vulvas (and penises) and thus perhaps the Sha'ar Hagolan 'coffee-bean' head (Plate 65) and torso (Plate 67) are ithyphallic; the profiles of Plates 65 and 66 certainly suggest this (in Garrard and Gebel (1988)).

8   Douglas Baird (pers. comm.) maintains that the PPNB collapse premiss is mistaken, and is in large part a construct based on imprecise periodization within the PPNB. While he accepts that large and long-lived villages could do a lot of local environmental damage, he maintains that given low overall population density at the time, villagers could simply move to other sites when they had degraded their locality too much. This possibility, he argues, is obscured by imprecise dating of the phases within the older sites in particular. Accordingly, rather than there being a real *hiatus palestinien* upon what is effectively the collapse of the PPNB, what occurs is a relatively normal process of social succession.

## 6   THE LAND THAT TWO RIVERS MADE

1   While the Ubaidian levels at Yarim Tepe III 'unearthed in all . . . eight big houses belonging to [i.e. continued over] different building levels and uniting over 90 rooms' (Bader, Merpert and Munchaev 1981: 56), those big houses (typically of $8 \times 8$ m in complex no. 8) are not the symmetrical T-form houses described in the next chapter. Perhaps this represents the adoption of elements of Ubaidian social organization by Halafian populations; or, more likely, is an 'extra-alluvial' adaptation by (northern) Ubaidian populations.

2   Huot (1989: 38) states that 'the Ubaid 0 phase is no doubt contemporary with the Samarra period, particularly on the basis of the architectural affinities which can be detected between the two cultures [J.-D. Forest]'. However, Michael Roaf in discussing this paper (op. cit.: 41) puts emphasis upon the Ubaid 0 ceramics as late Samarran or Choga Mami Transitional. I am obliged to Harriet Crawford for the reference to the publication of this symposium on the Ubaid (Henrickson and Thuesen 1989).

## 7   THE UBAIDIAN INHERITANCE

1   Of course it may not be actual people that move onto the alluvium, there forming Ubaidian culture, but merely their cultural traits which are adopted by populations already exploiting the alluvium in a mobile or sedentary, Epipalaeolithic or Neolithic fashion, and of course changing themselves and the received cultural attributes in the process. But this is most unlikely.

2   Note the important distinction between the *extended*, i.e. multi-generational household (found, for example, in China) and the *expanded* household or *oikos*. In the former household consisting of parents and siblings and wives, hierarchy is merely a matter of seniority; in the *oikos* by contrast hierarchy is based on the ownership of property.

3   Replacing the simpler stamp seal, cylinder seals – whose images were rolled into wet clay – came into use during the Uruk period (fourth millennium) to identify goods and verify documents. In origin a necessity of temple and palace

administration, as the economy became more diverse they were also acquired by private individuals.

It is probable that the earliest seals were carved on natural materials such as the distal ends of metapodial (lower leg) bones (Collon 1987: 14). Although most surviving Uruk seals are cut from limestone, a fairly soft material, soon hard and even precious materials, such as lapis lazuli, were employed. Accordingly, the imagery on the seals generally survives very well, and this glyptic is a considerable source of information, given that in Mesopotamia we do not have the range and clarity of mural painting, reliefs and statuary found in Egypt.

4  Further important discussion of the problems and potentials of this technique, especially in regard to estimating urban population size and density, is to be found in Postgate (1994).

## 8  THE HOUSEHOLD AS ENTERPRISE

1  For a detailed examination of Bronze Age society in Mesopotamia see Maisels (1990, 1998).

## 9  WHAT WE'RE GETTING TO KNOW AND WHAT WE NEED TO DO

1  There is, however, a British Archaeological Mission to Pakistan – based in London – which is grant-aided by the British Academy.
2  The question 'Why should the British taxpayer pay for archaeological excavation in foreign countries?' has the exactly the same answer as why they should support research in this country: to expand knowledge and to globalize it.
3  The Royal Canon of Turin is a largely ruined papyrus.
4  Harriet Crawford (pers. comm.) remarks that in fact *any* excavation is *destruction*. Techniques for recovery of information are improving all the time so the priority is really sites associated with development programmes. The longer we leave the others the better the chances of a high retrieval of information' (original emphasis).

# BIBLIOGRAPHY

Adams, R.McC. (1981) *The Heartland of Cities: Studies of Ancient Settlement and Land Use on the Central Floodplain of the Euphrates.* Chicago & London, University of Chicago Press.

Adams, R.McC. (1983) 'The Jarmo stone and pottery vessel industries'. In Braidwood *et al.*, pp. 209–32.

Adams, R.McC. (1989) Discussion on Nissen. In Henrickson and Thuesen (eds), pp. 250–5.

Akkermans, P.M.M.G. (1989a) 'The Neolithic of the Balikh Valley, northern Syria: A first assessment'. *Paleorient*, 15/1: 122–34.

Akkermans, P.M.M.G. (ed.) (1989b) *Excavations at Tell Sabi Abyad: Prehistoric Investigations in the Balikh Valley, Northern Syria.* Oxford, BAR 468.

Akkermans, P.M.M.G. (1989c) 'Halaf mortuary practices: A survey'. In Haex, Curvers and Akkermans (eds), pp. 75–88.

Akkermans, P.M.M.G. (1990) *Villages in the Steppe: Later Neolithic Settlement and Subsistence in the Balikh Valley, Northern Syria.* Leiden, Rijksmuseum van Oudheden.

Akkermans, P.M.M.G. (1991) 'New radiocarbon dates for the Later Neolithic of northern Syria'. *Paleorient*, 17/1: 121–5.

Albright, W.F. (1960) *The Archaeology of Palestine.* Harmondsworth, Penguin.

Algaze, G. (1989) 'The Uruk expansion: Cross-cultural exchange in early Mesopotamian civilization'. *Current Anthropology*, 30(5): 571–608.

Al-Adami, K.A. (1968) 'Excavations at Tell Es-Sawwan'. *Sumer*, 24: 54–94.

Al-Soof, B.A. (1968) 'Tell Es-Sawwan: Excavations of the fourth season (Spring 1967)'. *Sumer*, 24: 3–15.

Al-Soof, B.A. (1969) 'Excavations at Tell Qalinj Agha (Erbil)'. *Sumer*, 25: 3–42.

Bacon, E. (ed.) (1976) *The Great Archaeologists: The modern world's discovery of ancient civilizations as reported in the pages of the* Illustrated London News *from 1842 to the present day.* London, Secker & Warburg.

Bader, N. O. , Merpert, N.Ya. and Munchaev, R.M. (1981) 'Soviet expedition's surveys in the Sinjar Valley'. *Sumer*, 37(1–2): 55–110.

Baird, D., Campbell, S. and Watkins, T. (1991) *Excavations at Kharabeh Shattani*, Vol. II. Occasional Papers No. 18, Edinburgh University Department of Archaeology.

Ball, W. (1990) 'The Tell al-Hawa project. The second and third seasons of excavations at Tell al-Hawa, 1987–89'. *Mediterranean Archaeology*, 3: 75–92.

Bard, K. (1990) Review of B.J. Kemp's *Ancient Egypt: Anatomy of a Civilization. Journal of Field Archaeology*, 17: 481–5.

Bartl, K. (1989) 'Zur Datierung der *altmonochromen* Ware von Tell Halaf'. In Haex, Curvers and Akkermans (eds), pp. 257–74.

Bar-Yosef, O. (1989) 'The PPNA in the Levant - an overview'. *Paleorient*, 15/1: 57–63.

Bar-Yosef, O. and Belfer-Cohen, A. (1989) 'The origins of Sedentism and farming communities in the Levant'. *Journal of World Prehistory*, 3(4): 447–98.

Bar-Yosef, O. and Kislev, M. (1989) 'Early farming communities in the Jordan Valley'. In Harris and Hillman (eds), pp. 632–42.

Bar-Yosef, O. and Vandermeersch, B. (1989) *Investigations in South Levantine Prehistory*. Oxford, BAR Int. Series 497.

Bashilov, V.A., Bolshakov, O.G. and Kouza, A.V. (1980) 'The earliest strata at Yarim Tepe I'. *Sumer*, 36: 43–64.

Becker, C. (1991) 'The analysis of mammalian bones from Basta, a Pre-Pottery Neolithic site in Jordan: Problems and potential'. *Paleorient*, 17/1: 59–75.

Belfer-Cohen, A. (1989) 'The Natufian issue: a suggestion'. In Bar-Yosef and Vandermeersch (eds), pp. 297–307.

Binford, L.R. (1989) 'The "New Archaeology", then and now'. In Lamberg-Karlovsky (ed.), pp. 50–62.

Bintliff, J.L. (1982) 'Palaeoclimatic modelling of environmental changes in the east Mediterranean region since the last Glaciation'. In Bintliff and van Zeist (eds), pp. 485–527.

Bintliff, J.L. and van Zeist, W. (eds) (1982) *Palaeoclimates, Palaeo-environments and Human Communities in the Eastern Mediterranean Region in Later Prehistory*, Oxford, BAR Int. Series 133.

Blackham, M. (1996) 'Further investigations as to the relationship of Samarran and Ubaid ceramic assemblages'. *Iraq*, LVIII: 1–15.

Boehmer, R.M. (1991) 'Uruk 1980–1990: A progress report'. *Antiquity*, 65/248: 465–78.

Bokonyi, S. (1982) 'The climatic interpretation of macrofaunal assemblages in the Near East'. In Bintliff and van Zeist (eds), pp. 149–63.

Bottema, S. (1989) 'Notes on the prehistoric environment of the Syrian Djezireh'. In Haex, Curvers and Akkermans (eds), pp. 1–16.

Boudon, R. (1989) *The Analysis of Ideology*. Cambridge, Polity Press.

Braidwood, L.S. (1983) 'Appendix: Additional remarks on the Jarmo obsidian'. In Braidwood *et al.* (eds), pp. 285–8.

Braidwood, R.J. (1983) 'The site of Jarmo and its archaeological remains'. In Braidwood *et al.* (eds), pp. 155–208.

Braidwood, R.J. (1983b) 'Jarmo chronology'. In Braidwood *et al.* (eds), pp. 537–40.

Braidwood, R.J. (1983c) 'Miscellaneous analyses of materials from Jarmo'. In Braidwood *et al.* (eds), pp. 541–4.

Braidwood, R.J. (1989) 'Recollections'. In Daniel and Chippindale (eds), pp. 89–99.

Braidwood, R.J. and Howe, B. (1960) *Prehistoric Investigations in Iraqi Kurdistan*. Oriental Institute Publications No. 31. Chicago, The Oriental Institute of the University of Chicago.

Braidwood, L.S., Braidwood, R.J., Howe, B., Reed, C.A. and Watson, P.J. (eds) (1983) *Prehistoric Investigations along the Zagros Flanks*. Oriental Institute Publications No. 105. Chicago, The Oriental Institute of the University of Chicago.

Brice, W.C. (1966) *South-west Asia: A Systematic Regional Geography*. London, University of London Press.

Bueller, J. (1989) 'A microwear analysis of sampled borers from Netiv Hagdud, a PNNA settlement in the Jordan Valley'. In Haex, Curvers and Akkermans (eds), pp. 21–8.

Byrd, B.F. (1988) 'The Natufian of Beidha. Report on renewed field research'. In Garrard and Gebel (eds), Vol. I, pp. 175–97.

Byrd, B.F. (1989) 'The Natufian: Settlement variability and economic adaptations in the Levant at the end of the Pleistocene'. *Journal of World Prehistory*, 3(2): 159–97.

Calvet, Y. (1985–6) 'The new deep sounding ×36 at Tell el-'Oueili'. *Sumer*, 44(1–2): 67–87.

Campbell, S. and Baird, D. (1990) 'Excavations at Ginnig, the Aceramic to Early Ceramic Neolithic sequence in north Iraq'. *Paleorient*, 16/22: 65–77.

Campbell-Thomson, R. (1929) *A Century of Excavation at Nineveh*. London, The Religious Tract Society.

Carneiro, R.L. (1981) 'The chiefdom: Precursor of the state'. In Jones and Kautz (eds), pp. 37–75

Chang, K.-C. (1989) 'Ancient China and its anthropological significance'. In Lamberg-Karlovsky (ed.), pp. 155–66.

Childe, V.G. (1936) *Man Makes Himself*. London, Fontana (4th edn 1966).

Childe, V.G. (1969) 'Recollections'. In Daniel and Chippindale (eds), pp. 12–19.

Civil, M. (1987) 'Ur III bureaucracy: Quantitative aspects'. In Gibson and Biggs (eds), pp. 43–53.

Cleator, P.E. (1976) *Archaeology in the Making*. London, Robert Hale.

Clutton-Brock, J. (1981) *Domesticated Animals from Early Times*. London, British Museum/Heinemann.

Cohen, M.N. (1977) *The Food Crisis in Prehistory. Overpopulation and the Origins of Agriculture*. New Haven, Yale University Press.

Collon, D. (1987) *Cylinder Seals in the Ancient Near East*. London, British Museum Press.

Crawford, H.E.W. (1991) *Sumer and the Sumerians*. Cambridge, Cambridge University Press.

Curtis, J. (1982) *Fifty Years of Mesopotamian Discovery*. London, British School of Archaeology in Iraq.

Curtis, J. (ed.) (1993) *Early Mesopotamia and Iran: Contact and Conflict c. 3500–1600 BC*. London, British Museum Press.

Dalley, S. (1989) *Myths from Mesopotamia: Creation, The Flood, Gilgamesh and Others*. Oxford, Oxford University Press.

Daniel, G. (1964) *The Idea of Prehistory*. Harmondsworth, Penguin.

Daniel, G. (1967) *The Origins and Growth of Archaeology*. New York, Thomas J. Crowell Co.

Daniel, G. (1976) 'Stone, bronze and iron'. In Megaw (ed.), pp. 32–42.

Daniel, G. (ed.) (1981) *Towards a History of Archaeology*. London, Thames & Hudson.

Daniel, G. and Chippindale, C. (eds) (1989) *The Pastmasters: Modern Pioneers of Archaeology*, London, Thames & Hudson.

Davis, S. (1989) 'Hatoula 1980–1986: Why did prehistoric peoples domesticate food animals?' In Bar-Yosef and Vandermeersch (eds), pp. 43–59.

De Contenson, H. (1989) 'L'Aswadien, un nouveau facies du Néolithique Syrien'. *Paleorient*, 15/1: 259–62.

De Contenson, H., Cauvin, M.-C., van Zeist, W., Bakker-Heeres, J.A.H. and Leroi-Gourhan, A. (1979) 'Tell Aswad (Damascene)' *Paleorient*, 5: 153–2.

Delougaz, P. (1940) *The Temple Oval at Shafajah*. Oriental Institute Publications No. 53. Chicago, The Oriental Institute of the University of Chicago.

Delougaz, P. and Lloyd, S. (1942) *Presargonic Temples in the Diyala Region*. Oriental Institute Publications No. 58. Chicago, The Oriental Institute of the University of Chicago.

Delougaz, P., Hill, H.D. and Lloyd, S. (1967) *Private Houses and Graves from the Diyala Region*. Oriental Institute Publications No. 88. Chicago, The Oriental Institute of the University of Chicago.

Demarest, A.A. (1989) 'Ideology and evolutionism in American archaeology: looking beyond the economic base'. In Lamberg-Karlovsky (ed.), pp. 89–102.

Desmond, A. (1982) *Archetypes and Ancestors: Palaeontology in Victorian London*. London, Blond & Briggs.

Desse, J. (1985–6) 'Analysis of bones from Tell el-'Oueili, lower levels (Obeid 0, 1, 2, 3), 1983 campaign'. *Sumer*, 44(1–2): 123–34.

Diakonoff, I.M. (1969) 'The rise of the despotic state in ancient Mesopotamia'. In Diakonoff (ed.), pp. 173–203.

Diakonoff, I.M. (ed.) (1969) *Ancient Mesopotamia: A Socio-economic History. A Collection of Studies by Soviet Authors*. Moscow, Nauka.

Diakonoff, I.M. (1982) 'The structure of Near Eastern society before the middle of the second millennium BC'. *Oikumene*, 3: 1–100; Budapest, Akadamiai Kiado.

Donaldson, M.L. (1985) 'The plant remains'. In Rollefson *et al.*, pp. 96–104.

Dunnell, R. C . (1989) 'Aspects of the application of evolutionary theory in archaeology'. In Lamberg-Karlovsky (ed.), pp. 35–49.

Edelberg, L. (1966–7) 'Seasonal dwellings of farmers in northwestern Luristan'. *Folk*, 8–9: 373–401.

Edwards, P.C. (1989) 'Revising the broad spectrum revolution: And its role in the origins of Southwest Asian food production'. *Antiquity*, 63: 225–46.

Eidem, J. and Warburton, D. (1996) 'In the land of Nagar: A survey around Tell Brak'. *Iraq*, LVIII: 51–62.

Ellis, M. de J. (1989) 'Observations on Mesopotamian oracles and prophetic texts: Literary and historiographic considerations'. *Journal of Cuneiform Studies*, 41/2: 127–86.

el-Wailly, F. and Abu es-Soof, B. (1965) 'The excavations at Tell es-Sawwan. First preliminary report'. *Sumer*, 21: 17–32.

Evans, J.D. (1981) 'Introduction: On the prehistory of archaeology'. In Evans, Cunliffe and Renfrew (eds), pp. 12–18.

Evans, J.D., Cunliffe, B. and Renfrew, C. (1981) *Antiquity and Man: Essays in Honour of Glyn Daniel*. London, Thames & Hudson.

Evans-Pritchard, E.E. (1981) *A History of Anthropological Thought*. London, Faber & Faber.

Fairservis, W.A. (1989) 'An epigenetic view of the Harappan culture'. In Lamberg-Karlovsky (ed.), pp. 205–17.

Falconer, S.E. and Savage, S.H. (1995) 'Heartlands and hinterlands: Alternative trajectories of early urbanization in Mesopotamia and the Southern Levant'. *American Antiquity*, 60(1): 37–58.

Fisher, W.B. (1978) *The Middle East* (7th edn). London, Methuen.

Flannery, K.V. (1972) 'The origins of the village as a settlement type in Mesoamerica and the Near East: a comparative study'. In Ucko *et al.* (eds), pp. 23–53.

Flannery, K.V. and Wheeler, J.C. (1967) 'Animal bones from Tell es-Sawwan, level III (Samarran period)'. *Sumer*, 23: 179–82.

Forest, C. (1984) 'Kheit Qasim III: The Obeid settlement'. *Sumer*, 40(1–2): 119–21.

Forest, J.D. (1984) 'Kheit Qasim III - An Obeid settlement'. *Sumer*, 40(1–2): 85.

Forest, J.D. (1985–6) 'Tell el-'Oueili preliminary report on the the 4th season (1983): Stratigraphy and architecture'. *Sumer*, 44(1–2): 55–66.

Forest-Foucault, Ch. (1980) 'Rapport sur les fouilles de Kheit Qasim III – Hamrin'. *Paleorient*, 6: 221–4.

Foster, B.R. (1982) 'Archives and record-keeping in Sargonic Mesopotamia'. *Zeitschrift für Assyriologie*, 72(1): 1–27.

Freeman, D. (1984) *Margaret Mead and Samoa: The Making and Unmaking of an Anthropological Myth*. Harmondsworth, Penguin.

Friedman, J. and Rowlands, M.J. (eds) (1977) *The Evolution of Social Systems*. London, Duckworth.

Gardin, J-C. (1980) *Archaeological Constructs: An Aspect of Theoretical Archaeology*. Cambridge, Cambridge University Press.

Garfinkel, Y. (1987) 'Yiftahel: A Neolithic village from the seventh millennium BC in lower Galilee, Israel'. *Journal of Field Archaeology*, 14: 199–212.

Garrard, A.N. and Gebel, G. (eds) (1988) *The Prehistory of Jordan: the State of Research in 1986*, 2 parts. BAR International Series 396 (i, ii).

Garrod, D.A.E. (1932) 'A new Mesolithic industry: The Natufian of Palestine'. *Journal of the Royal Anthropological Institute*, 62: 257–70.

Garrod, D.A.E. (1942) 'Excavation at the cave of Shukbah, Palestine, 1928'. *Proceedings of the Prehistoric Society*, 8: 1–20.

Gebel, H.G. (1988) 'Late Epipalaeolithic - Aceramic Neolithic sites in the Petra area'. In Garrard and Gebel (eds), pp. 67–100.

Gebel, H.G., Muheisen, M.S., Nissen, H.J., Qadi N. and Starck, J.M. (1988) 'Preliminary report on the first season of excavations at the Late Aceramic Neolithic site of Basta'. In Garrard and Gebel (eds), I: 101–34.

Gelb, I.J. (1965) 'The ancient Mesopotamian ration system'. *Journal of Near Eastern Studies*, 24: 230–43.

Gelb, I.J. (1969) 'On the alleged temple and state economies in ancient Mesopotamia'. *Studi in Onore di Eduardo Volterra*, 6: 137–54; Rome, Guiffre Editore.

Gelb, I.J. (1979) 'Household and family in Ancient Mesopotamia'. In Lipinski (ed.), I: 1–98.

Gibson, McG. and Biggs, R.D. (eds) (1987) *The Organization of Power: Aspects of Bureaucracy in the Ancient Near East*. Studies in Ancient Oriental Civilization No. 46. Chicago, The Oriental Institute of the University of Chicago.

Gillispie, C.C. (1959) *Genesis and Geology*. New York, Harper & Row.

Goodman, S. (1985) *Gertrude Bell*. Leamington Spa, Berg.

Gould, R.A. (1980) *Living Archaeology: New Studies in Archaeology*. Cambridge, Cambridge University Press.

Gräslund, B. (1981) 'The background to C.J. Thomsen's Three Age System'. In Daniel (ed.), pp. 45–68.

Greener, L. (1966) *The Discovery of Egypt*. New York, Dorset Press [1989].

Hadidi, A. (ed.) (1987) *Studies in the History and Archaeology of Jordan III*. London & New York, Routledge.

Haex, O.M.C., Curvers, H.H. and Akkermans, P.M.M.G. (eds) (1989) *To the Euphrates and Beyond: Archaeological Studies in Honour of Maurits van Loon*. Rotterdam/Brookfield, A.A. Balkema.

Hall, H.R. (1930) *A Season's Work at Ur, Al-'Ubaid, Abu Shahrain (Eridu), and Elsewhere*. London, Methuen.

Halstead, P. (1990) 'Quantifying Sumerian agriculture: Some seeds of doubt and hope'. In Postgate and Powell (eds), pp. 187–95.

Harlan, J.R. (1967) 'A wild wheat harvest in Turkey'. *Archaeology*, 20: 197–201.

Harris, W.V. (1989) *Ancient Literacy*. Cambridge, Mass., Harvard University Press.

Harris, D.R. and Hillman, G.C. (eds) (1989) *Foraging and Farming: The Evolution of Plant Exploitation*. London, Unwin Hyman.

Hawkes, J. (1982) *Mortimer Wheeler: Adventurer in Archaeology*. London, Weidenfeld & Nicolson.

Hecker, H.M. (1982) 'Domestication revisited: Its implications for faunal analysis'. *Journal of Field Archaeology*, 9: 217–36.

Hegmon, M. (1985) 'Exchange in social integration and subsistence risk: A computer simulation'. Doctoral qualifying paper, Department of Anthropology, University of Michigan.

Hegmon, M. (1986) 'Sharing as social integration and risk reduction: A computer simulation involving the Hopi'. Manuscript, Museum of Anthropology, University of Michigan.

Helbaek, H. (1965) 'Early Hassunan vegetable food at Tell es-Sawwan near Samarra'. *Sumer*, 20: 45–8.

Helbaek, H. (1966) 'Pre-Pottery Neolithic farming at Beidha'. *Palestine Exploration Quarterly*, 98: 8–72.

Helbaek, H. (1972) 'Samarran irrigation agriculture at Choga Mami in Iraq'. *Iraq*, 34: 35–48.

Heltzman, S.F. (1975) 'Bachofen and the concept of matrilineality'. In Thoresen (ed), pp. 125–9.

Henrickson, E.F. (1981) 'Non-religious residential settlement patterning in the Late Early Dynastic of the Diyala region'. *Mesopotamia*, XVI: 43–140.

Henrickson, E.F. (1982) 'Functional analysis of elite residences in the Late Early Dynastic of the Diyala region'. *Mesopotamia*, XVII: 5–33.

Henrickson, E.F. and Thuesen, I. (1989) *Upon This Foundation – The 'Ubaid Reconsidered*. Copenhagen, Museum Tusculanum Press.

Henry, D.O. (1983) 'Adaptive evolution within the Epipalaeolithic of the Near East'. In *Advances in World Archaeology*, Vol. 2, F. Wendorf and A.E. Close (eds), New York, Academic Press, pp. 99–160.

Henry, D.O. (1985) 'Preagricultural sedentism: the Natufian example'. In Price and Brown (eds), pp. 365–81.

Henry, D.O. (1989) *From Foraging to Agriculture: The Levant at the End of the Ice Age*. Philadelphia, University of Pennsylvania Press.

Hepper, F.N. (1981) *Bible Plants at Kew*. London, HMSO.

Herzfeld, E. E. (1930) *Die Ausgrabungen von Samarra*, Band V: *Die vorgeschichtlichen Töpferein von Samarra*, Berlin.

Higgs, E.S. (ed.) (1972) *Papers in Economic Prehistory*. Cambridge, Cambridge University Press.

Higgs, E.S. (1973) Economy. In Noy, Legge and Higgs, pp. 95–6.

Hijara, I.H. (1973) 'Fouilles de Tell Qalinj Agha'. *Sumer*, 29: 13–34.

Hijara, I.H., Hubbard, R.N.L.B. and Watson, J.P.N. (1980) 'Arpachiya, 1976'. *Iraq*, 42: 131–54.

Hillman, G.C., Colledge, S.M. and Harris, D.R. (1989) 'Plant-food economy during the Epipalaeolithic period at Tell Abu Hureyra, Syria: dietary diversity, seasonality, and modes of exploitation'. In Harris and Hillman (eds), pp. 240–68.

Hillman, G.C. and Davies, M.S. (1990) 'Measured domestication rates in wild wheats and barley under primitive cultivation, and their archaeological implications'. *Journal of World Prehistory*, 4(2): 157–222.

Hole, F. and Flannery, K.V. (1967) 'The prehistory of south-western Iran: A preliminary report'. *Proceedings of the Prehistoric Society*, 33: 147–206.

Hongo, H. (1996) 'Fauna remains from Tell Aray 2, Northwestern Syria'. *Paleorient*, 22/1: 125–44.

Hopf, M. (1969) 'Plant remains and early farming in Jericho'. In Ucko and Dimbleby (eds), pp. 347–59.

Hopf, M. and Bar-Yosef, O. (1987) 'Plant remains from Hayonim Cave'. *Paleorient*, 13: 117–20.

Hubbard, R.N.L.B. (1980) 'Halafian agriculture and environment at Arpachiya'. *Iraq*, 42: 153–4.

Hunt, R.C. (1987) 'The role of bureaucracy in the provisioning of cities: A framework for analysis in the Ancient Near East'. In Gibson and Biggs (eds), pp. 161–92.

Hunt, R.C. (1988) 'Hydraulic management in southern Mesopotamia in Sumerian times'. In Postgate and Powell (eds), pp. 189–206.

Huot, J.-L. (1989) ''Ubaidian village of Lower Mesopotamia. Permanence and evolution from 'Ubaid 0 to 'Ubaid 4 as seen from Tell el'Oueili'. In Henrickson and Thuesen (eds), pp. 19–42.

Inizan, M.-L. (1985–6) 'Tell el-'Oueili: The knapped stone finds'. *Sumer*, 44(1–2): 120–2.

Jacobsen, T. (1957) 'Early political development in Mesopotamia'. *Zeitschrift für Assyriologie, Neue Folge*, 18(52): 91–140.

Jacobsen, T. (1976) *The Treasures of Darkness: A History of Mesopotamian Religion*. New Haven, Yale University Press.

Jacobsen, T. (1989) 'Lugalbanda and Ninsuna'. *Journal of Cuneiform Studies*, 41/1: 69–86.

Jasim, S.A. (1985) *The Ubaid Period in Iraq: Recent Excavations in the Hamrin Region*. Oxford, BAR International Series No. 267, 2 vols.

Jasim, S.A. (1989) 'Structure and function in an 'Ubaid village'. In Henrickson and Thuesen (eds), pp. 79–90.

Jones, G.D. and Kautz, R.R. (1981) *The Transition to Statehood in the New World*. Cambridge, Cambridge University Press.

Kafafi, Z.A. (1987) 'The Pottery Neolithic in Jordan in connection with other Near Eastern regions'. In Hadidi (ed.), pp. 33–9.

Kafafi, Z.A. (1988) 'Jebel Abu Thawwab. A pottery Neolithic village in north Jordan'. In Garrard and Gebel (eds), pp. 451–71.

Kaufman, D. (1986) 'A reconsideration of adaptive change in the Levantine Neolithic'. In *The End of the Palaeolithic in the Old World*, Lawrence G. Straus (ed.), BAR-S284, pp. 117–28.

Kaufman, D. (1988) 'New radiocarbon dates for the Geometric Kebaran'. *Paleorient*, 14/1: 107–9.

Kaufman, D. (1989) 'Observations on the Geometric Kebaran: a view from Neve David'. In Bar Yosef and Vandermeersch (eds), pp. 275–85.

Keeley, L.H. (1988) 'Hunter-gatherer economic complexity and "population pressure": A cross-cultural analysis'. *Journal of Anthropological Archaeology*, 7: 373–411.

Kehoe, A.B. (1991) 'The invention of Prehistory'. *Current Anthropology*, 32(4): 467–76.

Kirkbride, D. (1966) 'Five seasons at the Pre-Pottery Neolithic site of Beidha in Jordan: A summary'. *Palestine Exploration Quarterly*, 98: 8–61.

Kirkbride, D. (1967) 'Beidha 1965: An interim report'. *Palestine Exploration Quarterly*, 99: 5–13.

Kirkbride, D. (1968) 'Beidha: early Neolithic village life south of the Dead Sea'. *Antiquity*, 42: 263–74.

Kitchen, K.A. (1991) 'The chronology of ancient Egypt'. *World Archaeology*, 23(2): 201–8.

Klindt-Jensen, O. (1976) 'The Influence of ethnography on early Scandinavian archaeology'. In Megaw (ed.), pp. 43–8.

Klindt-Jensen, O. (1981) 'Archaeology and ethnography in Denmark: Early studies'. In Daniel (ed.), pp. 14–19.

Kohl, P. (1989) 'The use and abuse of world systems theory: The case of the "pristine" West Asian state'. In Lamberg-Karlovsky (ed.), pp. 218–40.

Kohler-Rollefson, I. (1988) 'The aftermath of the Levantine Neolithic in the light of ecological and ethnographic evidence'. *Paleorient*, 14/1: 87–93.

Kohler-Rollefson, I. (1989) 'Changes in goat exploitation at 'Ain Ghazal between the Early and Late Neolithic: A metrical analysis'. *Paleorient*, 15/1: 141–6.

Kohler-Rollefson I., Gillespie, W. and Metzger, M. (1988) 'The fauna from Neolithic 'Ain Ghazal'. In Garrard and Gebel (eds), II: 423–30.

Kozlowski, S.K. (1989) 'Nemrik 9, A PPN Neolithic site in northern Iraq'. *Paleorient*, 15/1: 25–31.

Kozlowski, S.K. and Kempisty A. (1990) 'Architecture of the Pre-Pottery Neolithic settlement in Nemrik, Iraq'. *World Archaeology*, 21(3): 348–62.

Kramer, S.N. (1981) *History Begins at Sumer*. Philadelphia, The University of Pennsylvania Press.

Kristiansen, K. (1981) 'A social history of Danish archaeology (1805–1975)'. In Daniel (ed.), pp. 20–44.

Kuijt, I., Mabry, J. and Palumbo, G. (1991) 'Early Neolithic use of upland areas of Wadi el-Yabis: Preliminary evidence from the excavations of 'Iraq ed-Dubb, Jordan'. *Paleorient*, 17/1: 99–108.

Lal, B.B. , Gupta, S.P. and Asthana, S. (eds) (1984) *Frontiers of the Indus Civilization: Sir Mortimer Wheeler Commemoration Volume*. New Delhi, Books & Books.

Lamberg-Karlovsky, C.C. (ed.) (1989) *Archaeological Thought in America*. Cambridge, Cambridge University Press.

Lambert, W.G. (1989) 'Notes on a work of the most ancient Semitic literature'. *Journal of Cuneiform Studies*, 41/1: 1–33.

Lapidus, I.M. (ed.) (1969) *Middle Eastern Cities*. Berkeley and Los Angeles, University of California Press.

Lebeau, M. (1985–6) 'A first report on pre-Eridu pottery from Tell el-'Oueili'. *Sumer*, 44(1–2): 88–119.

Lee, R.B. and DeVore, I. (eds) (1968) *Man the Hunter*. Chicago, Aldine.

Legge, A.J. (1973) 'Fauna'. In Noy, Legge and Higgs, pp. 90–1.

Le Miere, M. (1989) 'Les débuts de la céramique sur le Moyen-Euphrate (6500–5500 BC)'. In Haex, Curvers and Akkermans (eds), pp. 53–64.

Levine, P. (1986) *The Amateur and the Professional: Antiquarians, Historians and Archaeologists in Victorian England, 1838–1886*. Cambridge, Cambridge University Press.

Lieberman, D.E. (1991) 'Seasonality and gazelle hunting at Hayonim Cave: New evidence for "sedentism" during the Natufian'. *Paleorient*, 17/1: 47–57.

Limbrey, S. (1990) 'Edaphic opportunism? A discussion of soil factors in relation to the beginnings of plant husbandry in south-west Asia'. *World Archaeology*, 22(1): 45–52.

Lipinski, E. (ed.) (1979) *State and Temple Economy in the Ancient Near East*, 2 vols. Leuven, Orientalia Lovaniensa Analecta 6.

Lipman, V.D. (1988) 'The origins of the Palestine Exploration Fund'. *Palestine Excavation Quarterly*, 120: 45–54.

Lloyd, S. (1978) *The Archaeology of Mesopotamia: From the Old Stone Age to the Persian Conquest*. London, Thames & Hudson.

Lloyd, S. (1980) *Foundations in the Dust: The Story of Mesopotamian Exploration*, revised edn. London, Thames & Hudson.

Lloyd, S. (1989) 'Recollections'. In Daniel and Chippindale (eds), pp. 61–78.

Lloyd, S. and Safar, F. (1945) 'Tell Hassuna: Excavations by the Iraq Government Directorate General of Antiquities in 1943 and 1944'. *Journal of Near Eastern Studies*, 4: 255–89.

Lowie, R.H. (1937) *The History of Ethnological Theory*. New York, Holt, Rinehart & Winston.

Lubbock, J. (1870) *The Origin of Civilization and the Primitive Condition of Man*. London, Longmans, Green & Co.

Macalister, R.A.S. (1925) *A Century of Excavation in Palestine*. London, The Religious Tract Society.

Maisels, C.K. (1987) 'Models of social evolution: Trajectories from the Neolithic to the State'. *Man*, 22(2): 331–59.

Maisels, C.K. (1990) *The Emergence of Civilization: From Hunting and Gathering to Agriculture, Cities and the State in the Near East*. London, Routledge.

Maisels, C.K. (1991) 'Trajectory versus typology in social evolution'. *Cultural Dynamics*, IV(3): 251–69.

Maisels, C.K. (1998) *Early Civilizations of the Old World: The Formative Histories of Egypt, The Levant, Mesopotamia, India and China*. London, Routledge.

Malinowski, B. (1922) *Argonauts of the Pacific*. London, Routledge.

Mallowan, M.E.L. (1936) 'The excavations of Tell Chagar Bazar and an archaeological survey of the Habur region 1934–5'. *Iraq*, 3: 1–87.

Mallowan, M.E.L. (1977) *Mallowan's Memoirs: The Autobiography of Max Mallowan*. Glasgow, Collins.

Mallowan, M.E.L. and Rose, J.C. (1935) 'Excavations at Tell Arpachiyah, 1933'. *Iraq*, 2: 1–178.

Mandel, R.D. and Simmons, A.H. (1988) 'A preliminary assessment of the geomorphology of 'Ain Ghazal'. In Garrard and Gebel (eds), II: 431–6.

Martin, H. (1988) *Fara: A Reconstruction of the Ancient Mesopotamian City of Shuruppak*. Birmingham (UK), Chris Martin & Associates.

Matthews, R.J. (1991) 'Fragments of officialdom from Fara'. *Iraq*, 53: 1–15.

Matthews, R.J. (1996) 'Excavations at Tell Brak, 1996'. *Iraq*, LVIII: 65–77.

Matthews, R.J. and Wilkinson, T.J. (1991) 'Excavations in Iraq, 1989–1990'. *Iraq*, 53: 169–82.

Megaw, J.V.S. (ed.) (1976) *To Illustrate the Monuments: Essays Presented to Stuart Piggott on the Occasion of his 65th Birthday*. London, Thames & Hudson.

Meijer, D.J.W. (1989) 'Ground plans and archaeologists: On similarities and comparisons'. In Haex, Curvers and Akkermans (eds), pp. 221–36.

Mellaart, J. (1975) *The Neolithic of the Near East*. London, Thames & Hudson.

Merpert, N.Ya. and Munchaev, R.M. (1973) 'Early agricultural settlements in the Sinjar Plain, N. Iraq'. *Iraq*, 35: 93–119.

Merpert, N.Ya., Munchaev, R.M. and Bader, N.O. (1981) 'Investigations of the Soviet expedition in northern Iraq, 1976'. *Sumer*, 37: 22–54.

Merpert, N.Ya. and Munchaev, R.M. (1984) 'Soviet expedition's research at Yarim Tepe III settlement in northwestern Iraq, 1978–1979'. *Sumer*, 43(1–2): 54–68.

Merpert, N.Ya. and Munchaev, R.M. (1987) 'The earliest levels at Yarim Tepe I and Yarim Tepe II in northern Iraq'. *Iraq*, 49: 1–36.

Michalowski, P. (1987) 'Charisma and control: On continuity and change in early Mesopotamian bureaucratic systems'. In Gibson and Biggs (eds), pp. 55–68.

Moholy-Nagy, H. (1983) 'Jarmo artefacts of pecked and ground stone and of shell'. In Braidwood *et al.* (eds), pp. 289–346.

Moir, E. (1958) 'The English antiquaries'. *History Today*: 781–92.

Momigliano, A. (1966) 'Ancient History and the Antiquarian' [1950]. In *Studies in Historiography*. London, Weidenfeld & Nicolson, pp. 1–39.

Montet, P. (1964) *Eternal Egypt*. London, Weidenfeld & Nicolson.

Moore, A.M.T. (1989) 'The transition from foraging to farming in southwest Asia: Present problems and future directions'. In Harris and Hillman (eds), pp. 620–31.

Morales, V.B. (1983) 'Jarmo figurines and other clay objects'. In Braidwood *et al.* (eds), pp. 369–424.

Muheisen, M. (1988) 'The Epipalaeolithic phases of Kharaneh IV'. In Garrard and Gebel (eds), II: 353–67.

Muheisen, M., Gebel, H.G., Hanns, C. and Neef, R. (1988) 'Excavations at 'Ain Rahub, a final Natufian and Yarmoukian site near Irbid (1985)'. In Garrard and Gebel (eds), II: 473–502.

Munchaev, R.M., Merpert, N.Ya. and Bader, N.O. (1984) 'Archaeological studies in the Sinjar Valley, 1980'. *Sumer*, 43(1–2): 32–53.

Needham, J. (1969) *The Grand Titration: Science and Society i71 East and West*. London, George Allen & Unwin.

Nadel, D., Bar-Yosef, O. and Gopher, A. (1991) 'Early Neolithic arrowhead types in the southern Levant: A typological suggestion'. *Paleorient*, 17/1: 109–19.

Netting, R.McC. (1990) 'Population, permanent agriculture, and polities: unpacking the evolutionary portmanteau'. In Upham (ed.), pp. 21–61.

Netting, R.McC., Wilk, R.R. and Arnould, E.J. (eds) (1984) *Households: Comparative and Historical Studies of the Domestic Group*. Berkeley, University of California Press.

Nissen, H.J. (1988) *The Early History of the Ancient Near East*. Chicago, University of Chicago Press.

Nissen, H.J. (1989) 'The 'Ubaid Period in the context of the Early History of the Ancient Near East'. In Henrickson and Thuesen (eds), pp. 245–55.

Northedge, A., Wilkinson, T.J. and Faulkner, R. (1990) 'Survey and excavations at Samarra, 1989'. *Iraq*, 52: 121–47.

Noy, T. (1989) 'Gilgal 1 - a Pre-Pottery Neolithic Site, Israel - the 1985–1987 seasons'. *Paleorient*, 15/1: 11–18.

Noy, T. , Legge, A.J. and Higgs, E.S. (1973) 'Recent excavations at Nahal Oren, Israel'. *Proceedings of the Prehistoric Society*, 39: 75–99.

Noy, T., Schuldrein, J. and Tchernov, E. (1980) 'Gilgal, a Pre-Pottery Neolithic A site in the lower Jordan Valley'. *Israel Exploration Journal*, 30: 63–82.

Oates, D. (1982) 'Tell Brak'. In Curtis (ed.), pp. 62–71.

Oates, D. and Oates, J. (1976) 'Early irrigation agriculture in Mesopotamia'. In Sieveking, Londworth and Wilson (eds), pp. 109–35.

Oates, D. and Oates, J. (1981) 'The Near East: A personal view'. In Evans, Cunliffe and Renfrew (eds), pp. 28–34.

Oates, J. (1968) 'Prehistoric investigations near Mandali, Iraq'. *Iraq*, 30: 1–20.

Oates, J. (1969) 'Choga Mami, 1967–68: A preliminary report'. *Iraq*, 31: 115–52.

Oates, J. (1973) 'The background and development of early farming communities in Mesopotamia and the Zagros'. *Proceedings of the Prehistoric Society*, 39: 147–81.

Oates, J. (1977) 'Mesopotamian social organisation: Archaeological and philological evidence'. In Friedman and Rowlands (eds), pp. 457–85.

Oates, J. (1982) 'Choga Mami'. In Curtis (ed.), pp. 22–9.

Oates, J. (1983) 'Ubaid Mesopotamia reconsidered'. In Young *et al.* (eds), pp. 251–81.

Oppenheim, A.L. (1969) 'Mesopotamia - land of many cities'. In Lapidus (ed.), pp. 3–16.

Oppenheim, M. von (1931) *Tell Halaf: A New Culture in Oldest Mesopotamia*. London & New York, G.P. Putnam's Sons.

Oppenheim, M. von and Schmidt, H. (1943) *Tell Halaf (Erster Band): Die Prahistorischen Funde*. Berlin, Walter de Gruyter.

Oppenheim, M. von and Naumann, R. (1950) *Tell Halaf (Zweiter Band): Die Bauwerke*. Berlin, Walter de Gruyter.

Oppenheim, M. von and Moortgat, A. (1955) *Tell Halaf (Dritter Band): Die Bildwerke*. Berlin, Walter de Gruyter.

Oppenheim, M. von and Hrouda, B. (1962) *Tell Halaf (Vierter Band): Die Kleinfunde aus Historischer Zeit*. Berlin, Walter de Gruyter.

Parrot, André (1955) *Discovering Buried Worlds*. London, SCM Press.

Patterson, T.C. (1989) 'Pre-state societies and cultural styles in ancient Peru and Mesopotamia: A comparison'. In Henrickson and Thuesen (eds), pp. 293–321.

Pemberton, W., Postgate, J.N. and Smyth, R.F. (1988) 'Canals and bunds, ancient and modern'. In Postgate and Powell (eds), pp. 207–21.

Perrot, J. (1966) 'La troisieme campagne de fouilles à Munhatta (1964)'. *Syria*, 43: 49–63.

Petrie, W.M.F. (1932) *Seventy Years in Archaeology*. London, Sampson, Low, Marston & Co. Ltd.

Piggott, S. (1981) ' "Vast perennial memorials": The first antiquaries look at megaliths'. In Evans, Cunliffe and Renfrew (eds), pp. 19–25.

Piggott, S. (1989) *Ancient Britons and the Antiquarian Imagination: Ideas from the Renaissance to the Regency*. London, Thames & Hudson.

Plog, S. (1990) 'Agriculture, sedentism, and environment in the evolution of political systems'. In Upham (ed.), pp. 177–99.

Possehl, G. (ed.) (1982) *Harappan Civilization: A Contemporary Perspective*. Warminster, Aris & Phillips.

Postgate, J.N. (1982) 'Abu Salabikh'. In J. Curtis (ed.), pp. 48–61.

Postgate, J. N. (1990) 'Excavations at Abu Salabikh, 1988–9'. *Iraq*, 52: 95–106.

Postgate, J.N. (1994) 'How many Sumerians per hectare? – probing the anatomy of an early city'. *Cambridge Archaeological Journal* 4(1): 47–65.

Postgate, J.N. and Moon, J. (1984) 'Excavations at Abu Salabikh, a Sumerian city'. *National Geographic Reports* 17 (Year 1976): 721–43.

Postgate, J.N. and Powell, J.A. (eds) (1988) *Irrigation and Cultivation in Mesopotamia*, part 1. Cambridge, Bulletin on Sumerian Agriculture, vol. 4.

Postgate, J.N. and Powell, J.A. (eds) (1990) *Irrigation and Cultivation in Mesopotamia*, part 2. Cambridge, Bulletin on Sumerian Agriculture, vol. 5.

Powell, M.A. (1996) 'Money in Mesopotamia'. *JESHO*, 39(3): 224–42.

Price, T.D. and Brown, J.A. (eds) (1985) *Prehistoric Hunter-Gatherers: The Emergence of Cultural Complexity*. London & New York, Academic Press.

Raikes, R.L. (1966) 'Beidha: Prehistoric climate and water supply'. *Palestine Exploration Quarterly*, 98: 68–72.

Redman, C.L., Berman, M., Curtin, F., Langhorne, W., Versaggi, N. and Wanser, J. (1978) 'Social archaeology: Beyond subsistence and dating'. London & New York, Academic Press.

Roaf, M.D. (1982) 'The Hamrin Sites'. In Curtis (ed.), pp. 40–7.

Roaf, M.D. (1989) ' 'Ubaid social organization and social activities as seen from Tell Madhhur'. In Henrickson and Thuesen (eds), pp. 91–146.

Roaf, M.D. (1990) *Cultural Atlas of Mesopotamia and the Near East*. New York & Oxford, Equinox.

Roaf, S. (1982) 'Tell Madhhur: Isometric partial reconstruction'. In Curtis (ed.), p. 43.

Rodden, J. (1981) 'The development of the Three Age System: Archaeology's first paradigm'. In Daniel (ed.), pp. 51–68.

Rollefson, G.O. (1988) 'Stratified Burin classes at 'Ain Ghazal: Implications for the desert Neolithic of Jordan'. In Garrard and Gebel (eds), II: 437–49.

Rollefson, G.O. and Simmons, A.H. (1988) 'The Neolithic settlement at 'Ain Ghazal'. In Garrard and Gebel (eds), II: 393–421.

Rollefson, G.O., Kafafi, Z.A. and Simmons, A.H. (1991) 'The Neolithic village of 'Ain Ghazal, Jordan: Preliminary report on the 1988 season'. Basor Supplement No. 27, pp. 95–116; published by Johns Hopkins University Press for ASOR. Preliminary Reports of ASOR-sponsored Excavations 1982–89, E. Rast and M. Zeiger (eds).

Rollefson, G.O., Simmons, A.H., Donaldson, M.L., Gillespie, W., Kafafi, Z.A., Kohler-Rollefson, I.U., McAdam, E., Rolston, S.L. and Tubb, M.K. (1985) 'Excavation at the Pre-Pottery Neolithic B village of 'Ain Ghazal (Jordan), 1983'. Mitteilungen der Deutschen-Orient-Gesellschaft (MDOG), 117: 69–134.

Saggs, H.W.F. (ed. and intro.) (1970) Nineveh and its Remains: With an Account of a Visit to the Chaldaean Christians of Kurdistan, and Yezidis, or Devil-worshippers, by Austen Henry Layard. London, Routledge.

Sahlins, M. (1974) Stone Age Economics. London, Tavistock.

Sanlaville, P. (1996) 'Changements climatiques dans la région Levantine à la fin du Pleistocene Superieur et au début de l'Holocene. Leurs relations avec l'évolution des sociétés humaines'. Paleorient, 22/1: 7–30.

Selz, G.J. (1990) 'Studies in Early Syncretism: The development of the Pantheon in Lagas'. Acta Sumerologica, 12: 111–42.

Sieveking, G. de G., Longworth, I.H. and Wilson, K.E. (1976) Problems in Economic and Social Archaeology. London, Duckworth.

Sklenar, K. (1983) Archaeology in Central Europe: The First 500 Years. Leicester, Leicester University Press.

Stampfli, H.R. (1983) 'The fauna of Jarmo, with notes on animal bones from Matarrah, the Amuq and Karim Shahir'. In Braidwood et al. (eds), pp. 431–4.

Starck, J.M. (1988) 'Stone rings from Baga and Basta: Geographical and chronological implications'. In Garrard and Gebel (eds), I: 137–74.

Stein, G. (1990) 'On the Uruk expansion' [critique of Algaze 1989]. Current Anthropology, 31(1): 66–7.

Steinkeller, P. (1987) 'The administrative and economic organization of the Ur III State'. In Gibson and Biggs (eds), pp. 19–41.

Stekelis, M. (1972) The Yarmoukian Culture of the Neolithic Period. Jerusalem, Magnes Press.

Stekelis, M. and Yizraeli, T. (1963) 'Excavations at Nahal Oren, preliminary report'. Israel Exploration Journal, 13: 1–12.

Stocking, G.W. Jnr (1975) 'Scotland as the model of mankind: Lord Kames' philosophical view of civilization'. In Thoresen (ed.), pp. 65–89.

Stocking, G.W. Jnr (1987) Victorian Anthropology. New York, The Free Press.

Stronach, D. (1982) 'Ras al'Amiya'. In Curtis (ed.), pp. 37–9.

Thoresen, T.H.H. (1975) (ed.) Toward a Science of Man: Essays in the History of Anthropology. The Hague/Paris, Mouton.

Trigger, B.G. (1980) Gordon Childe: Revolutions in Archaeology. London, Thames & Hudson.

Trigger, B . G. (1983) 'The rise of Egyptian civilization'. In Trigger, Kemp, O'Connor and Lloyd (eds), pp. 1–70.

Trigger, B.G. (1989) 'History and contemporary American archaeology: A critical analysis'. In Lamberg-Karlovsky (ed.), pp. 19–34.

Trigger, B.G. (1990a) *A History of Archaeological Thought*. Cambridge, Cambridge University Press.

Trigger, B.G. (1990b) 'The 1990s: North American archaeology with a human face?' *Antiquity*, 64: 778–87.

Trigger, B.G., Kemp, B.J., O'Connor, D. and Lloyd, A.B. (1983) *Ancient Egypt: A Social History*. Cambridge, Cambridge University Press.

Tsuneki, A. and Miyake, Y. (1996) 'The earliest pottery sequence of the Levant: new data from Tell el-Kerkh 2, northern Syria'. *Paleorient* 22/1: 109–23.

Tubb, M.K. (1985) 'Preliminary report on the 'Ain Ghazal statues'. In Rollefson *et al. (MDOG*, 117), pp. 117–34.

Turnbull, P. and Reed, C.A. (1974) 'The fauna from the terminal Pleistocene of Palegawra Cave: A Zarzian occupation site in northeast Iraq'. *Fieldiana: Anthropology*, 63: 81–146.

Turville-Petrie, F. (1932) 'Excavations in the Mugharet el Kebarah'. *Journal of the Royal Anthropological Institute*, 62: 270–6.

Tylor, E.B. (1871) *Primitive Culture*. P. Radin (ed.), 1958, New York, Harper Torchbooks.

Ucko, P.J. and Dimbleby, G.W. (eds) (1969) *The Exploitation and Domestication of Plants and Animals*. London, Duckworth.

Ucko, P.J., Tringham, R. and Dimbleby, G.W. (eds) (1972) *Man, Settlement and Urbanism*. London, Duckworth.

Unger-Hamilton, R. (1989) 'The Epi-Palaeolithic southern Levant and the origins of pastoralism'. *Current Anthropology*, 30(1): 88–103.

Upham, S. (1990) *The Evolution of Political Systems*. Cambridge, Cambridge University Press.

Vanstiphout, H.L.J. (1990) 'The Mesopotamian debate poems. A general presentation (part 1)'. *Acta Sumerologica*, 12: 271–318.

Van Wijngaarden-Bakker, L.H. (1989) 'The animal remains of Tell Sabi Abyad – Square P14'. In Akkermans (ed.) (1989b), pp. 301–23.

Van Zeist, W. (1969) 'Reflections on prehistoric environments in the Near East'. In Ucko and Dimbleby (eds), pp. 35–46.

Van Zeist, W. and Bakker-Heeres, J.A.H. (1979) 'Some economic and ecological aspects of plant husbandry at Tell Aswad'. *Paleorient*, 5: 161–9.

Van Zeist, W. and Bakker-Heeres, J.A.H. (1982) 'Archaeobotanical studies of the Levant. I: Neolithic sites in the Damascus Basin: Aswad Ghoraife, Ramad'. *Palaeohistoria*, 24: 165–256.

Van Zeist, W. and Bottema, S. (1982) 'Vegetational history of the eastern Mediterranean and the Near East during the last 20,000 years'. In Bintliff and van Zeist (eds), pp. 277–321.

Van Zeist, W. and Waterbolk-van Rooijen, W. (1989) 'Plant remains from Sabi Abyad'. In Akkermans (ed.) (1989b), pp. 325–35.

Vertesalji, P.P. (1989) 'Transitions and transformations: 'Ubaidizing tendencies in Early Chalcolithic Mesopotamia'. In Henrickson and Thuesen (eds), pp. 227–55.

Watkins, T. (1990) 'The origins of house and home?' *World Archaeology*, 21(3): 336–47.

Watkins, T., Baird, D. and Betts, A. (1989) 'Qermez Dere and the early Aceramic Neolithic of N. Iraq'. *Paleorient*, 15/1: 19–24.

Watson, J.P.N. (1980) 'The vertebrate fauna from Arpachiyah'. *Iraq*, 42: 15–3.

Watson, P.J. (1978) 'Architectural differentiation in some Near Eastern communities, prehistoric and contemporary'. In Redman *et al.* (eds), pp. 131–58.

Watson, P.J. (1983a) 'The Halafian culture: A review and synthesis'. In Young *et al.* (eds), pp. 231–50.

Watson. P.J. (1983b) 'A note on the Jarmo plant remains'. In Braidwood *et al.* (eds), pp. 501–4.

Wattenmaker, P. (1990) 'On the Uruk expansion' [critique of Alagaze 1989]. *Current Anthropology*, 31(1): 67–9.

Weinstein-Evron, M. (1991) 'New radiocarbon dates for the Early Natufian of El-Wad Cave, Mt Carmel, Israel'. *Paleorient*, 17/1: 95–8.

Wheeler, M. (1955) *Still Digging: Interleaves from an Antiquary's Notebook.* London, Michael Joseph.

Whitehouse, R.D. (ed.) (1983) *The Macmillan Dictionary of Archaeology.* London, Macmillan.

Wigley, T.M.L. and Farmer G. (1982) 'Climate of the eastern Mediterranean and the Near East'. In Bintliff and van Zeist (eds), pp. 3–37.

Wilkinson, T.J. (1990a) 'Soil development and early land use in the Jazira region, Upper Mesopotamia'. *World Archaeology*, 22(1): 87–103.

Wilkinson, T.J. (1990b) 'The development of settlement in the north Jazira between 7th and 1st millennia BC'. *Iraq*, 52: 49–62.

Wilkinson, T.J., Monahan, B.H. and Tucker, D.J. (1996) 'Khanijdal East: A small Ubaid site in northeastern Iraq'. *Iraq*, LVIII: 17–50.

Willey, G.R. (1961) Review of *Evolution and Culture*, M.D. Sahlins and E.R. Service (eds). *American Antiquity*, 26: 441–3.

Wilshusen, R.H. and Stone, G.D. (1990) 'An ethnoarchaeological perspective on soils'. *World Archaeology*, 22(1): 104–11.

Winstone, H.V.F. (1990) *Woolley of Ur: The Life of Sir Leonard Woolley.* London, Secker & Warburg.

Woolley, C.L. (1982 edn) *Ur 'of the Chaldees'.* P.R.S. Moorey (ed.), London, The Herbert Press.

Wortham, J.D. (1971) *Britsh Egyptology 1549–1906.* Newton Abbot, David & Charles.

Wright, K. (1991) 'The origins and development of ground stone assemblages in Late Pleistocene southwest Asia'. *Paleorient*, 17/1: 19–45.

Yasin, W. (1970) 'Excavations at Tell es-Sawwan, 1969'. *Sumer*, 26: 3–20.

Young, D.F. (1973) *Beyond the Sunset: A Study of James Leslie Mitchell* [Lewis Grassic Gibbon]. Aberdeen, Impulse Books.

Young, T.C., Smith, P.E.L. and Mortensen, P. (eds) (1983) *The Hilly Flanks and Beyond: Essays on the Prehistory of Southwestern Asia (Presented to Robert J. Braidwood).* Studies in Ancient Oriental Civilization, No. 36. Chicago, The Oriental Institute of the University of Chicago.

Zagerell, A. (1989) 'Pastoralism and the early state in Greater Mesopotamia'. In Lamberg-Karlovsky (ed.), pp. 268–301.

Zettler, R.L. (1987) 'Administration of the Temple of Inanna at Nippur under the Third Dynasty of Ur: Archaeological and documentary evidence. In Gibson and Biggs (eds), pp. 117–31.

Zohary, D. (1962) *Plant Life of Palestine.* New York, Roland.

Zohary, D. (1969) 'The progenitors of wheat and barley in relation to domestication and agricultural dispersal in the Old World'. In Ucko and Dimbleby (eds), pp. 47–66.

Zohary, D. (1972) 'The wild progenitor and place of origin of the cultivated lentil: *Lens culinaris'. Economic Botany*, 26: 326–32.

Zohary, D. (1989) 'Domestication of the Southwest Asian Neolithic crop assemblage of cereals, pulses, and flax: The evidence from the living plants'. In Harris and Hillman (eds), pp. 358–73.

# INDEX

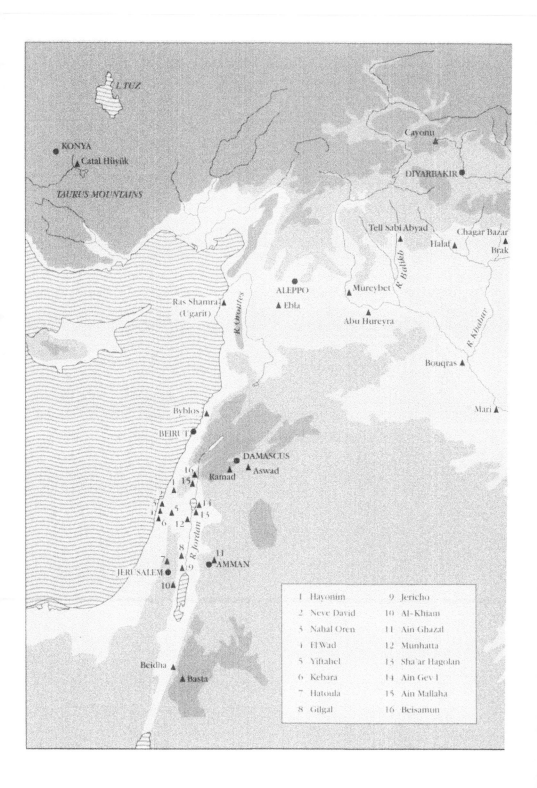

| | | | |
|---|---|---|---|
| 1 | Hayonim | 9 | Jericho |
| 2 | Neve David | 10 | Al-Khiam |
| 3 | Nahal Oren | 11 | Ain Ghazal |
| 4 | El Wad | 12 | Munhatta |
| 5 | Yiftahel | 13 | Sha'ar Hagolan |
| 6 | Kebara | 14 | Ain Gev I |
| 7 | Hatoula | 15 | Ain Mallaha |
| 8 | Gilgal | 16 | Beisamun |

Map labels:
L. TUZ
KONYA
Çatal Hüyük
TAURUS MOUNTAINS
Çayönü
DIYARBAKIR
Tell Sabi Abyad
Chagar Bazar
Halaf
Brak
ALEPPO
Ebla
Mureybet
R. Balikh
Ras Shamra (Ugarit)
R. Orontes
Abu Hureyra
R. Khabur
Bouqras
Mari
Byblos
BEIRUT
16
1
15
3
4  5
6  12
DAMASCUS
Ramad
Aswad
14
13
R. Jordan
8
7
11  AMMAN
9
JERUSALEM
10
Beidha
Basta

*9 7 8 0 4 1 5 1 8 6 0 7 0 *

An environmentally friendly book printed and bound in England by www.printondemand-worldwide.com

PEFC Certified

This product is
from sustainably
managed forests
and controlled
sources

www.pefc.org

PEFC/16-33-415

This book is made of chain-of-custody materials; FSC materials for the cover and PEFC materials for the text pages.

#0218 - 080216 - C0 - 234/156/14 - PB - 9780415186070